T0325559

ADVANCE PRAISE

"Pandit and Marmanis have made a significant contribution to the strategic supply management literature. The book is exceptionally well written and covers all aspects of spend management. It is an indispensable book for every manager and executive responsible for improving the bottom line. Domain knowledge and technology considerations are masterly presented. The seasoned supply management professional, and academics alike, will find it to be a great reference and full of insight. People just entering the field could not ask for a better introduction in this critical area of supply management."

—**Avner Schneur,** *CEO, Emptoris*

"In my experience, the term 'spend analysis' means a lot of things to a lot of people. Typically, it conjures up images of a few reports that show spend for each commodity or supplier. In reality, spend analysis is much more insightful than that, in terms of the complexity involved in analyzing spend data, and also how one can use the data to identify problems and opportunities within the sourcing value chains.

"Spend analysis is evolving. It is evolving from 'rear-view' analysis to predictive modeling capability by integrating with financial processes like budgeting, demand planning, invoice analysis, and compliance visibility.

"This is a very well-written book that covers all topics of spend analysis in sufficient detail. Both practitioners and academicians will find the topics interesting and educational. The authors have positioned spend analysis within the overall context of a supply management program and have made a compelling case for why it is important to implement a robust spend analysis program as a strong foundation for strategic sourcing."

—**Jay Reddy,** *Former CEO, MindFlow Technology*

ADVANCE PRAISE

SPEND ANALYSIS
The Window into Strategic Sourcing

Kirit Pandit, M.S., M.B.A
Vice President of Content Strategy
Head of Product Management for Spend Analysis
and Compliance Solutions
Emptoris, Inc.

H. Marmanis, Ph.D.
Director of Research
Chief Architect of Spend Analysis
and Compliance Solutions
Emptoris, Inc.

Copyright ©2008 by Emptoris, Inc. and Kirit Pandit and Haralambos Marmanis

ISBN-10: 1-932159-93-6
ISBN-13: 978-1-932159-93-6

Printed and bound in the U.S.A. Printed on acid-free paper
10 9 8 7 6 5 4 3 2 1

Library of Congress Cataloging-in-Publication Data

Pandit, Kirit, 1967-
  Spend analysis : the window into strategic sourcing / by Kirit Pandit and
Haralambos Marmanis.
    p. cm.
  Includes index.
  ISBN-13: 978-1-932159-93-6 (hardcover : alk. paper)
  1. Industrial procurement--Management. 2. Business logistics--Management.
3. Data warehousing. I. Marmanis, Haralambos, 1970- II. Title.

  HD39.5.P36 2008
  658.7'2--dc22   2007045937

Phone: (954) 727-9333
Fax: (561) 892-0700
Web: www.jrosspub.com

CONTENTS

Foreword xiii

Preface xv

Acknowledgments xvii

About the Authors..xix

Web Added Value™ xxi

PART I

Chapter 1. Fundamentals of Spend Analysis 3
What Is Spend Analysis? 5
    Basics 5
History of Spend Analysis 10
    Specialist Vendors 11
    Consolidation 12
Similarities/Differences between Spend Analysis and Data Warehousing 12
Characteristics of an Ideal Spend Analysis Application 15
    Data Definition and Loading (DDL) 15
    Data Cleansing, Structure, and Enrichment (DE) 17
    Spend Data Analytics (SA)...19
    Knowledgebase Management (KB) 20
Summary 22
References..22

Chapter 2. Business Imperative and Return on Investment 23
Spend Leakage and Compliance Multiplier 23
    Importance of Spend Analysis within Supply Management 25
Benefits to Businesses 26
Estimation of Spend Analysis Return on Investment 27
    Savings Opportunity 30
Case Study 1—Highly Decentralized Purchasing 30
    Overview and Objectives 30
    Methodology 31
Case Study 2—Global Procurement Challenges 31
    Methodology 34
    Results 35
Case Study 3—Merger Planning and Integration 39
    Overview 39
    Situation 40
    Methodology 40
    Conclusion 43
Summary 44
References 45

Chapter 3. How to Implement a Successful Spend Analysis Program 47
Set Objectives 48
Lead from the Top 48
Establish a Focused Center of Excellence 49
Carefully Evaluate Choices 50
    Commodity Classification 50
    Data Enrichment 50
Take a Limited-Scope, Phased-Rollout Approach 50
    Requirements Scoping 50
    Multicube Approach 51
    Data Scoping 52
    Refresh Requirement 52
Know Your Data 53
Technology Should Support Business, Not Drive Business 53
Align the Team to Support the Organization 54
Increase Organizational Visibility 54
Measure Constantly, Report Frequently 54
Engage with Your Application Provider 55
Sample Project Plan 55

Case Study 1—Procurement Transformation for an $8 Billion
    Agrochemical Business...55
    Overview 55
    Background 57
    Implementation and Key Learning 57
    Spend Analysis Program Success 58
    Sourcing Program Success 58
    The Future—Managing Supplier Relationships 59
Case Study 2—A Fortune 500 Provider in the Healthcare Industry 59
    Overview 59
    Implementation 60
    Challenges 60
    Results after One Year...61
Case Study 3—A Company with Global Procurement Locations 61
    Overview 61
    Implementation 62
    User Adoption..62
    Next Steps 62
Summary 62
References..63

Chapter 4. Opportunity Identification **65**
Spend-Level Opportunities..67
    Supplier Rationalization..67
    Demand Aggregation (or Disaggregation) 67
    Bypass of the Preferred Purchasing Process 69
        Non-PO Spend..69
        Off-Contract Spend 69
    Diversity Spend Compliance 70
    Supplier Performance..70
        Spend with Poorly Performing Suppliers 71
        Approved versus Nonapproved Spend 71
        Spend by Payment Type 72
Transaction-Level Opportunities 72
    Contractual Term Opportunities..72
        Unrealized Discounts and Rebates 73
        Quantity Violations 74
        Delivery Date Violations 76
    Payment Term Opportunities 76
    Invoice Processing Opportunities 77

Consolidated Payments 77
Frequent Charges and Credits...77
PO Approval Limits 78
Prioritizing Opportunities 79
Step 1—Conduct Buyer Interviews..79
Step 2—Create a Segmentation Framework..........................80
Step 3—Segment the Categories 80
Step 4—Assign Category to Implementation Waves 80
Summary 81

PART II

Chapter 5. The Anatomy of Spend Transactions **85**
Types of Spend...85
Direct...85
Indirect 86
MRO 87
Procurement Processes 88
Procure-to-Pay (P2P) 88
Purchasing Cards (P-Cards)..88
Travel and Entertainment (T&E) 88
Information and Approval Flow in P2P Processes 89
Data Requirements for P-Cards 93
Data Requirements for T&E 93
Source Systems and Data Extracts 94
Accounts Payable 94
Purchasing/e-Procurement 94
Receiving 95
Materials Management...95
Freight Transactions 95
Corporate P-Cards 96
Travel and Entertainment 96
Contract Management 96
Material Requirements Planning or Manufacturing
Resource Planning Systems...96
Contract Manufacturer Data 96
Other (External Sources) 96
Quality of Data 97
Item Description..98

Vendor Name 99
Cost Center and GL Code 99
Summary 100

Chapter 6. Spend Analysis Components.................................**101**
Introduction..101
Data Definition and Loading (DDL) 103
Data Cleansing 105
DDL Considerations..107
Data Assessment 108
Data Enrichment (DE) 110
Overview 110
Classification..115
Clustering 116
Business Rules and Manual Editing....................................116
Dimensional Enrichment..116
Classification 119
Clustering 120
Transactional Enrichment 120
Business Rules 120
Transactional Classification..123
Knowledge Acquisition and Management 125
Concepts 126
Attributes...127
Instances 127
Knowledgebase Essential Functionality.............................127
Browsing...127
Editing 128
Knowledge Assimilation 128
Spend Reporting and Analytics...129
Business Intelligence Key Capabilities...............................131
Reporting 131
Analytics...131
Scorecarding...132
Dashboards...132
Business Event Management..132
Basic OLAP Reports 133
Pivot Tables..133
Cross-tabular Reports 133
Graphical Reports 135

Specialized Charts...141
    Waterfall Chart...141
    Pareto Chart 142
    Treemap 142
    Multidimensional Report 144
    Map Report 144
  Ad Hoc Analytics 144
  What-If Analysis 147
  Dashboards 148
Summary 148
References..150

Chapter 7. Taxonomy Considerations..151
Ontologies and Taxonomies 151
Popular Industry Standard Commodity Taxonomies 153
UNSPSC 154
  Design 154
  Advantages of UNSPSC 155
  Disadvantages of UNSPSC..156
eOTD 157
  Design 157
  Advantages of eOTD 165
  Disadvantages of eOTD 166
eCl@ss...166
  Design 166
  Advantages of eClass 168
  Disadvantages of eClass 169
RUS..170
  Design 171
  Advantages of RUS 172
  Disadvantages of RUS 173
Quantitative Comparison of Taxonomies 173
  Size and Growth 174
  Hierarchical Order and Balance of Content 175
  Quality of Property Libraries..175
Conclusion and Summary...177
References..178

Chapter 8. Technology Considerations 179
Technical Considerations in the SA Module 179

Online Analytic Processing (OLAP) 179
What Is Your OLAP Schema?..180
What Do Your Dimensions Look Like?..181
Precooked Data or On-the-Fly Calculations? 182
Continental or International Deployment? 182
Pivoting or Multidimensional Navigation?................................183
Technical Considerations in the DDL Module 184
Representative Sampling 185
Missing Values..185
Balanced Dimensional Hierarchies 187
Detection of Systematic Errors 189
Technical Considerations in the DE Module 190
String Matching 190
Classification..191
Statistical Algorithms..193
Distance-Based Algorithms 194
Decision Tree-Based Algorithms..194
Neural Networks-Based Algorithms 195
Rule-Based Algorithms 196
Clustering 196
Classifier Evaluation 198
ROC Graph Details 200
Association Rules 201
Summary 203
References..203

PART III

Chapter 9. Tracking and Monitoring **209**
Introduction...209
Spend Under Management 212
Integrated Supply Management..212
External Integration Using Web Services 214
Using Spend Analysis for Measuring Benefits 214
Summary 217

Chapter 10. Spend Analysis and Compliance **219**
Introduction...219
Control Violations in the Procurement Process 220
Supplier Assessment 220

Supplier Selection 221
Contract 221
Procurement or Requisition..222
Fulfillment..222
Invoicing 222
Payment 222
Implementing Controls in Procurement 222
Commonly Implemented Controls 222
Payment Controls via 3-Way Match...224
Authorizations 224
P-Card Control...224
Travel and Entertainment 224
Spend Leakage 225
Contract Compliance 225
Vendor Compliance 226
Fraud 226
Case Study 227
The Future of Procurement Compliance 228
Measurement 228
Prevention 228
Summary 229
References..229

Chapter 11. The Future of Spend Analysis **231**
Supplier Discovery..232
Spend Forecasting 232
What-If Spend Analysis..232
Microanalysis 233
New Product Target Cost Analysis 233
Real-Time Classification 233
Relevance Search 234
Price Benchmarking 235
Summary 235

Index **237**

FOREWORD

Earnings per share, return on invested capital, and risk management are among the topics that consume the attention of most senior executives, which is entirely appropriate, given the consequences—both corporate and personal—for failing to stay "on top of your game" year after year in the business world.

Slowly but surely more and more senior executives are coming to the realization that strategic supply management can be a significant driver of improved corporate performance and better risk management. In my corporate career, and while interacting with my peers at other companies, this growing realization was noticeable and encouraging. Now as an advisor to companies large and small, I can personally attest to the keen interest that many senior executives have in understanding the potential of world class supply management to dramatically improve the performance of their companies. Once they understand the potential, the next logical step becomes developing a transformation plan to accomplish the targeted benefits.

One of the foundation blocks for transforming an organization's practices to *world class* supply management is the business process known as strategic sourcing—and one of the requirements for enabling *world class* strategic sourcing results is rigorous spend analysis. Of course, you can start strategic sourcing without rigorous spend analysis. Many companies, in the years before the development of modern spend analysis tools, had to "bootstrap" their sourcing efforts with crude, manual spend analyses. In fact, many sourcing programs based on preliminary, manual spend analyses still get underway.

Yet if the objective is to achieve truly world class and sustainable results, the effort will necessitate implementing a rigorous spend analysis methodology sooner rather than later. Spend analysis can help improve several areas: the identification of cost reduction opportunities; the prioritization of sourcing projects; the negotiated results; and the tracking and monitoring to ensure that negotiated results make it to the bottom line. Spend analysis can also play an important role in improving compliance in this world of Sarbanes-Oxley.

Spend Analysis: The Window into Strategic Sourcing, written by leaders in the field of spend analysis, is the definitive text on this important subject. I encourage you to read it, to discuss it with your colleagues, and to make its ideas a core part of your transformation plan.

— **Robert A. Rudzki**
President, Greybeard Advisors LLC
(www.GreybeardAdvisors.com)
Former SVP and CPO, Bayer Corporation,
and Procurement Executive,
Bethlehem Steel Corporation
Co-author of *Straight to the Bottom Line®:
An Executive's Roadmap to World Class
Supply Management* (2006) and *On-Demand
Supply Management: World Class Strategies,
Practices and Technology* (2007)
Author of *Beat the Odds: Avoid Corporate
Death and Build a Resilient Enterprise* (2007)

PREFACE

Twenty years ago, most companies manufactured what they sold. One of the defining aspects of our new economy is the reliance on "outsourcing" of labor and goods to suppliers all over the globe. Strategic sourcing has thus become a weapon that forward-thinking companies are using to differentiate themselves from their peers. Spend analysis is the starting block for building a successful strategic sourcing program. If implemented correctly, spend analysis can provide holistic, detailed visibility into spend patterns, creating a foundation from which opportunities for savings can be identified and action on them can be taken. If implemented incorrectly, a spend analysis implementation program can become easily misdirected and fall short of delivering all of the potential savings.

This book is both a text and a reference book on spend analysis. It explores all aspects of spend analysis in detail. Six questions that are most frequently asked by our prospects and customers are:

- How can I build a business case for spend analysis—and how can I sell it to my CFO?
- Should I build an application in-house or buy off-the-shelf?
- What should I look for in an application?
- What are the best practices for implementing spend analysis?
- Once implemented, how can I ensure user adoption?
- How can I measure ROI on an on-going basis?

Spend Analysis: The Window into Strategic Sourcing will provide answers to all of these questions. In most cases, we provide important tips that are gleaned from actual customer success stories. In some instances, we provide case studies. This type of presentation should provide enough material for the reader to think about and then be able to apply some or all of the concepts to his or her situation.

The choice of whether you should build your own application or obtain a license depends on a large number of factors. Furthermore, if you decide to build, a secondary set of factors will determine the characteristics and requirements of the application. Although this book will not tell you exactly how to build an application, all of the important functions that each module must possess will be provided. We will also list some critical requirements and the corresponding choices that you will face when you determine which function to implement.

Part I presents the most relevant material at an easy-to-understand level. Chapter 1 explores the definition of spend analysis and provides a high-level overview of its components. Chapter 2 provides guidelines and examples for building a business case for spend analysis. In Chapter 3, the important factors that ensure a successful implementation are enumerated. Chapter 4 presents various examples of savings opportunities revealed by spend analysis.

In Part II, we take a deep dive and explore many of these areas in greater detail. Both implementers and practitioners will find this information to be very useful. Chapter 5 provides detailed information on transaction data and source systems that are used in spend analysis. Chapter 6 explores the various components of a spend analysis application in detail. Chapter 6 also provides insight, based on information theory, into theoretical treatment of some commonly encountered questions, such as "How rich is my transactional information?" Chapter 7 compares some commonly used industry standard commodity taxonomies. This information is important because the taxonomy you choose will play an important role not only in spend analysis, but also across the entire enterprise resource planning footprint. Chapter 8 provides important background material on some of the technological issues and challenges that you will encounter.

Part III presents advanced concepts in spend analysis. Chapter 9 describes how spend analysis can be used in conjunction with other applications, Chapter 10 is about how spend analysis can drive better compliance, and Chapter 11 concerns the future of spend analysis.

Readers do not need specialized knowledge of database systems, information technology, or any other field. The material is intended for nonexperts and experts alike. However, readers who are only interested in the business aspects of spend analysis might choose to read only Parts I and III.

The data used in some of the customer case studies have been changed to ensure confidentiality. The conclusions drawn based upon them remain, of course, the same.

ACKNOWLEDGMENTS

Thanks are due to the marketing team at Emptoris for providing a variety of case studies and analyst articles. We also want to extend our earnest acknowledgments to Avner Schneur and Ammiel Kamon for their support. In addition, both authors deeply appreciate the interactions that we have had with all of our colleagues and customers, past and present, at Intigma, Zeborg, and Emptoris. These colleagues and customers have been a constant source of invaluable information and we are privileged to have worked with them.

Thanks are also due to Drew Gierman at J. Ross Publishing for all of the valuable time he spent with us.

The writing of this book would not have been possible without the love, patience, and support of our families. We thank them with the deepest sense of gratitude and unstinting devotion.

A very special note of appreciation goes to Bob Rudzki for encouraging, mentoring, and guiding us.

ABOUT THE AUTHORS

Kirit Pandit is Vice President of Content Strategy and the Head of Product Management for the Spend Analysis and Compliance Solution at Emptoris, Inc. He has over twelve years of experience in the areas of procurement transformation, supply chain optimization, and content management. Since 2000, he has been working to design and elicit value from procurement processes and data to enable better spend visibility and savings.

Kirit has been with Emptoris since early 2005 when Emptoris acquired Intigma, a spend data management company that he co-founded in 2000. Intigma was one of the first companies to offer a disruptive technology for automating the conversion and enrichment of spend data so as to offer complete and accurate spend visibility. In 2004, Intigma was providing spend data management services to four of the top six spend analysis providers. In addition to being the CEO at Intigma, he played important roles in product management, key customer and channel relationships, and governance and financing efforts.

Prior to starting Intigma, Kirit spent four years at Deloitte Consulting, where he implemented supply chain optimization and e-procurement solutions for Fortune 500 customers. Prior to joining Deloitte, he spent six years at National Instruments in Austin, Texas as a Senior Design Engineer, where he developed cutting-edge products for the test and measurement industry.

He has published papers in scientific and business journals and has spoken at investor and industry forums. In 2006, he was the recipient of the "Pros to Know" award from *Supply and Demand Chain Magazine*.

Kirit holds a B.Tech. in Electrical Engineering from the Indian Institute of Technology, Bombay, and an M.S in Electrical Engineering as well as an M.B.A. from The University of Texas at Austin.

Haralambos Marmanis is Director of Research and Chief Architect of Spend Analysis and Compliance Solutions at Emptoris, Inc., where he introduced and implemented machine learning and data mining techniques in sourcing, content management, and spend analysis.* His work experience is quite diverse, ranging from network protocols, cardiovascular flow simulations, and microelectromechanical systems (MEMS) to trading applications, electronic marketplaces, and supply chain management.

Dr. Marmanis is a recipient of the Sigma Xi Outstanding Research Award (1999). His scientific work has received support from the National Science Foundation and his work on visualizing multivalued data has been featured on the cover page of the *Visualization '99* Conference Proceedings. He was an invited lecturer in the Joint Conference on Information Sciences (2007) and is the author of numerous publications in peer-reviewed international scientific journals and conference proceedings as well as in technical periodicals.

He holds a Ph.D. degree in Applied Mathematics from Brown University, an M.Sc. degree in Theoretical and Applied Mechanics from the University of Illinois at Urbana-Champaign, and a B.Sc. and an M.Sc. degree in Civil Engineering from the Aristotle University of Thessalonica.

---

* In 2004 Emptoris was the recipient of the INFORMS Franz Edelman award, presented by The Institute for Operations Research and the Management Sciences (INFORMS). In 2005, Forrester Research ranked the spend analysis solution of Emptoris as the "Best of the Best" with a perfect 5.0 score.

Web
Added
Value™

Free value-added materials available from
*the Download Resource Center at **www.jrosspub.com***

At J. Ross Publishing we are committed to providing today's professional with practical, hands-on tools that enhance the learning experience and give readers an opportunity to apply what they have learned. That is why we offer free ancillary materials available for download on this book and all participating Web Added Value™ publications. These online resources may include interactive versions of material that appears in the book or supplemental templates, worksheets, models, plans, case studies, proposals, spreadsheets, and assessment tools, among other things. Whenever you see the WAV™ symbol in any of our publications, it means bonus materials accompany the book and are available from the Web Added Value™ Download Resource Center at www.jrosspub.com.

Downloads available for *Spend Analysis: The Window into Strategic Sourcing* consist of spend analysis report templates for conveying complex multidimensional information and additional case studies on spend analysis return on investment.

PART I

PART 1

FUNDAMENTALS OF SPEND ANALYSIS

Every CFO's dream is to be able to cut millions of dollars in costs, not on a one-time basis, but annually—and to keep raising the bar for the procurement and operations teams to squeeze out additional savings year after year. Over the last few decades, most CEOs have focused on driving frontline revenue growth as a means of increasing EPS (earnings per share) and have often ignored or neglected the other side of the equation, namely, the cost. Now, the focus is slowly shifting. In today's global economy, in which more than half of your products and services might be sourced from suppliers in different countries, the ability to systematically manage a large and diverse supply base could well prove to be the single most important differentiator between leaders and laggards over the next 10 years.

Companies who understand this have already implemented strategic sourcing initiatives and are reaping handsome rewards. Take the example of Dave Picarillo, VP of Sourcing at BrainTree Sourcing, a division of Royal Ahold.[1] Ahold, as you might know, is responsible for sourcing goods and services for 6 grocery brands and more than 1200 supermarkets in the United States. Dave also oversees sourcing for Ahold's divisions that operate 85 warehouses which provide goods and equipment to restaurants throughout the United States. In the United States alone, Ahold spends more than $3 billion annually on indirect goods and services.

Ahold launched its strategic sourcing program in 2003. In 2 years, the program had yielded a mouth-watering savings of $350 million just on indirect procurement! What's more, the savings have kept growing each year. Ahold now expects to expand the program to private label goods, expecting to save 5 to 10%. So how did Dave accomplish this? What did he do that others should be paying attention to?

Ahold's biggest problem prior to this new strategic sourcing program was getting good visibility into their category spend. Ahold's traditional methods relied on distributed category teams submitting spreadsheets to the procurement team. Because of different standards and the differing quality of data, the spreadsheets and the data were not tightly organized at the corporate level. Therefore, Ahold was never able to get a clear, corporate-wide view of what it spent. Without this visibility, Ahold could not identify overall efficiencies and weaknesses of its sourcing process. With this in mind, the first step that Dave took was implementing a Web-based spend analysis application. With the new system, procurement and category managers at Ahold could get corporate-wide spend visibility through a Web browser from anywhere in the world. Managers could "slice and dice" the spend data in real time, identify opportunities for vendor consolidation and other savings, and generate actionable reports on a continuous basis, which gave Dave the foundation to implement an integrated Web-based supply management system which could be used to create and manage savings programs that could be monitored on a continuous basis.

In short, Dave replaced the ad hoc, disconnected sourcing processes with an integrated strategic program, which not only produced lower spending on goods and services, but also shortened the production conception to reception time in stores. The spend analysis application empowered category managers to review more spending projects in less time. The RFx (request for information/quote) portal allowed buyers and suppliers to collaboratively finalize requests for quotes, thus replacing the emails- and spreadsheets-based point-to-point system. Furthermore, the new system also made it possible to score supplier performance. Managers in different divisions can now rate the same supplier across different categories. Finally, Ahold can now leverage the optimized bidding and allocation capabilities of the tool to ensure that contracts for certain categories such as washing windows are given to local providers.

The payoff from such systems has been staggering to those on the cutting edge. According to a 2005 ROI leadership report in *Baseline Magazine*,[2] GlaxoSmithKline (GSK), a drug maker and distributor in the healthcare industry, boasts of an annual return of 5451% from its sourcing programs—and this is just the beginning. As companies gain more visibility and control in sourcing, they can hold suppliers more accountable, negotiate for better terms and conditions, and channel the learning process across the entire supply base. Managers at Ahold went through about 3 days of training, followed by biweekly meetings on best practices. Ahold incurred about $1 million in costs to implement the complete system. Thus the benefits of $350 million in savings far exceeded the cost.

WHAT IS SPEND ANALYSIS?

Spend analysis is the starting point of strategic sourcing and creates the foundation for spend visibility, compliance, and control. Spend analysis organizes procurement information via supplier hierarchies, commodity alignment, and spend amount, in order to:

- Ascertain true category spend
- Identify strategic sourcing opportunities through demand aggregation and supplier rationalization
- Identify expense reduction through increased compliance—in the form of vendor rebates, maverick spend, contract compliance, and budget variance

The savings can range from 2 to 25% of total spend.

Basics

Let us simplify the above definition even more. Put simply, spend analysis is a process of systematically analyzing the historical spend (purchasing) data of an organization in order to answer the following types of questions:

- What was the corporate-wide spend associated with each cost center last year? Does the aggregate amount enable me to increase leverage with suppliers?
- What are the top commodities? What has the spend trend been over the last few years? Which of these commodities represent opportunities for spend reduction?
- Which suppliers are the most valuable and strategic?
- How much am I spending with preferred suppliers? How much am I spending with poorly performing suppliers?
- What percentage of spend is associated with contracts?

The idea is to be able to examine these reports and identify opportunities for savings. For example, if the spend associated with nonpreferred suppliers is high, this category is clearly where spend "leakage" is occurring because the prices and terms negotiated with preferred suppliers are usually better than the prices and terms that are in effect with nonpreferred suppliers. Similarly, if a particular commodity is fragmented (i.e., is being sourced from many suppliers), this commodity could be consolidated into fewer suppliers and better prices could be negotiated by channeling a higher volume of spend through them.

If your purchasing or finance department can readily provide accurate answers to the above questions, then your company has perhaps already implemented a good spend analysis solution. If the latter is not the case, then you should challenge the accuracy of the answers. Chances are, though, that your purchasing department will not be able to provide the answers. In fact, there is a high likelihood that you will not receive even one answer. If that is the case, you are not alone. A vast majority of enterprises have not yet implemented spend analysis.

At this point, you might wonder what is so difficult about analyzing purchasing data. The above questions seem simple enough to answer. To understand this situation, take a look at Figure 1.1, which shows a few transactions pulled from the AP (accounts payable) systems of two divisions of a corporation. Examine these transactions and try to quickly answer the following questions:

1. How much did the company spend on personal computers?
2. How much did the company spend with IBM on software?
3. What was the spend associated with IT and professional services in Q3 and Q4 of 2006?

You will quickly figure out the challenges in analyzing this data. The two divisions have separate cost centers and separate GL (general ledger) codes, which have not been integrated. You may also have noticed that all of the transactions belong to IBM, but this might not be easily apparent if you did not know that Lotus Corporation, Ascential, and MRO Software are subsidiaries of IBM. You might also have noticed the many different variations of the name IBM. Also, the various fields in the two extracts are not identical. Division 2 transactions do not show commodity codes or SIC (standard industrial classification) codes. They do contain descriptions, but they are not very good.

In short, the data residing in business systems are many times not cleansed, enriched, consolidated, and organized at the corporate level. This makes it very difficult to make like comparisons. Moreover, the information is finance-centric. The various GL, cost center, and other codes were created to facilitate accounting, not purchasing. Figure 1.2 shows a procurement-centric view of the same spend, in which spend is aggregated by categories. This view is so much more meaningful! A few facts immediately catch your attention—Division 1 is spending much more money on IBM IT consulting than division 2 even though it is buying no servers from IBM and is spending less on maintenance than division 2. Why does division 1 have more consulting needs than division 2? Another fact that jumps out is that division 1 is not buying any servers from IBM and division 2 is not buying any personal computers from IBM. If they could consolidate their individual demand and source both these from IBM, could they negotiate better prices?

Division 1

Vendor Name	GL Name	Cost Center Name	SIC Code	Commodity	Date	Amount
IBM	Maintenance	Data Center	NULL	IT equipment and services	1/1/2006	$4,123,421
International Business Machines	Capital outlays	Internal IT Services	PCs	IT equipment and services	4/5/2006	$5,894,639
IBM.COM/SHOP	Capital outlays	Internal IT Services	PCs	IT equipment and services	5/6/2006	$4,452,621
Intl Biz Machines	Professional services	Department 44	NULL	IT equipment and services	7/20/2006	$15,191,821
IBM Consulting	Professional services	Trading Desk Europe	NULL	IT equipment and services	9/1/2006	$11,231,611
IBM Global Services	AP/Other	Network Project	NULL	IT equipment and services	9/24/2006	$31,480,165
Lotus Notes	Capital outlays	Internal IT Services	NULL	IT equipment and services	10/1/2006	$17,204,865
Total						**$89,579,143**

Division 2

Vendor Name	GL Name	Cost Center Name	Description	Date	Amount
IBM	MRO	IT	External Hard Drives	1/3/2006	$74,804
Intl Bus Machines	Capital expenses	IT	Server x3550	4/4/2006	$2,155,250
IBM Asia	Capital outlays	IT	System x3850 Express	5/6/2006	$3,453,890
IBM Asia	IT maintenance	IT	SW renewal	7/15/2006	$10,620,000
IBM Glob Serv	IT services	Telecom	Network audit	8/8/2006	$8,250,400
IBM Glob Serv	IT services	Telecom	Network audit	9/2/2006	$2,541,629
Ascential	Capital expenses	Catalog operations	SW maintenance 15%	10/6/2006	$2,229,990
MRO Soft	IT maintenance	Catalog operations	Integration consulting	10/15/2006	$4,150,115
MRO SW	Capital expenses	Catalog operations	Maximo implementation	11/4/2006	$6,666,330
Total					**$40,142,408**

Figure 1.1. Transactions from the AP systems of two divisions.

Category	Division 1	Division 2
Computer maintenance	$4,123,421	$13,022,019
Personal computers	$10,347,260	$0
IT consulting	$57,903,597	$10,816,445
Software	$17,204,865	$10,620,000
Servers		$5,683,944
Total	**$89,579,143**	**$40,142,408**

Figure 1.2. A procurement-centric presentation of the spend in Figure 1.1 which has been aggregated by category.

Now extend this analysis to millions of transactions across hundreds of systems and you will begin to appreciate the challenges as well as the power of spend analysis. For example, Figure 1.3 illustrates a report that shows the top ten commodities by spend. This report is very useful because it immediately shows the commodities that you should be focusing on for cost reduction based on spend volume alone. However, this report does not give you much information as to whether the opportunities are related to supplier consolidation, maverick spend, contract compliance, or others. This report also does not tell you how easy or complex it will be to source these commodities. Thus, you would need to overlay other reports on this report in order to pinpoint the exact opportunities.

A glance at Figure 1.4 immediately reveals the fact that professional services is the most fragmented commodity. Professional services might represent a better opportunity for supplier consolidation than electronic components, even though it has a lower spend.

If spend analysis is so useful, why haven't companies widely implemented it? In a survey of 400 procurement professionals conducted by *Supply and Demand Chain Magazine*, just one third (32%) of respondents reported that their companies use spend analysis all the time to help set a baseline for sourcing activities, and only 20% reported that they currently use spend analysis software.[3]

What are the reasons for such low adoption? First of all, we are talking about analyzing not a few hundred or a few thousand transactions or even a few million. We are talking about tens or hundreds of millions of transactions. The sheer volume of data makes this an enterprise-class application. Yet there is more to the complexity of the situation than just the volume of the data. A total of 41% of the respondents ranked their inability to get data from disparate systems as the greatest challenge to effectively gathering the raw information necessary for spend

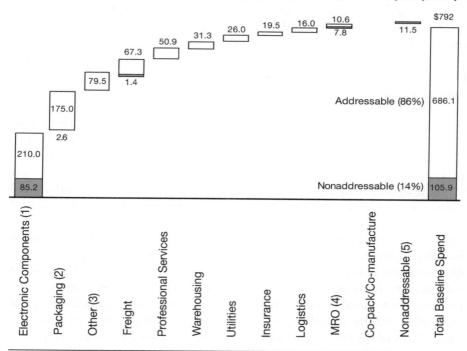

Figure 1.3. The top ten commodities by spend (addressable spend of $600 million). MM, millions.

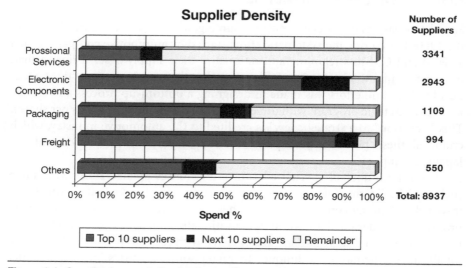

Figure 1.4. Supplier fragmentation for the top five commodities.

analysis, and 31% said that they lacked the analytical tools necessary to identify savings opportunities. Consequently, 74% of respondents said they are still using desktop software such as spreadsheets and databases moderately or extensively for spend analysis.

The challenges are not all technical. A majority of respondents (54%) cited the absence of a strategic sourcing process and the mindset within their organizations as key limitations to improving their procurement processes, while 32% pointed to a lack of organizational know-how as a limiting factor.

It is not surprising, then, that 56% of the respondents reported that use of spend analysis at their companies was limited either to individual locations or to a single division, while just 44% reported being able to use spend analysis on a cross-divisional basis.

In Chapter 3 (*How to Implement a Successful Spend Analysis Program*), we will discuss all of the challenges and best practices for implementing a successful spend analysis program. To embark on that journey, perhaps it might be beneficial to review the history of spend analysis, which will give us a general sense of how the requirements in this area, and the corresponding complexity in the spend analysis applications, have evolved. Then, we will examine the data warehouse approach and investigate if ETLA, or the "Extract→Transform→Load→Analyze" process, which is used to build a traditional data warehouse, is applicable to spend analysis. As it turns out, the spend analysis requirements present various challenges that make it rather difficult for traditional data warehousing to support.

HISTORY OF SPEND ANALYSIS

Spend analysis has its roots in strategic sourcing, which is a term coined loosely in the 1980s to describe the systematic effort started by automotive companies such as Ford and GM to streamline and rationalize their supply base.[4] Prior to that, most companies were pursuing similar goals, but these goals were mostly at a tactical level, and no effort was made in designing a bottom-up process and elevating it to a strategic program with direct influence on the EPS (earnings per share). This "elevation" to a strategic level is credited to the automotive industry, which endorsed these practices perhaps as a direct response to the success of the Japanese companies.

Soon, a number of specialized consulting houses opened shop, with some such as A.T. Kearney at one time having hundreds of consultants worldwide involved in helping companies reduce their purchasing costs. Most of the early programs were designed around supplier rationalization in key commodities. The idea was to identify aggregate spend associated with each supplier, and then to use intelligent segmentation techniques to retain some suppliers and consolidate/

eliminate others that were not deemed to be strategically important. Most of the "spend analysis" was thus done only at a supplier level and sometimes at the division and/or cost center level. Often, the DUNS (Dun and Bradstreet, D&B) classification was used to categorize suppliers.

This approach to spend analysis yielded enormous success by the early and mid 1990s, and early supply chain and ERP vendors tried to enter the area with elementary offerings. Most work in the mid to late 1990s was being done by consultants who were targeting indirect spend commodities. With the enormous success of FreeMarkets in their reverse auctions strategy for direct materials, this discipline was formalized into SRM (supplier relationship management) with the emergence of a new class of enterprise vendors such as Ariba and Emptoris that offered integrated modules such as RFx, reverse auctions, bid optimization, supplier performance, and spend analysis for creating and managing an end-to-end supply management program.

In the early 2000s, there was a "horizontal" shift in categories. The early successes in the indirect spend categories paved the way for expansion into MRO (maintenance, repair, and operations) and direct materials. In the last few years, we have also seen "vertical" movement. The low-hanging opportunities in vendor consolidation had already been addressed. Companies now wanted a deeper, granular "look" to identify opportunities such as product consolidation (products that are functionally equivalent), item price variance, unrealized rebates and volume discounts, and others. This desire for a deeper, granular look created the need for much more advanced enrichment platforms (identifying functionally duplicate items is not a very easy exercise) on the one hand and a more demanding application to identify these opportunities on the other hand. Spend analysis thus became the "window" into strategic sourcing—it was the front end that helped identify opportunities and also a back end that helped monitoring and tracking of these savings. In other words, spend analysis became a "must have" for any sensible strategic sourcing program.

Specialist Vendors

The year 2001 marked the arrival of specialist "automated spend analysis" application vendors—Zeborg and Verticalnet in 2001, followed by Softface. In 2002, Aentropy and Zycus appeared with slightly different offerings. Specialist consulting outfits such as Tigris and Silver Oak Solutions used analytic tools along with consultants to address the all-manual approach used in the past.

There was also movement on the pure content side. D&B and Austin-Tetra started offering services for supplier intelligence. Pure content providers such as Intigma developed cutting-edge technology for classification and offered subcontracting services to major spend analysis providers.

Consolidation

Ketera acquired Aentropy in 2002. Emptoris bought Zeborg in September 2003 and Intigma in early 2005. In January 2004, Verticalnet acquired Tigris to gain its vendor and product classification expertise and consultants. Ariba picked up Softface in February 2004. Procuri purchased Truesource (a new entrant) in late 2006, followed by the acquisition of Austin-Tetra by Equifax. Expectations are that the ERP vendors will soon follow suit in this phase of consolidation.

SIMILARITIES/DIFFERENCES BETWEEN SPEND ANALYSIS AND DATA WAREHOUSING

Most companies that decide to implement a spend analysis solution go through a build-or-buy decision, which is usually influenced by (if not made by) the IT department which is required to support the applications. Many companies, having already invested millions of dollars in implementing a data warehouse solution, seek to extend these solutions in order to support spend analysis. After all, data warehousing involves pulling periodic transactional data from ERP and other business systems into a dedicated database and running analytical reports on that database. It seems logical to think that this approach can be used effectively to capture and analyze purchasing (spend) data.

Indeed, using this approach is possible. However, from both a technical and a process perspective, spend analysis offers unique challenges that must be understood, and the solutions must be properly designed in order to make this work. The authors have heard about a few success stories, but many more failed implementations, when customers have tried to use existing data warehouses for spend analysis.

Some of the reasons why many data warehousing initiatives fail to deliver on spend analysis include:

- Raw transactional data are loaded "as is." The data are not cleansed or enriched in any way, resulting in inaccurate spend classification and reports that lack credibility.
- Scope creep causes report and data requirements to increase, resulting in performance issues (reports take a long time to run), which in turn causes low adoption.
- Knowledge assimilation is not designed into the system. Therefore, the incremental variable cost of analyzing new spend data does not decrease and that, in turn, negatively affects the ROI, which especially impacts M&A (merger and acquisition) activity because post-merger cost of spend analysis ends up being more expensive.

From a technical perspective, most data warehouse implementations use an ETLA (Extract→Transform→Load→Analyze) approach:[5]

- Extract—Extract the information from the various IT systems.
- Transform—Normalize and enrich the data.
- Load—Load the data into a database.
- Analyze—Create a library of reports to mine the data.

At a high level, spend analysis also uses an ETLA approach: spend transaction data need to be Extracted and Transformed, Loaded into a database, and Analyzed. However, there is more to it than that. Let us examine the ETLA process in more detail to see where and how spend analysis differs.

Let us start with "E" or Extract. Here, the requirements are quite similar. Spend data are very rarely in one system. Spend data reside in different IT systems that are spread out across various divisions that are geographically dispersed and in many different languages. For example, a company such as Tyco has over a hundred divisions, each having multiple IT systems. These systems are managed by different groups that might not report into a centralized IT department. They are seldom integrated. For example, we have done implementations in which the spend transaction feeds come from over a hundred different systems on tens of ERP platforms including legacy systems across tens of subdivisions on four continents. Synchronization of the data extracts often becomes tricky in such situations.

Let us move on to the "T'" or Transform. In spend analysis, the end goal is to aggregate and organize spend (i.e., transaction amounts) in order to facilitate the analysis that is based on supplier, category, division, etc. We call this process "transforming." In spend analysis, this process has some unique considerations:

Quality of vendor data. The same vendor might be entered differently in different transactions. For example, we saw how a company like IBM might be entered as I.B.M., International Business Machines, IBM Global Services, or any one of many other variations. Furthermore, due to M&A activities, two different suppliers (e.g., Lotus Corp. and IBM) might in fact be one and the same supplier (IBM). Thus, there is a need to consolidate this spend and associate it with a "parent" company.

Quality of transactional data. Transactional data are invariably poorly formatted and incomplete. Duplicate records are common. Commodity code assignments might be missing, be incorrect, or not be detailed enough. Item descriptions might be blank or of poor quality. Unless these fields are cleansed, assigning proper commodity codes to these transactions (i.e., classifying these transactions to a commodity schema) becomes difficult.

Quality of category schema. A good commodity schema is at the heart of a good spend analysis program because most opportunities are found by commodity managers who have years of experience in procuring items in their commodities. Unfortunately, commodity codes used in the material master files are often at too high a level for purposes of detailed spend analysis, which means the schema needs to be modified. What is more, this modification is not a one-time exercise. Good commodity schemas evolve constantly. They grow both horizontally (i.e., new commodities are added) and vertically (commodities are broken down into sub-commodities); therefore, this process of maintaining the schema is a continuous exercise. Many companies are now adopting industry standard schemas (more on that later) so that they can utilize the learning from the peers and enable benchmarking exercises.

Type of data enrichment needed. It might not be enough to clean up the vendor files. It might also be necessary to enrich the vendor lists with additional information, such as diversity, credit ratings, quality ratings, etc. Similarly it might not be possible to accurately classify transactions to the commodity schema without improving the quality of the descriptions by incorporating product data sheets.

The "T" in spend analysis is thus of critical importance because the effectiveness of spend analysis is determined largely by how accurately and quickly transactions (that have poor information) are classified to an evolving commodity structure. This means that the commodity managers *must* have some control in approving the schema evolutions, as well as the assignment of commodity codes. What is even more important is that this information must be stored and leveraged in processing new transactions. This continuous feedback cycle is what enables the spend application to "learn" as it grows and become increasingly more accurate over time. Most traditional data warehouse approaches rely on static metadata schemas that have very rigid security and access controls. They are built to capture periodic data from transaction systems that can be analyzed. Good spend analysis applications are "knowledgebase systems" and not pure analytical systems. This is not to say that data warehouses cannot be designed to meet these requirements. In fact, most database applications today have a powerful library of data mining and analysis functions and have been successfully used in a variety of knowledge management functions.

Now let us look at the "A" or Analyze. Assuming enrichment is somehow achieved and the data are loaded into a database, appropriate reports will need to be run. Many companies who have attempted to analyze spend by implementing a reporting engine on top of a data warehouse have reported several limitations. The initial reports prepared by the IT department fall short on delivering the required information. Often, they are finance-centric and not procurement-centric. The turnaround time to get the reports modified can be weeks and sometimes months. Moreover, the clarity and accuracy of the reports are often questionable because the data have not been enriched. Experienced strategic sourcing professionals know that identifying savings opportunities is really an art rather than a science. The "aha" moment usually comes when the user has a procurement-centric view of the data and is "slicing and dicing" the data and looking at all spend patterns (by supplier, by geography, by commodity, by buyer, etc.) simultaneously. Running a number of static reports one by one does not yield this "discovery" experience. Instead, specialized visualization tools that aid in this "explore and discover" process are what is needed. These powerful analyzers can present both a high-level and a transactional-level view of the data in near real time. This topic will be covered in more detail in Chapter 8 (*Technology Considerations*), but suffice it to say that designing such visualization tools with a good response time that scales to hundreds of concurrent users is a fairly tricky technological challenge.

CHARACTERISTICS OF AN IDEAL SPEND ANALYSIS APPLICATION

The ETLA process can help us understand the components that make up a good spend analysis application:

1. Data definition and loading (DDL)
2. Data cleansing, structure, and enrichment (DE)
3. Spend data analytics (SA)
4. Knowledgebase management (KB)

These components will be revisited in several chapters in Part II. Chapter 6 (*Spend Analysis Components*) is devoted to a detailed discussion of each of these components. In this chapter, we will present a brief overview.

Data Definition and Loading (DDL)

Deciding what data are required for your spend analysis program is the first decision that you have to make. You will certainly want to have some critical information available to you, such as transaction date, transaction description, vendor name, and spend amount. However, there is usually an abundance of additional data that can be extremely valuable for the success of your spend analysis.

The data are typically located on many different systems. Thus, the extraction of the data will be performed by integrating multiple heterogeneous data sources, such as delimited files, relational databases, Excel files, and so on. All of these data have different schemas and, quite frequently, different semantics. Consistency of

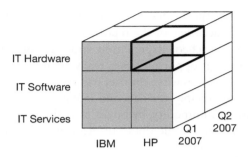

Figure 1.5. A simple three-dimensional cube.

the data, across the sources and over time, is critical during the data identification and extraction phase. Once the data have been identified, the goal is to extract them so that they are inserted in a common schema. Data warehouses for spend analysis are usually structured as multidimensional data models. The latter models are, in essence, a collection of multidimensional functions.[6]

Let us clarify this point. Dimensional modeling divides the world into measurements and context. Measurements are actual numerical quantities that are associated with one or more contexts. So, for instance, in the world of spend analysis, at a high level, you might want to see your spend in United States dollars (USD) aggregated by supplier, commodity, cost center, division, geography, and time. Thus, in this case, spend is the "measurement" or "measure" or "fact." Supplier, commodity, cost center, division, geography, and time are contexts or "dimensions." (Other examples of measures are supplier count, transaction count, and budget variance.) In the remainder of the book, we will use the terms "dimensions" and "measures." The word "dimension" is actually very fitting because it lets you envision a spend hypercube whose intersection points correspond to a spend measure. Thus, the total spend (also called the "top of the cube" spend) could be, say, $4 billion. To find the spend associated with specific commodities and suppliers, you can "enter" the cube and start traversing the intersection points of these commodities with the different suppliers. We call this process "drilling" into the cube. We call the points of intersection "drill points." Note also, that for convenience, in the rest of the book, we will refer to a "hypercube" simply as a "cube" even though a hypercube has more than three dimensions.

Figure 1.5 shows how a simple three-dimensional cube looks. The commodity dimension has three records or "nodes"—IT Services, IT Hardware, and IT Software. The vendor dimension has two nodes—HP and IBM. The time dimension has two nodes—Q1, 2007 and Q2, 2007. Thus, the spend associated with HP's IT Hardware in Q1, 2007 corresponds to the subcube highlighted in the top right corner. Figure 1.6 shows the structure of the flattened cube. Only the dimen-

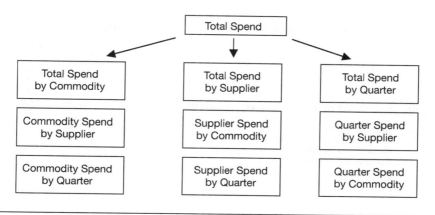

Figure 1.6. A flattened cube.

sions are depicted. If we decide to show individual "nodes" in each dimension, the total number of boxes will increase to 15 (12 for each point of intersection plus the 3 boxes that show the total spend for each dimension).

The reader can now expand this to a hypercube with more dimensions and understand conceptually how the dimensional/measure model is constructed. Dimensional models are represented in various ways. The simplest and most widely used is called the "star" schema, which consists of a table that contains the transactions and a set of dimensional tables that are linked to it by standard foreign key relationships. If you spread the dimensional tables around the transaction table, and you possess a certain degree of imagination, the graph will look like a star; hence, the name of the schema. Figure 1.7 shows such a schema for our simple example of a three-dimensional cube. Each record in the transaction table contains the measurements on the points of intersection in the cube. This model will be covered in more detail in Chapter 6 (*Spend Analysis Components*).

Data Cleansing, Structure, and Enrichment (DE)

An application that addresses this stage of spend analysis must have the following features:

Web-centric with Admin and restricted access privileges. The content enrichment team might be a distributed team, with some members of the team located offshore and some members working at the division and plant levels. User access might need to be restricted to particular commodities or cost centers, so users do not accidentally go beyond their domain of expertise.

Data cleansing and enrichment. As we saw earlier, in order to get accurate spend visibility, vendors need to be "familied" and clustered and transactions need

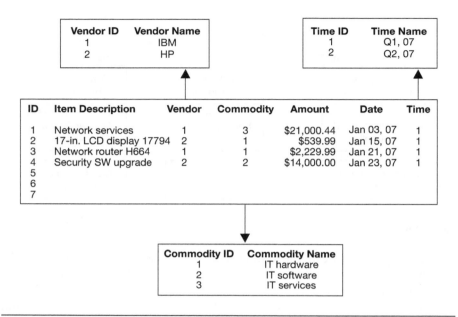

Figure 1.7. A star schema for a simple three-dimensional cube.

to be classified to an appropriate commodity structure. These tasks can be accomplished through application of rules. For example, a simple rule could be "If vendor = IBM, classify spend to IT Services." Rules could be created manually, or they could be synthesized by computers through an approach known as machine learning. Rules could end up conflicting with each other. For example, the rule "If vendor = IBM and cost center = data center, classify spend to IT Hardware" would conflict with the previous rule.

Thus, the data enrichment function should be comprised of:

- Vendor enrichment
- Transaction classification
- Rules engines with conflict resolution

Figure 1.8 shows the results after vendor consolidation. Figure 1.9 shows commodity spend after transactional classification.

Hierarchy and dimensional editing. Commodity, supplier, cost center, and other schemas evolve over time. Moreover, there might be multiple administrators of each schema. For example, each commodity manager might have partial control of the structure of his or her commodity. Distributed, restricted, and controlled editing of the dimensional structures is needed to ensure proper evolution of these schemas.

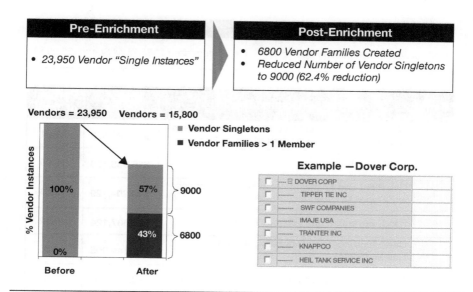

Figure 1.8. Vendor "familying," an important step in showing true vendor spend.

Job scheduling. Because spend datasets are very large in size, the job run times are usually in hours and not minutes, thus making job scheduling and event notification an important function.

Import of feedback from end users of the system. We have mentioned how important it is for users to collectively and iteratively improve the accuracy of spend categorizations. This function should be able to collect all feedback, resolve conflicting feedback, generate rules, and autoprocess those rules.

Spend Data Analytics (SA)

An application that addresses the SA stage of spend analysis must be able to perform the following functions:

1. Web-centric application with Admin and restricted access privileges
2. Specialized visualization tools
3. Reporting and dashboards
4. Feedback submission for suggesting changes to dimensional hierarchy
5. Feedback submission for suggesting changes to classification
6. Immediate update of new data
7. "What-if" analysis capability

Pre-Classification	Post-Classification
• $1060MM Uncategorized Spend	• Categorized $885.7MM Spend (92.99%)

Rank	UNSPSC Commodity	Spend	Percent of Total
1	Material Handling and Conditioning and Storage Machinery and Their Accessories and Supplies	$27,182,570	25.64
2	Published Products	$16,958,170	16.00
3	Live Plant and Animal Material and Accessories and Supplies	$10,204,129	9.63
4	Food, Beverage, and Tobacco Products	$9,667,124	9.12
5	Chemicals including Biochemicals and Gas Materials	$5,149,995	4.86
6	Industrial Production and Manufacturing Services	$3,043,181	2.87
7	Building and Construction and Maintenance Services	$2,696,808	2.54
8	Farming and Fishing and Forestry and Wildlife Machinery and Accessories	$2,534,392	2.39
9	Management and Business Professionals and Administrative Services	$2,476,937	2.34
10	Distribution and Conditioning Systems and Equipment and Components	$1,844,712	1.74

Figure 1.9. Transactional classification reveals true commodity spend. MM, millions.

The applications that are employed in this stage allow users to "slice and dice" the data; run, export and share reports; and perform any kind of analysis that might be required.

Knowledgebase Management (KB)

At the heart of a good spend analysis solution is the ability to "learn" and classify spend more accurately. This is accomplished via a closed-loop technique, wherein the information associated with every "click" made by a user is fed back into a knowledgebase or lexicon of industry-specific information. The idea is to leverage this information and improve classification accuracy over time. For example, consider a simple case of an item with a description "SCR 4-40 × 1/8." Based simply on the abbreviation SCR, a classifier might interpret this part to be a screw, a silicon controlled rectifier, a satellite channel router, a single cable router, or several other items. Obviously, the reason why the classifier fails the first time around with a 75% probability is because the knowledgebase did not know about this abbreviation relative to the industry domain. Neither did it know how to interpret the string "4-40 × 1/8." If this new information is recognized as attributes of a screw and is stored, the classifier accuracy will improve the next time it encounters such a description.

The lexicon consists of three entities—concepts, instances, and relationships:

- Concepts are abstract notions such as nouns, qualifiers, attributes, UOMs (units of measure), etc.

- Instances are specific occurrences in real life. For example, use of "Dell 17" Plasma Monitor" is an instance of a description that has concepts such as proper nouns (Dell), common nouns (plasma and monitor), an attribute (17), and a UOM (inches).

- Relationships are structural and semantic connections between concepts. Certain relationship libraries are commonly available. For example, natural language (NL) relationships govern how concepts can be concatenated together. Thus, "Plasma Monitor" and "Monitor Plasma" have completely separate meanings. Similarly, the items "waste paper basket" and "trash can" can have an association if the words "waste" and "trash" are listed as synonyms of each other. Such NL libraries can be purchased off the shelf. Relationships can also be created manually. For example, the concept "Dell" could be associated with the concept "information technology." Finally, relationships can be derived or synthesized using various techniques. For example, by analyzing historic commodity assignments, probabilistic associative rules can be constructed.

The classifiers in spend analysis use the relationships information in the lexicon to enrich and classify the spend data. The richer the lexicon, the more accurate the classifications will be.

Knowledgebase managers are applications that allow the management of the entries in the knowledgebase. Change management is critical, so an approval workflow should be incorporated in such systems. In Chapter 8 (*Technology Considerations*), we will discuss classification techniques and knowledgebases in detail.

SUMMARY

In this chapter, we laid down the basics of spend analysis—its definition, its scope, the differences between spend analysis and data warehousing, and key features of good spend analysis applications. We reviewed the history of spend analysis in order to better understand how the requirements have morphed and how the vendors have beefed up their offerings in order to support them. We also looked at the requirements in spend analysis that need special data enrichment and which make it difficult to successfully implement spend analysis using classic data warehousing programs. Most transactions have poor-quality information that needs to be cleansed and enriched in order to be accurately classified. Most vendor master files also need to be processed. Parent corporations need to be linked to their subsidiaries in order to provide corporate-level spend visibility. We also briefly examined the main components of a spend analysis application, namely, data definition and loading (DDL), data enrichment (DE), spend analytics (SA), and knowledgebase management (KB). Each of these subjects will be explored in greater detail in Part II.

REFERENCES

1. *Internet Retailer.* The new reality of sourcing—how Ahold saves $350 million through web based sourcing—for starters, that is. February 2005.

2. *Baseline Magazine.* 2005 ROI Leadership Awards. July 2005.

3. Andrew K. Reese. Spend analysis a top priority, but not widely adopted ... yet. *Supply and Demand Chain.* March 2004.

4. Forrester Research. *Spend Analysis: Key App, Few Vendors.* July 2004.

5. Warren Thornthwaite. *From Bauhaus to Warehouse: Understanding Data Warehouse Architecture Requirements.* Phoenix, AZ: DCI Data Warehouse Summit; December 1998.

6. Ralph Kimball. Fact tables and dimension tables: the logical foundations for dimensional modeling. *Intelligent Enterprise.* January 1, 2003.

BUSINESS IMPERATIVE AND RETURN ON INVESTMENT

In order to achieve ongoing cost reduction targets, companies systematically launch high-impact savings initiatives to leverage purchasing volume, consolidate suppliers, and reduce off-contract spend. However, without a comprehensive understanding of corporate-wide spending patterns, effectively identifying and prioritizing such savings opportunities will be impossible. In other words, you will not know where to save unless you know where you are spending. Therefore, managers, executives, and analysts need quick and easy access to a consolidated, accurate, and granular view of corporate spend.

SPEND LEAKAGE AND COMPLIANCE MULTIPLIER

In the supply management best-seller, *Straight to the Bottom Line™: An Executive's Roadmap to World Class Supply Management*, authors Robert A. Rudzki, Douglas Smock, Michael Katzorke, and Shelley Stewart list the savings that are possible in some of the more common commodities (reproduced in Figure 2.1).[1] After examining Figure 2.1, the obvious question to ask is—"So where do these savings come from?" Three main components contribute to these savings:

- Strategic sourcing that includes identifying strategic vendors and moving toward vendor consolidation for purposes of volume discounts and higher quality

What Is Possible in Cost Reduction?

Category	Benchmarks
Raw materials	2–5% + Better Risk Management
Packaging	10–20%
Indirect materials and services	10–20%
Information technology	15–30%
Professional services	8–15%
Capital projects	7–15%
Other indirects	5–15%
Media, marketing, promotional items	10–20%
Logistics/transportation	7–15%

Figure 2.1. Possible savings in some common commodities. (© 2006 by Rudzki, Smock, Katzorke, and Stewart. Reprinted with permission.)

- Reducing maverick spend through preferred suppliers and better processes
- Avoiding spend leakage by monitoring compliance to negotiated terms

The last component is especially important because if the proper controls are not put in place, any negotiated savings captured in the contracts might leak out. These three components need to be iterated into a continuous cycle—call this cycle the spend management program. A properly executed spend management program can, over a period of time, deliver continuous savings in all of the major categories.

Figure 2.2a (a hypothetical example) shows the impact of contract compliance on the savings goal.[1] The percent of noncompliance is multiplied by the total potential benefit from the contract to arrive at a figure for dollars of lost opportunity. To illustrate the sensitivity of contract compliance to savings, Rudzki et al. introduce the notion of the compliance multiplier, which is illustrated in Figure 2.2b.[2] The idea behind this concept is that if you can negotiate a 10% cost reduction with your supplier, the actual savings that are realized really depend on how much contract compliance is achieved. If only 25% compliance is achieved, then the net savings per $10 million in spend is only $250,000. Increase this compliance to 85% and you get an $850,000 reduction in spend. Chapter 10 (*Spend Analysis*

Contract	Percent of Noncompliance	Percent of Annual Spend	Contract Benefit	Lost Opportunity
Office supplies	30%	$5,000,000	30%	$450,000
PCs	15%	$3,000,000	15%	$67,500
Services X	40%	$7,000,000	10%	$280,000
Raw materials Y	10%	$10,000,000	5%	$50,000
Average noncompliance				
• Simple average	26.25%			
• $ Weighted average	23%			
Lost $ Opportunity/Year				$847,500

Figure 2.2a. Lost opportunity calculator. (© 2006 by Rudzki, Smock, Katzorke, and Stewart. Reprinted with permission.)

Percent of Cost Reduction	25%	50%	75%	85%	95%
5	$125,000	$250,000	$375,000	$425,000	$475,000
10	$250,000	$500,000		$850,000	$950,000
15	$375,000	$750,000	$1,125,000	$1,275,000	$1,425,000
20	$500,000	$1,000,000	$1,500,000	$1,700,000	$1,900,000
25	$620,000	$1,250,000	$1,875,000	$2,125,000	$2,375,000
30	$750,000	$1,500,000	$2,250,000	$2,550,000	$2,850,000

($ to the Bottom Line for Each $10 Million of Spend)

Best Practices + Good Compliance = $ to the Bottom Line

Figure 2.2b. Compliance multiplier. (© Greybeard Advisors LLC. Reprinted with permission.)

and Compliance) discusses contract and payment compliance in more detail and addresses the areas which need to be monitored more carefully.

Importance of Spend Analysis within Supply Management

All of the above-described savings are not just theoretically possible—they have been achieved by deploying advanced supply management solutions by some of the leading companies in the world. In these deployments, spend analysis plays a pivotal role because no real spend management program can effectively commence until you know where your current spend is.

In many companies, the purchasing departments have a working knowledge of which commodities are ripe for vendor consolidation or price improvements. Thus, in the last 5 years, many companies have used such domain expertise and have achieved savings in certain key commodities by directly performing reverse auctions.

While such tactical opportunities can be exploited, they can only take you so far. While they might yield a one-time price reduction, you might not know if there are other commodities that have bigger opportunities because of a recent acquisition that your company has made—or how many of the same vendors are supplying the same goods or services to another division within your organization under a different contract. You also might not know whether you have enough controls in place today to ensure that the negotiated savings will actually be realized. Thus, in the absence of clear, complete, and precise spend visibility, such savings are opportunistic at best and should be avoided.

On the back side, spend analysis also forms the basis of monitoring and measuring your progress in reaching your savings targets. Each month you can track how much maverick spend is being driven through preferred suppliers, price, volume, and budget variances and calculate where you are relative to the final savings target. If preferred vendor spend is not increasing, it might mean a faulty order process, wherein the buyers are not being steered to using preferred vendors. If the price discounts are not being captured, this means contract compliance is not being monitored. Monitoring and measuring your progress will allow you to take corrective actions early in the process to plug the spend leakages.

BENEFITS TO BUSINESSES

Web-based spend analysis solutions provide the foundation for viewing corporate-wide spend data while relieving the manual tasks associated with creating reports and trends. Information is directly accessible by end users and updated regularly, thus providing an accurate and consistent view of spend over time. A typical solution provides the capability to view predefined reports and create ad hoc analyses through multidimensional filtering, cross-tabular reports, pivot tables, and charts along various dimensions, such as commodity, vendor, cost center, geography, etc.

Specific benefits include:

- Comprehensive visibility into all corporate spend
- Vastly improved data accuracy and consistency
- Quality and depth of analysis that usually improves dramatically over time

- Reduction in cycle time for creating custom reports and ad hoc analyses from up to 2 weeks to near instantaneous
- Reduction of off-contract spend to leverage volume savings (up to 15% savings from preferred rates)
- Elimination of full-time data extraction specialists to format and cleanse data and create custom reports ($60,000 per year each)
- Reduction of corporate purchasing card bypass, reducing administrative costs for processing a PO (purchase order) or check. (Industry data indicates a savings range of $20 to $100 per PO.)
- Rapid identification and prioritization of the largest savings opportunities
- Incremental savings through supplier consolidation and volume purchasing
- Additional savings through identification of contract negotiation opportunities
- Elimination of supplier overpayments and guaranteed capture of rebates
- Continuous compliance improvement and additional savings by monitoring actual versus targeted savings
- Reduction of procurement's reliance on an overextended IT staff to provide purchasing data
- Elimination of disagreements over data quality with a credible "source of truth" for all spend

The matrix in Figure 2.3 summarizes these benefits.

ESTIMATION OF SPEND ANALYSIS RETURN ON INVESTMENT

Spend analysis is used to identify opportunities for savings. The actual savings are realized through use of advanced sourcing techniques such as Web-based RFI, RFQ, optimized bidding, etc. Depending on the sourcing complexity of the various commodities, not all estimated savings can be realized. Because of these dependencies and uncertainties, it is often difficult to calculate the ROI associated with a spend analysis implementation (by itself). However, with some assumptions, you can calculate a fairly accurate ROI as described below. The following discussion illustrates how to estimate ROI by reducing unapproved supplier spend.

Benefit Category	Benefits
Sourcing savings	Increased understanding of spend by category, by supplier and supplier parent, and by business unit
Supplier management	Rebate management
	Volume commitment risk management
	Contract and price audits
	Best price comparisons
Reduction of maverick buying	Identify user groups buying from unapproved suppliers and through nonapproved channels or off-deal
	Ensure company achieves volume commitments
Savings tracking and enforcement	Ability to ensure negotiated savings and demand management initiatives puts savings on the bottom line by identifying affected G/L accounts and categories and tracking expenditures over time (e.g., you can track spend by category or G/L code and business unit to see if spending is actually going down or if users are just buying more at a cheaper price)
e-Procurement system rollout support	Identify spend outside of e-procurement system by category and business area — can target noncompliance and track progress
Corporate card and P-card program support	Identify candidate suppliers and categories to move to a card program
	Identify users not taking advantage of the card program
General ledger coding cleanup	Improved financial reporting and budget preparation — review and rationalize what G/L code each business area is using for similar purchases — quickly identify areas for corrective action
Management reporting	Quick access to aggregate and detailed information organized around multiple dimensions
	Elimination or reassignment of staff performing manual or Excel-based spend and financial analysis
	Ability to balance P&L statement expenses to the A/P — requires a custom enhancement as discussed in the letter to DA dated Feb 25/03
e-Billing and invoicing consolidation	Identify opportunities to reduce the number of POs processed and checks cut by identifying suppliers who should consolidate invoices or move to e-billing
Customer relationship management	Enables relationship management clarity for the commercial side of the bank where a supplier is also a customer (or should be a customer)

Figure 2.3. Various benefits associated with spend analysis.

Benefit Type	Savings Calculation
Enables savings	Other clients estimate an additional 6–10% savings on sourcing through better information
Direct savings	Ability to track when volume-based rebates should apply
Cost avoidance	Track progress against volume commitments to reduce risk of paying penalties
Direct savings	Ensure suppliers are meeting pricing commitments (when unit price detail is available)
Direct savings	Compare prices paid for like goods and services (when unit price detail is available)
Enables savings	Maverick spend can be as high as 33% Savings from buying on negotiated contract are 5–15%
Enables savings	Ensure volume goes to suppliers with a commitment
Cost avoidance	Ensure sourcing savings and demand management savings are realized
Enables savings	Savings from buying on negotiated contract are 5–15%
Soft dollars	Increased penetration and speed of rollout
Direct revenue	Increased card revenue (if it is a bank-issued card)
Soft dollars	Improved financial reporting and budget preparation — improved analysis
Direct savings or soft dollars	Reduced labor costs or reassignment to more productive tasks
Direct savings or soft dollars	Reduced labor costs or reassignment to more productive tasks
Direct savings or soft dollars	Reduced labor costs or reassignment to more productive tasks
Enables savings	Savings of the cost for processing a PO or check; industry data indicates range of $20–$100 per PO
Soft dollars	Better decision making

Conservative Scenario	Input	Calculation
Spend on indirect goods and services	$1,000,000,000	
Percentage of spend with approved suppliers defined	25%	$250,000,000
• Portion of this spend through bypass suppliers	33%	$82,500,000
Bypass reduction through spend analysis	33%	$27,225,000
Savings from reducing bypass		
• Savings from using approved versus unapproved suppliers	10%	$2,722,500
• Savings from additional volume discounts with suppliers	2%	$544,500
Internal costs from effort to change spending behavior	($200,000)	
Savings through Spend Analysis		**$3,067,000**

Figure 2.4. ROI calculation illustration.

Savings Opportunity

This scenario illustrates the value of the ability of spend analysis to change spending behavior and assumes that a company has defined approved supplier lists for about 25% of their total spending and that unapproved supplier prices are 10% higher than negotiated prices. (AMR Research estimates this amount to be as high as 15%.) Also assumed is that shifting spend from unapproved suppliers to approved suppliers will qualify the company for an additional 2% in volume discounts. As shown in Figure 2.4, if a third of purchases in "defined" spending categories are considered to be bypass spending and the company can use spend analysis to reduce bypass spending by 33%, doing so will yield a return of $3.07 million savings on a baseline of $1 billion in spend.

A similar calculation could be done for off-contract spend, poorly performing spend, supplier rationalization, etc. Figure 2.5 shows expected savings from various opportunities.

We will now review three case studies that illustrate how leading companies have achieved high ROI in sourcing by leveraging spend analysis.

CASE STUDY 1—HIGHLY DECENTRALIZED PURCHASING

Overview and Objectives

A $1.3 billion manufacturer of food products had a highly decentralized buying organization. The manufacturer was looking at improving spend visibility and institutionalizing a world class supply management process. The company had six divisions with each division having multiple plants. Purchasing was fairly decentralized because there were no standards in place preventing the divisions and/or plants from purchasing off-contract or with "nonapproved" vendors. The company had grown through acquisitions and therefore had a number of different ERP and decision support systems scattered throughout their divisions and plants.

When questioned, the executive management listed the following as their objectives:

1. Gain visibility to spend in order to develop sourcing strategies.
2. Identify low-hanging fruit.
3. Identify minority- and women-owned business enterprises (MWBE). (USDA requirements mandated that a certain minimum amount of business must be awarded to MWBEs.)
4. Monitor compliance to contracts.
5. Import the enriched spend data (vendor, items) into the ERP system as a single source of truth.
6. Support M&A growth.

Methodology

Spend analysis was first performed on all MRO and direct materials. Transactions were classified into a custom commodity structure, and addressable and nonaddressable spends by commodities were identified. Figure 2.6 shows a waterfall chart for the top ten commodities.

Once spend visibility was attained, the next step was to supplement that data with actual interviews with buyers to find out real sourcing opportunities. Figure 2.7 shows the assessment model, which involved conducting buyer interviews and using previous sourcing experience. Based on this analysis, commodities were segmented based on size of opportunity and difficulty/complexity of implementation.

This assessment was followed with a six-step sourcing process. The processes were launched in "waves" in which each wave targeted sets of commodities. Savings of 81% were forecasted for 2 years in wave 1 which included these categories: corrugated packaging, fruit, temporary labor, and travel (hotels, car rentals, and agencies). Of the forecasted savings, 8.3% went toward licensing the spend analysis application. Another 10% was paid to consultants over 2 years. Thus, a net savings of 62% was anticipated over 2 years.

CASE STUDY 2—GLOBAL PROCUREMENT CHALLENGES

One of the largest pharmaceutical firms in the world with annual sales of £20 billion and £7.9 billion in spend had 725 procurement professionals across 90 manufacturing locations in 39 countries.[2] The company had £8.5 billion global spend

| | | | | Projected Cost Savings as Percentage of Impactable Spend Base | | | |
Savings Category	Description	CPC Analytics Configuration Required to Support Capture of Savings	Diagnostic Question to Evaluate Prospect's Savings Opportunity from CPC Analytics	Low	Medium	High	Prospect
Strategic sourcing	Detailed analysis of requirements, selection of lowest-cost suppliers, fact-based negotiation, and implementation of best-in-class contracts	Customized	Are you currently able to develop an enterprise-wide picture of organizational demand patterns and requirements and existing supply strategies by commodity?	5%	10%	15%	10%
Buyer compliance	Identification and reduction of spend volumes which bypass existing preferred supplier contracts	Basic	Are you able to identify all spend that bypasses existing approved contracts and also identify the specific buying locations responsible?	1%	3%	5%	3%
Supplier compliance	Identification of supplier pricing errors relative to contract and receipt of retroactive compensation and penalties	Customized	Are you able to identify all supplier pricing errors relative to contract?	1%	2%	3%	2%
Incumbent rebates and renegotiation	Receipt of retroactive rebates and/or immediate renegotiation of pricing with incumbent suppliers resulting from a detailed knowledge of spend with these suppliers; also includes any increased discounts with incumbents due to increased volumes and leverage	Basic	Do you have a consolidated picture of total spend with incumbents who supply many different cost centers in your company or who sell through different business units or subsidiaries?	1%	2%	4%	2%

Price reduction

		Configuration	Question				
Process cost reduction	Purchasing	Move paper-based requisition and purchasing processes to e-procurement	Basic	Are you able to segment all enterprise-wide transactions by purchase process to identify opportunities for migration to e-procurement?	0.07%	0.15%	0.25%	0.15%
	Payment	Move paper invoices to P-cards	Basic	Are you able to segment all enterprise-wide transactions by payment process to identify opportunities for migration to P-cards?	0.20%	0.45%	0.75%	0.45%
Demand management	Purchase volume	Maintain usage within budget requirements and avoid overbuying due to easier buying processes and price reductions	Customized	Are you able to track item-level volume usage patterns by buying location?	1%	3%	5%	3%
	Specifications	Ensure ability to monitor and challenge user specifications as appropriate	Customized	Are you able to track item-level specifications by buying location?	1%	3%	5%	3%

Total Savings Opportunity (%)	23.60
Total Impactable Indirect Spend ($MM)	250.00
Total Savings Opportunity ($MM)	**59.00**
Savings Available with Basic CPC Analytics Configuration ($MM)	**14.00**

Figure 2.5. Expected savings from sourcing initiatives driven by spend analysis. MM, millions.

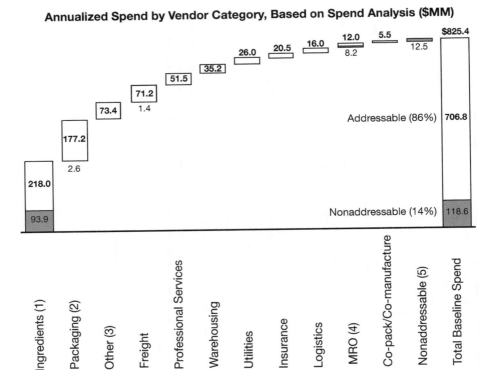

Figure 2.6. Spend visibility (addressable spend of $708 million). MM, millions.

via 33 SAP, 50 JDE, and 38 manual systems. The company wanted to free up cash through savings and use it to fund R&D activities. A secondary goal was to ensure that the suppliers were meeting their regulatory requirements.

Methodology

Spend analysis was first conducted and four key reports were generated (spend analysis was performed in U.S. dollars):

- Commodity spending trend report (Figure 2.8)
- Supplier spending trend report (Figure 2.9)
- Preferred supplier compliance report by commodity (Figure 2.10)
- Spend concentration report by commodity (Figure 2.11)

The compliance report shows approved spend for each category. The concentration report shows the vendor fragmentation for each commodity being sourced. Based on these two reports, key commodities were identified as candidates for savings.

| **Spend Analysis:**
• Total paid and sourceable spend
• Vendor density
• Buyer density
• Savings opportunities

Buyer Interviews:
• Meet with buyers across divisions to develop deep understanding of spend patterns
• Identify sourceable commodities based upon buyer feedback

Past Project Experience:
• Average savings achieved
• Spend trends
• Historic data analysis
• Company's commodity expertise | **Opportunity Assessment Model**

• Excel-based
• Annualized spend data
• Weight-based scoring
• Category prioritization
• Manual overrides on opportunity savings and effort level | • Identified opportunity savings by category

• Calculated effort-level score by category

• Assigned categories to quadrants based on opportunity and effort score
  — Q1: high savings, low effort
  — Q2: high savings, high effort
  — Q3: low savings, low effort
  — Q4: low savings, high effort |

Figure 2.7. Opportunity assessment model.

Results

In 3 years, over 250 categories were sourced through 2000 sourcing events, yielding an 18 to 26% cost reduction across key categories. The net result was $1 billion in cumulative savings over 3 years.

Prior to spend analysis, the procurement group had instituted a number of policies that were receiving less than ideal adoption. Now, the procurement group was able to track compliance to procurement policies. For example, its IT organization is now in line with a "No PO, No Pay" policy. By using spend analysis the procurement group was able to document IT spend going from 47% compliance to 92% compliance.

Another key win was a corporate-wide initiative to increase spending with preferred suppliers. This program allowed the company to move an additional 5% of its spend to preferred suppliers. A key enabler was the ability of the spend analysis tool to not only identify and track compliance, but also to act as the system of record for the establishment and management of preferred supplier status.

In the next chapter (Chapter 3, *How to Implement a Successful Spend Analysis Program*), we will discuss the processes and steps used to ensure success in such a massive and complex undertaking.

Commodity	2006					
	2006 q1 Spend ($)	2006 q2 Spend ($)	2006 q3 Spend ($)	2006 q4 Spend ($)	Total Spend ($)	Percent of Total
Technology	302,507,256	327,193,637	112,749,826	57,323,973	799,774,693	19
Facilities	188,493,028	266,374,462	92,436,427	52,171,334	599,475,251	14
Professional services	142,663,152	173,521,387	64,507,551	28,093,264	408,785,354	10
Marketing	51,030,358	115,990,980	42,274,155	21,238,724	230,534,21	75
Human resources	75,427,091	97,327,785	36,566,702	15,769,169	225,090,748	5
Supplies	41,532,568	61,673,254	40,549,979	41,316,143	185,071,94	44
Capital equipment	58,274,801	60,393,845	27,203,744	36,164,213	182,036,602	4

Figure 2.8. Commodity trend report.

Supplier	2006				Total			
	2006 q1 Spend ($)	2006 q2 Spend ($)	2006 q3 Spend ($)	2006 q4 Spend ($)	Spend ($)	Transactions	Percent Spend	Commodities
IBM	132,891,325	52,213,393	11,340,945	7,033,319	203,478,981	3,056	4.8	8
US West	10,074,575	12,779,854	4,285,204	2,265,587	29,405,220	688	0.7	4
Marsh & McLennan	13,285,816	10,780,441	3,171,652	1,874,579	29,112,488	104	0.7	3
Imperial Chemical	6,044,220	7,374,650	4,647,947	4,920,393	22,987,209	17	0.5	3
MetLife, Inc.	10,246,920	6,688,047	1,998,108	1,075,647	20,008,721	238	0.5	2
SIG Pack Services, Inc.	17,901,533	—	1,262,124	—	19,163,658	25	0.5	2
Totals	190,444,389	89,836,384	26,705,979	17,169,525	324,156,277	4,128		

Figure 2.9. Supplier trend report.

	2006									Row Totals Spend in USD
	2006 q1		2006 q2		2006 q3		2006 q4		
Commodity	Approved Spend ($)	Approved Percent of Total	Approved Spend ($)	Approved Percent of Total	Approved Spend ($)	Approved Percent of Total	Approved Spend ($)	Approved Percent of Total	
Technology	203,808,835	24	169,859,695	15	64,708,925	16	27,262,166	11	799,774,693
Facilities	105,029,254	12	159,868,787	15	58,264,181	14	22,615,379	9	599,475,251
Professional services	94,473,646	11	110,282,155	10	44,836,517	11	8,595,240	3	408,785,354
Marketing	13,046,837	2	77,706,423	7	27,694,584	7	6,966,48	13	230,534,217
Human resources	26,877,337	3	78,876,779	7	30,527,455	7	3,095,042	1	225,090,748
Supplies	41,380,473	5	93,681	0.01	234,878	0.06	41,035,825	16	185,071,944
Capital equipment	57,057,884	7	444,257	0.04	126,942	0.03	36,145,502	14	182,036,602

Figure 2.10. Preferred supplier compliance report by commodity.

Spend Concentration Report – 2006

2006 Goal — 90% Spend with 10% or Less Active Suppliers

Commodity	Technology	Facilities	Professional Services	Marketing	Human Resources	Supplies	Capital Equipment
Spend in USD	799,774,693	599,475,251	408,785,354	230,534,217	225,090,748	201,236,608	190,608,135
Number of suppliers	338	264	182	43	179	351	406
Number of suppliers accounting for 90% spend	62.699	14.3352	19.656	10.5608	15.6983	52.4043	31.7492
Percent of suppliers accounting for 90% spend	18.55	5.43	10.8	24.56	8.77	14.93	7.82
Variance from goal	-8.55	4.57	-0.8	-14.56	1.23	-4.93	2.18

Figure 2.11. Spend concentration report by commodity.

CASE STUDY 3—MERGER PLANNING AND INTEGRATION

Overview

With roughly half of all mergers failing to achieve expected results, procurement is increasingly asked to deliver significant cost savings in merger situations. With proper execution, both service and manufacturing companies are able to realize significant savings quickly by consolidating suppliers, leveraging increased purchasing power, and rationalizing prices paid for like goods and services. To capture these savings, they need not only visibility into the spend of the two companies, but also an integrated view to analyze their combined spending patterns. With this, they will know how much each company (and the new combined entity) spends by category, vendor, item, geography, etc. and will be armed to identify the quickest, most substantial savings opportunities to pursue. Furthermore, as they execute on their new sourcing strategy, they are armed to monitor the effectiveness of the merger-related consolidation and sourcing.

Because about half of all mergers also fail to achieve expected business value, companies are under immense pressure to quickly demonstrate results and deliver value.[1] While strategic benefits are often realized over time, cost savings are seen by executives and investors as a source of low-hanging fruit that can quickly deliver significant cost savings. As a result, a CEO looks to procurement to deliver value in a "deal" and help meet investors' short-term expectations. There are many opportunities that procurement can leverage to meet these expectations, including:

Price rationalization. The companies typically find that they have negotiated and are paying different prices for the same items and can realize immediate savings by shifting purchasing to the lower cost supplier or, armed with a new source of leverage, by negotiating better prices with the higher cost suppliers.

Supplier consolidation. If the companies are using the same suppliers, they can typically negotiate better terms and prices with their increased buying power. In categories in which the companies are using different suppliers, they can benefit from consolidating the supply base to both simplify supplier management and negotiate better prices.

Purchasing leverage. Gaining visibility into and aggregating demand across categories, business units, regions, and plant locations, for example, can give the combined company greater leverage in supplier negotiations.

The benefits are significant for both service and manufacturing firms. Examples abound across industries and include food processing companies saving 22 to 58%, automobile and truck companies saving 38 to 50%, transportation companies saving 38 to 50%, and financial services firms saving 7 to 20% of total spend. To realize these benefits, what each company buys by supplier for how much, where the companies overlap in supplier usage, and what the new combined company's spending profile will look like must be known. Then, the spend of the new company must be analyzed to identify new savings opportunities and to monitor the effectiveness of the merger-related consolidation and sourcing.

The following disguised case study describes how two Fortune 500 banks leveraged spend analysis during their merger planning and integration. The case study focuses on a financial services merger.

Situation

Stone Bank, a large regional bank, had been acquired by Blue Bank, a larger national bank. Stone had been using spend analysis for about 2 years to gain better spend visibility and was recognizing significant cost savings as a result. Blue was not using spend analysis. Before regulators approved the merger, procurement professionals at Stone described the value of the solution to their peers at Blue. Together, procurement professionals at both banks identified that the spend analysis solution could be a critical enabling tool to assist with consolidating spend and integrating the banks.

The overall merger plan set aggressive savings targets that procurement was expected to meet. The new company, Blue Stone, would have to work quickly to identify the biggest and best opportunities to quickly demonstrate results to Wall Street.

The day that regulators approved the merger, a senior vice president at Blue created a plan to create a spend analysis dataset for Blue and then to combine the datasets from the two companies. The plan included a three-phase implementation to get data into the hands of commodity managers in plenty of time to facilitate strategic decision making.

Methodology

Phase 1. Aggregate Blue spend data. Spend data from Blue (with permission) was obtained and merged with the existing Stone datasets.

Phase 2. Enrich Blue data and integrate with Stone data. Blue's spend data was cleansed, enriched, and categorized to the same commodity structure used by Stone. The data from both companies were loaded into a single dataset. By using a single commodity structure, the team could easily analyze joint spend on commodities, as well as how the spend was divided by company. Figure 2.12 shows how Stone and Blue were quickly able to gain spend visibility and identify spending patterns across the two companies and prioritize savings opportunities.

Commodity	Subcommodity	Blue Bank	Stone Bank
	Distributed IT	$111,644,081	$7,731,384
	Contract labor	$106,403,677	$8,613,365
Technology	Networking	$36,885,856	$2,801,642
	Software	$21,885,349	$1,841,595
	Mainframe	$20,593,451	$1,919,272
	Facilities management/ operations	$119,445,836	$5,343,873
	Construction	$48,374,878	$412,619
Facilities	Rent	$31,320,830	$22,577
	Utilities	$17,749,629	$59,111
	Food service	$17,509,468	—
	Office furniture	$11,158,750	$9,104
	Security	$7,801,889	$137,854
	Consulting	$111,268,070	$3,651,889
Professional services	Legal fees	$28,866,846	$8,800,426
	Audit and tax services	$16,492,769	$1,624,113
	Contract labor	$155,428	—
	Equipment	$45,108,098	$4,059,180
Telecom	Local	$40,474,685	$4,504,384
	Long distance	$28,343,528	$5,655,957
	Cellular PCS/wireless/pagers	$2,356,710	$295,111
Financial services	Market services	$83,496,012	$2,685,803
	Market data	$38,117,861	$43,363

Figure 2.12. Common commodity structure allows comparison of the two datasets.

Figure 2.13 shows how spend analysis revealed that Stone was spending heavily on logistics, travel, and marketing relative to Blue and helped to guide Stone to categories with large savings potential.

Phase 3. Categorize spend to new commodity structure. The combined spend was categorized to a new, jointly devised commodity structure and the suppliers were "grouped" across both companies. The supplier grouping shown in Figure 2.14 enabled the procurement team to easily analyze combined spend with suppliers. In this phase, the spends for each company and for the combined entity were analyzed.

With the more granular analysis and recategorization, the two companies gained visibility at the vendor level to support vendor consolidation and leverage volume spend.

Armed with complete spend visibility, cross-company planning teams identified many savings opportunities by:

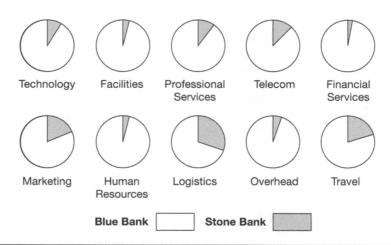

Figure 2.13. Joint spend analysis revealed that Stone bank was spending heavily on some commodities relative to Blue Bank and showed where consolidation could yield savings.

- Finding suppliers with whom both companies had contracts to identify the lowest cost contracts to use after the merger
- Finding suppliers with whom both companies had significant spend to request larger discounts and better terms based on the higher spend volume
- Rationalizing the supply base by commodity to only use suppliers with the lowest costs
- Identifying sourcing opportunities with the largest potential savings
- Modeling the spend profile for emerging organizational structures

In many cases, the cross-company planning teams negotiated new contracts prior to the finalization of the merger. This enabled real cost savings to begin on day one. Going forward, Blue Stone will develop a new organizational structure consisting of both new cost centers and some existing ones from both companies. This will further assist with budgeting and planning spend levels for the emerging entity.

Figure 2.15 shows how Blue Stone gained pre-merger spend visibility within the two companies and gained post-merger spend visibility across the combined enterprise to enable holistic procurement planning.

The merger went through more quickly and smoothly than anticipated due to the use of innovative spend analysis technology.

—CFO of Blue Bank

Supplier	Blue Bank		Stone Bank	
	Transaction Spend	Count	Spend	Transaction Count
IBM Corporation	$40,171,273	283	$1,034,821	34
Facilities Management Ltd.	$31,289,983	79	$22,577	2
Deloitte Touche Tohmatsu	$19,076,935	67	$1,274,510	1
Hewlett Packard	$18,724,184	1638	$702,657	82
International Print and Design Group	$16,788,657	989		
Verizon	$11,924,946	3115	$3,215,395	58
MCIWorldcom	$13,265,072	888	$1,688,642	35
KPMG	$14,434,171	48	$14,889	2
US West Communications	$12,338,670	216		
Federal Express	$4,748,812	1786	$7,012,861	550
Nortel	$11,317,121	42		
Accenture	$11,049,953	62		
ACME Warehouse	$10,275,233	1176		
Putnam Fiduciary Trust Cmpany	$10,269,540	14		
EKO Office Systems	$8,770,729	213	$145,008	20
BTR Media and Marketing	$8,313,234	347	$62,185	4
Harvard Maintenance, Inc.	$7,981,825	177	$11,670	4
Tye Time Marketing	$3,315,966	72	$4,341,790	40
Bird Maintenance	$7,515,669	404	$47,400	2
Green Momba Print Shop	$7,426,696	51		
Avalon Consulting Group, Inc.	$7,244,664	12		

Figure 2.14. Spend by supplier across Stone and Blue Banks.

Conclusion

Mergers and integrations are expected to deliver significant value. Procurement plays a key role in enabling the merged company to quickly demonstrate results by meeting high cost-reduction goals. Using spend analysis, Stone and Blue were able to achieve the level of spend visibility they needed to meet these goals. The solution helped them quickly align their procurement strategies and realize savings. The pressure to demonstrate results was high, and by acting early in the merger planning process, Blue and Stone were able to maximize savings in many ways, including:

- Analyzing spend with common vendors to leverage combined purchasing power

| | 2002 Spend | 2003 Spend | 2004 | | | |
			2004 Q1 Spend	2004 Q2 Spend	2004 Q3 Spend	2004 Q4 Spend
Blue Bank	$1,144,731,386	$1,260,729,779	$301,531,797	$311,184,841	–	–
Blue Stone	–	–	–	–	$350,307,269	$350,526,608
Stone Bank	$101,053,900	$111,077,796	$29,956,937	$27,413,881	–	–

Figure 2.15. Pre- and post-merger spend visibility across Stone and Blue Banks and across the combined enterprise.

- Analyzing common commodities and leveraging purchasing power by rationalizing vendors so that no overlap occurred
- Pre-negotiating contracts so that savings could be obtained sooner (i.e., when the merger was finalized)
- Monitoring post-merger compliance to ensure that negotiated savings were realized

Greater spend visibility can play a critical role in enabling merged enterprises to rationalize their supply base and spending. Companies face formidable challenges realizing such visibility, but those that do are better able to identify and capture the most significant savings opportunities. They can quickly drive bottom-line savings, contributing to the overall success and viability of the new enterprise.

SUMMARY

The total ROI tied to spend analysis along with supply management can exceed 1000% in just a few years. In this chapter, we have presented three case studies and have also itemized specific benefits of conducting systematic spend analysis. A number of good books are available that treat the ROI topic at great length (one such book has been cited in this chapter). A properly executed spend management program can dramatically increase the ROIC (return on invested capital) by decreasing expenses through price reductions and by negotiating better payment terms.

REFERENCES

1. Robert A. Rudzki, Douglas A. Smock, Michael Katzorke, Shelley Stewart, Jr. *Straight to the Bottom Line™: An Executive's Roadmap to World Class Supply Management.* J. Ross Publishing, Inc., Ft. Lauderdale, FL; 2006.
2. Robert Rudzki, Greybeard Advisors LLC. *Take It Straight to the Bottom Line— Drive Outstanding ROIC and EPS through World Class Supply Management.* © 2001–2006 Emptoris.

HOW TO IMPLEMENT A SUCCESSFUL SPEND ANALYSIS PROGRAM

After a prolonged RFI, pilot demonstrations, and negotiations, you have finally selected a vendor for your spend analysis solution. Now comes the real challenge! How can you ensure that your implementation is successful?

Spend analysis, in conjunction with other sourcing applications, is known to deliver staggering ROIs, sometimes exceeding 1000% in under a year. Yet, like all ERP class implementations, a successful spend analysis implementation goes far beyond implementing an IT application and training the purchasing department on how to use the application. If the correct organizational structure, executive support and visibility, appropriate levels of sponsorship, proactive support from the IT group, and corporate-wide visibility and adoption are not achieved in tandem, then even a good application can fall flat or deliver only marginal ROI.

Having the benefit of hindsight gained from delivering many successful implementations, the authors suggest the following guidelines:[1-3]

1. Set objectives.
2. Lead from the top.
3. Establish a focused center of excellence.
4. Carefully evaluate choices (commodity schema, data enrichment).
5. Take a limited-scope, phased-rollout approach.
6. Know your data.
7. Ensure that technology supports business.
8. Align the team to support the organization.

9. Increase organizational visibility to spend and sell internally.
10. Measure constantly and report frequently.
11. Engage with your application provider.

SET OBJECTIVES

Most strategic sourcing initiatives begin when executive management makes a decision to be "best in class" and to leverage procurement to improve enterprise performance by increasing margins, increasing growth, and improving customer satisfaction—in short, to establish procurement excellence as a core value in order to sustain high performance and improve enterprise value.

The management team needs to create a list of annual goals—quantifiable action items to support the "best-in-class" goal, such as:

- Achieve overall savings of 5% per year through:
  - Reducing spend by 5% across the top five commodities
  - Increasing supplier and contract compliance by 10%
  - Increasing internal process compliance by 20%

as well as a list of supporting goals:

- Reorganize cost centers appropriately.
- Elevate control of key decisions.
- Leverage all types of spend across the enterprise.
- Standardize procurement processes.
- Increase organizational visibility to spend.
- Realize synergies within the whole procure-to-pay process.

LEAD FROM THE TOP

The importance of securing executive support is critical to the success of the implementation. This is especially true if success depends on participation of groups other than sourcing such as IT. Many implementations that begin at the middle management level without any executive support and visibility either die or remain at the departmental level, thus not delivering on the full ROI potential of the implementation. The executive committee needs to mandate that procurement has one mission, one strategy, and one platform that will be used to manage and evaluate the purchasing of every commodity at every operating company within the organization. We suggest an executive steering committee as shown in Figure 3.1, to which the vice president of the supply chain or the vice president of procurement reports on a quarterly basis.

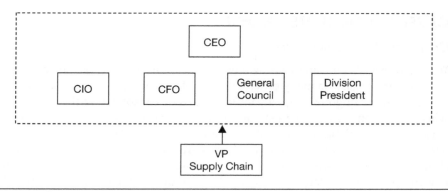

Figure 3.1. Executive steering committee.

Steering committees should empower the vice president of the supply chain (or the CPO) to make the following changes:

- Designate all corporate spend as being available for consideration by procurement.
- Effect procurement accountability for the attainment of annual savings goals.
- Empower the policy and organizational changes that are necessary for enabling procurement to reach the established goals.
- Assign responsibility for the creation of management reporting to track results and calculate impact on shareholder value.

On a quarterly basis, the vice president of the supply chain should report the progress made against attainment of these goals to the steering committee.

ESTABLISH A FOCUSED CENTER OF EXCELLENCE

Create a competency center that combines application specialists with seasoned buyers to facilitate cross-pollination of knowledge. This group will assume the role of "trainer" across the broad organization. The knowledge and enthusiasm shown by this group will determine the credibility and hence adoption of the application across the procurement and other departments. In the first (limited) rollout of the application, spend classification accuracy is typically less than 90%. Thus, it is easily possible for skeptical users to "poke holes" and undermine the credibility of the data. It is the role of the competency center to turn this situation around and "preach" to the broader user community that individual corrections submitted by all of the users will cause spend accuracies to increase over time. The continuous championing of this message and relentless measuring of adoption will guarantee overall success.

CAREFULLY EVALUATE CHOICES

Commodity Classification

You might have been using your own internal commodity codes so far (especially for direct materials) or many different types of commodity schemas across divisions. Rather than go through a painful process of consolidating these disparate schemas into one schema, you should seriously consider using an industry standard schema such as the UNSPSC (United Nations Standard Products and Services Code®). Industry standard schemas are often not used for direct materials in many industries, but this is slowly changing. Using an industry standard will free you from the burden of managing the evolution of the schema. Also bear in mind that you will want to retain your old category schemas in addition to UNSPSC. In such cases, you will want to establish mapping (cross-walks) between your old schemas and the new industry standard schema. Standardization means you might be able to leverage any commodity benchmarking information that research firms could provide in the future. It is difficult to change the mindset of hundreds of material planners and buyers to transition from a legacy commodity code that they are used to. The spend analysis implementation can serve as an opportunity to roll out the new schema and let the user community get comfortable with it. Once they understand the new structure, the old commodity schema can be slowly phased out.

Data Enrichment

The level of data enrichment should be tied to business requirements. For example, in performing vendor enrichment, at a basic level, vendors from multiple vendor master files need to be grouped and normalized. In addition, you can also assign SIC (standard industrial classification) codes, diversity, and credit ratings to the suppliers. These are special services that will cost extra. Evaluate your need for all of these services. If diversity compliance is a big issue for you, then you should consider this service. Similarly, item master files can be enriched at various levels—basic scrubbing, commodity code assignment, description normalization, description enrichment, and functional equivalency. Depending on your commodity, you might not need higher levels of enrichment. For example, most indirect commodities do not need description enrichment or normalization.

TAKE A LIMITED-SCOPE, PHASED-ROLLOUT APPROACH

Requirements Scoping

Correct scoping of a company's requirements is an important and often underestimated task. To meet their savings targets, many companies err on the side of tackling all opportunities at once. For example, they want to rationalize the supply base, increase supplier compliance, increase contract compliance, and decrease part duplication all at the same time. To achieve this, these companies would need to extract and deliver many different files, including contract parameters and part line item details, a process which takes a long time for the IT department to complete. Moreover, the spend cube would begin to become very large due to dimensional redundancies, leading to performance issues and poor spend quality. Thus, instead of a big bang approach, consider an approach for scoping the phases as "business releases" that ties each release to a specific business objective. Attack the low-hanging fruit such as supplier rationalization first. You might prioritize your objectives as:

1. Improve supplier rationalization
2. Increase compliance to preferred suppliers (i.e., reduce maverick spend)
3. Increase contract compliance
4. Increase compliance with respect to MWBE (minority- or women-owned business enterprises)
5. Reduce item price variance

Thus, you can simplify the first release by not having to extract and tie contract information to AP transactions. You can also reduce vendor enrichment time by not incorporating diversity and credit ratings. Finally, you can eliminate all information at the individual part level. By simplifying the scope of the first release, you can deliver it quicker and the information presented in the spend analyzer will be simple to understand and more credible. In subsequent releases, you can introduce the additional dimensions—contracts, MWBE, etc.—in order to support the other objectives.

Multicube Approach

Some companies are taking the approach of creating different cubes for different users, rather than packing all possible information in a single cube for all users (the latter can create performance issues). For example, all users might not be interested in auditing P-card information. Rather than include all of the details related to P-card transactions in the main cube, you can simply model the top-level information (supplier, cost center) in the main cube. Then, you can create a separate "microcube" that has all of the detailed transactional information, such as transaction ID, item description, approver, etc. The two cubes can be linked, and the audit team can be granted access to the microcube. The multicube approach can be rolled out in a phased manner consistent with the business and savings requirement.

Data Scoping

In addition to prioritizing your opportunities, you should also prioritize your data. To gain visibility to 100% of spend, you will have to extract transaction data from all of the systems across all of the divisions, thus taxing the IT department's ability and enthusiasm. Targeting 100% of spend should be the end goal, not the initial goal. Most successful implementations apply the 80/20 rule across source systems and divisions. They pick the divisions that account for 80% of the spend. Within that group, they pick the source systems that account for 80% of the spend. Typically, that means including the AP system, but excluding the P-card and T&E (travel and entertainment) systems. Finally, they target the 20% of suppliers that usually make up 80% of the spend.

Once you have visibility into the top 80% of spend, you can then expand to include other divisions and source systems. Such phased rollouts are quicker, cleaner, and easier to sell internally. Part of the savings delivered by earlier rollouts can be used to fund subsequent releases.

One drawback of the business release strategy is that it can become a chicken and egg problem, i.e., you might not know which opportunity to focus on until you can gain complete visibility into all of these areas. Typically though, most companies have a fairly good idea as to where they stand relative to these opportunities and thus can decide on a reasonable prioritization of objectives. Another factor to consider is whether IT prefers to tackle the extraction as a big bang process or as an incremental process. IT might, for instance, prefer to establish a one-time extraction/normalization process that does not change over time.

Refresh Requirement

Also important is for you to determine early on how frequently you want to refresh your spend cube. Many companies prefer monthly refreshes, while some prefer quarterly refreshes, but you should also consider if weekly refreshes would provide much more value than monthly refreshes. Obviously, the more current the data are, the more useful the data will be. However, the age of the data needs to be balanced against the cost and complexity of pulling, validating, and enriching it.

If the spend being addressed is indirect (such as in financial services or insurance companies), and the goal is to run sourcing events for supplier rationalization, then quarterly refreshes might be fine. On the other hand, if you are a manufacturing company, and you are analyzing direct material in your spend cube and want to measure compliance to preferred process and/or contracts, you might want to consider monthly refreshes. Your spend vendor will be able to make recommendations.

KNOW YOUR DATA

The accuracy of your spend is only as good as the quality of your data. Ensure that you spend time evaluating the quality of the data so you know beforehand what to expect. IT will not know this. The job of IT is to pull the data. IT will not know (nor will IT be concerned) that many transactions do not have good descriptions or that dates or vendor names are missing. Prior to loading the data into the spend cube, it is the responsibility of the sourcing team (along with the AP group) to preview the data and to try to address the gaps in the data. The more data quality control and cleansing that you perform internally, the better your end accuracy will be. Chapter 6 (*Components of Spend Analysis*) will present the notion of an information quality index and some methods to gauge the quality of your data.

The decision about whether to enrich the data in-house or to outsource this task to the spend analysis vendor is an important one. Some companies prefer to do the enrichment themselves because they have a developed sourcing program and have historically been doing this themselves; they do not trust an outside company to classify their transactions accurately; they have an internal group that, for HR reasons, they want to keep utilized; and they have data privacy issues. If you have never done data enrichment in-house before, and you do not have data privacy issues, seriously consider outsourcing for several reasons:

1. Unless you license specialized applications, data scrubbing can be a very manual, time-consuming activity which requires a team of content specialists. Do you want to invest in creating this team? Will the members serve other projects? Once the spend implementation reaches steady state, will the team be utilized 100%?
2. For vendor enrichment, you will need to subscribe to vendor databases that capture information on diversity and credit ratings. These databases have fairly high annual subscription costs.
3. You might have to deal with multiple languages if you have divisions in other countries. Do you have in-house translation capabilities?

In short, the scrubbing and enriching of transactions are laborious activities whose nitty-gritty details might best be left in the hands of a spend analysis provider.

TECHNOLOGY SHOULD SUPPORT BUSINESS, NOT DRIVE BUSINESS

Just as happens with all software applications, you will not use all features and functions in the application. There will be a key set of functions (reporting, opportunity identification, feedback, etc.) that you need to focus on in order to increase adoption. Focus on these core functions and ensure that the user base is comfortable using them. Ensure that your IT group is capable of supporting the application. Let the business requirements drive which features to focus on. Focus training sessions on what the users will actually need to use.

ALIGN THE TEAM TO SUPPORT THE ORGANIZATION

Each person in the spend core team should be assigned to support different buyers by businesses. This one-on-one attention will ensure early adoption of spend analysis across all commodities. It will also enable the core group to collect user feedback early in the process and work with the application provider to customize the user interface or to provide enhancement in subsequent releases that address the gaps. Finally, getting the commodity managers to submit corrections on spend mapping is critical to ensuring that the accuracy improves over time.

INCREASE ORGANIZATIONAL VISIBILITY

Nothing "sells" like success. Organize weekly "Webinars" and encourage more users, such as those in finance and operations, to use spend analysis. Ensure that C-level executives describe project successes in their discussions and speeches. Trumpet savings and any of the other benefits through company bulletin boards and newsletters. The core team and center of excellence staff should be agents of change, cross-pollinating ideas and spreading the gospel of spend analysis.

MEASURE CONSTANTLY, REPORT FREQUENTLY

Most C-level executives are interested in looking at metrics. For example, they might want to review opportunity identification reports to be convinced that the program is moving in the right direction and the savings target goals are indeed achievable. They might also want to look at how you stack up against your industry peers, which can be done by leveraging benchmarking information if it is available. Standardize on a set of reports that you want to use for purposes of reporting to the steering committee. Ensure that these reports are constantly updated and are available to the VP of the supply chain or the head of the sourcing project who reports to the steering committee. Present the steering committee with a report package at each quarterly meeting. Once executives understand the opportunities, they will be engaged and committed to achieving the savings.

ENGAGE WITH YOUR APPLICATION PROVIDER

The spend analysis application will have features and functions that support the top 90% of use cases. However, you will always have some unique workflows and requirements that might not be addressed in the application. These "last-mile" requirements might best be achieved by utilizing common productivity tools such as Excel. This is perfectly OK. Yet, at the same time, if you strongly believe that some particular feature that you want in the application will benefit other customers (perhaps a new type of report), then bring this up with your application provider. Application providers want feedback and are usually very receptive to new ideas. Urge your provider to create an advisory group and sign yourself up. Attend user conferences and establish one-on-one relationships with key people in the application provider's organization. You might be surprised about how quickly you see your feature request make its way into the next release.

SAMPLE PROJECT PLAN

Figure 3.2 shows a sample project plan for implementing a spend analysis program. Three case studies will now be presented to bring home the importance of all of the suggestions previously mentioned.

CASE STUDY 1—PROCUREMENT TRANSFORMATION FOR AN $8 BILLION AGROCHEMICAL BUSINESS

Overview

A little more than six years ago, two global pharmaceutical companies spun off their agrochemical businesses to form a new company. Today, that company is an $8 billion business with more than 19,000 employees and more than 200 operational sites in some 90 countries.

Recognizing from the outset that purchasing was a central part of the organization, the senior executives of the new company tasked the procurement team with designing and implementing a purchasing organization which would support a modern global company.

Any effective organization or program starts with a set of principles. The procurement team established (and was guided by) key principles from the very outset. First, the procurement team wanted the purchasing group to act entrepreneurially and to take responsibility and actions to ensure that the company acquired the best goods and services at the best value. To achieve this, the procurement group wanted to have an operation that employed not only best-in-class sourcing principles, but also one that was enabled by best-in-class technologies.

Launch project
- Kick-off meeting
- Establish teams
- Define key requirements
- Define project plan

Define spend model
- Confirm commodity structure
- Confirm dimensions
- Confirm organization hierarchy
- Confirm custom requirements

Data collection and assessment
- Define data requirements
- Sample data received
- Final dataset received

Data staging
- Confirm control totals
- Stage spend data
- Stage dimension data
- Document customer-specific data transformation rules

Custom requirements
- Calculated dimensions
- Approved vendor dimension

Update project plan enrichment
- Vendor familying
- Commodity mapping

Internal quality assurance cycle
- Publish to QA server
- Internal QA review

Reports
- Build standard reports
- Review reports

Training and communications
- Prepare training materials
- Plan training agenda
- Plan communication
- Conduct training session—feedback
- Conduct training session—end user

Define users and roles
- Identify users
- Define roles and user permissions
- Identify standard reports
- Configure feedback
- Configure dataset page

Production preparation
- Order needed equipment
- Environment setup
- Identify network issues
- Create user accounts

Publish process for feedback cycle
- Production development
- Validate production

Launch customer feedback
- Provide feedback
- Receipt of feedback
- Incorporate feedback changes

Publish process
- Production development
- Validate production

Figure 3.2. Spend analysis project plan.

With those requirements as a baseline, the essential principles of supply management employed by the company were defined as:

- Taking a global, holistic view of spend
- Making information both easy to find and insightful
- Transforming raw data into actionable information
- Creating and using a closed-loop supply management process
- Understanding the supply markets and cost drivers within each category of spend

In addition, the company has always had a focus on the importance of effective knowledge management. Knowledge sharing has been part of daily work and individuals and groups are encouraged and rewarded for sharing of knowledge within and across departments.

Background

As the sourcing function evolved, the procurement team increasingly sought out spend data to better inform its sourcing priorities and decisions. The thought was that the more *data-driven* that procurement and sourcing operations could be, the more strategic and effective procurement would be.

Of course, getting clear spend visibility across a disparate, global organization, with multiple ERP systems and hundreds of categories of spend, can be an immense challenge. At first, the group used a global data warehouse and an Oracle database, with a business intelligence tool on top. As it scaled, this method proved insufficient, with growing data accuracy problems and the lack of a procurement-centric, user-friendly interface negatively affecting end-user adoption.

The team quickly came to the conclusion that if it was going to be serious about global procurement and truly strategic in sourcing, it would need detailed, accurate spend visibility across the global operation. A solution dedicated to just that is a key component of delivering on such a principle.

Implementation and Key Learning

Thus, the goal now mandated that one centralized spend analysis tool be used for both direct and indirect spend across all areas of business—and a solution that would house both supply chain and indirect data and prove to be both insightful and easy to use.

The challenge then became data collection and enrichment. It is a tremendous effort to extract data from multiple systems in acceptable data formats. Just retrieving data into the database is not enough, the data must be structured and harmonized in such way that users can use it and get realizable value from it. There can be massive data gaps in existing transactional systems, such as when invoices do not have preceding orders or an allocation to spend categories.

Identifying prime sourcing opportunities tends to be the primary motivation for employing spend analysis. However, the company learned that leading organizations were using spend analysis capabilities and best practices to gain complete global visibility to the levels of depth needed to capitalize on an array of savings opportunities which can otherwise be untapped in an organization. For direct materials, the company was fortunate to have an internal codification system for products which had survived the last 20 years and all mergers and acquisition activities, but the data analysis in indirect spend was not so easy because the usage of POs was incomplete.

Detailed spend reports and on-the-fly analysis allowed buyers and cost center owners to support strategic and operational purchasing activities, providing the framework for savings measurement and tracking as well as enabling more effective spend control by cost center managers.

As an example of the high-value functions of spend analysis, the company sourced a number of "small-value components"—items that it does not order in significant quantities, but that are of significant importance to operations. Such items can only be ordered once or twice a year, but at a volume of 5 or 10 tons and usually with a purchase price of under $10,000.

These purchases reflect low spend levels, but they are classed as critical elements of the company's direct spend. There are about 500 such purchases each year. In the past the procurement group has handled them reactively, often at the last minute. Spend analysis is helping to bring this sourcing under better management, giving a view into small, yet critical purchases that the organization makes and allowing the team to manage their opportunity pipeline more effectively.

To ensure these higher levels of spend analysis capabilities, the chosen solution must be able to "slice and dice" data to a very detailed level in real time. The solution chosen by the company allowed them to have the ability to analyze spend on up to 30 different dimensions or axes, including category, cost center, GL account, geography, time, payment terms, UNSPSC code, supplier diversity status, and more. The solution also allowed the company to aggregate data from over 45 countries retrieved from more than 15 different types of systems, including every major ERP platform.

Spend Analysis Program Success

Whereas the procurement team formerly had only visibility dating back a year or more, now the team knows exactly what the company is spending at any given time—and with what suppliers. The spend analysis solution is used globally by more than 180 trained users at the company across purchasing and finance and at the cost center level.

Sourcing Program Success

Today, the company has successfully used its spend opportunities and has applied e-sourcing to all categories of spend. Doing so was a significant factor in the procurement organization meeting and exceeding all its pre-merger "synergy" goals. In the following operational efficiency program that started in 2004, procurement significantly contributed a year earlier than the promised delivery. When talking about some billion dollars in spend across 45,000 suppliers and 6 continents, this is an accomplishment worth boasting about. The success hinged on three factors: internal recognition and support of the sourcing program; a focus on change management and adoption; and selection of the right solution partner.

In terms of evaluating solution providers, the final vendor was selected because of their track record of success with other leading global organizations—because their solution offered a road map, a full suite of solutions, that the procurement organization could grow into as it extended its capabilities.

The Future—Managing Supplier Relationships

Today the company continues to evolve its procurement operations—and those operations continue to be central to the success of the broader organization. So where are they looking for the next wave of value from supply management?

To continue along its path, future projects will focus on enhancing supplier relationship management capabilities and enhanced contract management. The global economy and procurement have changed rapidly in recent years, and therefore normal supplier negotiation will also need to change. As a result, the company will be embracing and engraining supplier relationship management principles across the organization, segmenting and categorizing suppliers based on multiple attributes that define relationships, and ensuring proactive, best-in-class management of contractual relationships throughout their life cycle. Again, the forward-thinking, freshness of the new company spirit stands in good stead to deliver on this next challenge.

CASE STUDY 2—A FORTUNE 500 PROVIDER IN THE HEALTHCARE INDUSTRY

Overview

A Fortune 500 provider of products, services, and technology for the healthcare industry with annual revenues of $75 billion did not have a centrally managed strategic sourcing program. Business units primarily sourced independently (because of growth through acquisitions) and therefore buying power was not fully utilized. As part of its drive to move from a holding company to an integrated operating company, the provider decided to focus on strategic sourcing. This was a challenge—28 financial systems were being used; there were no requisition systems for indirect spend and no vendor master data; and decentralized purchasing meant multiple and disconnected policies. The requisition records were thus all independent and not normalized and hence not classified into any central commodity schema. Attempts at classification and enrichment were proving to be too tedious and labor intensive. Analytical capabilities were limited and untimely. Because of these reasons, there was virtually no aggregate spend visibility.

The director of strategic sourcing identified spend visibility as an important component of strategic sourcing. The following were identified as key drivers for the spend analysis implementation:

- To be able to view aggregate spend
- To find opportunities for savings
- To measure compliance
- To bring transparency to relationships with suppliers

Because of their limited internal success, the company decided to partner with a spend analysis solutions provider for both the application and the data enrichment services. After careful analysis, the following features were deemed most important in selecting the vendor:

- Tool capabilities—Specialized exploration tools (beyond ordinary reports) to identify opportunities and the ability for individual users to reclassify (remap) spend were very important.
- Supplier enrichment (diversity, credit ratings, etc.) and classification were very important.
- Overall spend accuracy was important for gaining credibility with users; thus the vendor needed to demonstrate autoclassification technology that was repeatable and that could scale to accommodate millions of transactions.
- The vendor had to be experienced and demonstrate a strong, lasting commitment for success.

Implementation

A monthly data refresh (load) frequency was established. To begin with, only the transactions that came from suppliers that made up 95% of the spend were enriched and classified. To iteratively improve classified spend accuracy, over 300 financial and operational users were trained to use the tool to suggest remapping of spend that looked incorrect. Such a distributed, iterative mapping process was the only process that ensured that the accuracy steadily improved.

Challenges

The data coming out of the systems were often of poor quality and had to be internally rationalized. Wherever internal rationalization was not done, the commodity code assignment suffered and the spend amounts appeared to be misclassified, which reduced the credibility of the data, leading to poor initial adoption. To address this problem, the director of spend analysis embarked on an aggressive program to increase the spend accuracy by training and encouraging the commodity managers to suggest remapping spend feedback. The future success of spend analysis hinged on the success of this "remapping feedback" program.

Results after One Year

In less than a year, spend accuracy in key commodities such as temporary labor and consulting services had increased significantly. The sourcing team suggested several vendors for on-boarding to P-cards from invoices. The number of users (adoption) steadily improved and ultimately the spend analysis system was accepted as the primary source of information for the procure-to-pay program. The group responsible for diversity programs has now come to depend on the spend analyzer for gaining visibility into enterprise-wide diversity spend. The spend analysis team is currently working with the finance team to structure the data cube such that expenses can be viewed as either capital expenses (i.e., expenses which can be capitalized on the balance sheet) as opposed to SG&A (sales, general, and administrative) expenses (i.e., expenses which appear on the income statement). Savings opportunities associated with SG&A expenses have a direct impact on earnings per share.

CASE STUDY 3—A COMPANY WITH GLOBAL PROCUREMENT LOCATIONS

Overview

The same company presented in Case Study 2 in Chapter 2 will be studied here. One of the largest pharmaceutical firms in the world with annual sales of £20 billion, the company had 725 procurement professionals across 90 manufacturing locations in 39 countries. The company had £8.5 billion global spend via 33 SAP systems, 50 JDE, and 38 manual systems. The company wanted to free up cash through savings and use it to fund R&D activities. A secondary goal was to ensure that suppliers were meeting their regulatory requirements.

However, spend visibility was a big hurdle. There was very little spend visibility at the item, GL, and cost center levels. Part of the reason was that the there were no standards imposed on the various divisions. AP transactions were classified to different GL and commodity standards. Suppliers were commodity coded (i.e., mapped to individual commodity taxonomies), but their spend (transactions) was not. The strategic sourcing teams relied on the procurement department to code and group suppliers.

Implementation

The head of procurement gave the go-live mandate for the spend analysis initiative. This was to be the Holy Grail for all compliance, category, and supplier spends. A phased deployment spanning 3 months was planned. Suppliers accounting for 80% of overall spend were initially targeted.

User Adoption

The spend analysis deployment team performed road shows and Web seminars globally in which they introduced the new system and touted its merits. These activities were followed by an internal workshop which was conducted in 3 cities over 3 weeks and was attended by 85 sourcing group managers. These workshops provided a "boot camp" course on how to use the applications. How-to guides and self-help documents were also distributed. Approximately 5% of the total spend was found to be initially misclassified. It was critical to train the managers on how to suggest corrections using the distributed feedback mechanism. The progress was communicated daily. The workshop agendas and goals were summarized in global communication sessions across the enterprise.

Next Steps

The success of the initial phase was followed by a deeper deployment strategy. In this phase, visibility of low spend suppliers (which accounted for 90% of supplies, but merely 1% of spend) was targeted. Spend analysis was integrated into the broader sourcing modules as the source of truth. For example, the preferred supplier data from spend analysis started being used in requisitioning systems. Spend deployment was also extended to the contract manufacturing group.

Currently, deployment addresses about 90% of the spend. There are on-going efforts to get even more data under spend and eventually under supply management.

Since 1999, the company has run 2000 sourcing events by identifying opportunities through spend analysis, accounting for about 40% of the total spend. The total system is being used by 140 internal customers.

SUMMARY

Like all enterprise class applications, the success of a spend analysis program hinges critically on leadership, setting objectives, executive management support, and scoping the implementation in manageable chunks that are pegged to business releases. Also important is to get buy-in from all of the stakeholders early on in the process. Finally, the only way to increase user adoption is to internally sell the success stories and use the user-generated feedback to increase the data accuracy over time. The case studies presented some of these strategies for implementing successful spend analysis programs.

REFERENCES

1. Lora Cecere. GlaxoSmithKline. *Using Sourcing to Add Billions to the Bottom Line.* Boston: AMR Research; March 2005.

2. Mickey North Rizza. *Con-way takes Procurement Transformation Journey.* Boston: AMR Research; January 2007.

3. Mickey North Rizza. *Great News for Procurement: Spend Analytics Capabilities are Improving.* Boston: AMR Research; February 2007.

OPPORTUNITY IDENTIFICATION

The value that spend analysis delivers is directly tied to how many opportunities for savings you can find. In addition, these opportunities need to be "actionable," meaning that the underlying savings should be readily obtained through a series of transformations or changes. The example in Figure 4.1 shows some of the savings opportunities uncovered in a Fortune 500 organization.

In this chapter we will list the typical opportunities for savings that most corporations identify. We will group these into two buckets—aggregate spend-level opportunities and transaction-level opportunities. Aggregate spend reports are readily available in many spend analysis applications, so the corresponding opportunities are easily identified. However, transaction-level opportunities are difficult to uncover. You will need specialized reports to uncover them. We will first present these two categories and then explore each of them in detail.

Spend-level opportunities. These are opportunities that can be identified simply by viewing the aggregate amounts (by commodity, supplier, cost center, etc.) without having to go down to the level of individual transactions:

1. Supply rationalization
    -   Vendor fragmentation per commodity
2. Demand aggregation
    -   Commodity/business unit fragmentation per supplier
    -   Contract consolidation across business units
3. Preferred purchasing process bypass
    -   Purchases from nonpreferred/unapproved suppliers
    -   Non-PO purchases

Opportunity	Finding	Action	Savings
Purchasing leverage	In a $500 million MRO category, 10 individual suppliers providing parts to each of the plants	Used aggregate demand as leverage to negotiate better process with vendors; realized average 6% price reduction across supplier	$30 million
Supplier consolidation	In a $155 million indirect category, over 350 suppliers	Consolidated the supply base to select preferred suppliers; leveraged increased spending with these vendors to negotiate better terms and prices; reduced supply base by 75% and realized a 4% savings across the category	$6 million
Part rationalization	Identified 15 duplicate parts representing $385 million in spend being sourced to support 3 different product lines across 20 plants	Consolidated supply around a single part and negotiated an average 3% price reduction with the preferred supplier	$12 million
Maverick spend reduction	65% of $120 million of contract labor spend by data center with nonapproved vendors	Shared findings with data center manager and reduced off-contract spending to 5%; realized 7% savings on spend shifted to approved vendors	$5 million
Unleveraged spend	$80-million indirect goods category not previously sourced	Conducted sourcing events for the category to establish approved pricing and suppliers; realized 18% savings across the category	$14 million
Total			**$67 million**

Figure 4.1. Savings opportunities in a Fortune 500 company.

- PO limit approval violations
- On-boarding for e-procurement and P-cards
- Off-contract spend

4. Diversity spend compliance
5. Supplier performance
   - Spend with poorly performing suppliers
   - Spend with suppliers with bad credit ratings

Transaction-level opportunities. These are opportunities that require transaction-level visibility and intelligence to identify:

1. Contract compliance violations
   - Unrealized discounts and rebates (contract compliance)

- Contract start and expiration date violations
- Delivery date violations
2. Item unit price variance—Are we paying more than our peers?
3. Payment terms opportunities—Are we paying too early or too late?
4. Invoice processing opportunities
   - Consolidated payment processing opportunities
   - Frequent charges and credits
   - Recurring invoices
5. Quality of GL assignments

SPEND-LEVEL OPPORTUNITIES

Supplier Rationalization

Vendor rationalization, perhaps the lowest-hanging fruit in terms of opportunities, has been the pivotal theme surrounding strategic sourcing for the last several years. The idea is that over time, through organic growth or M&A, the supply base grows to be too "fat." When that happens, spend becomes very fragmented. The same part is often sourced by different divisions from multiple suppliers, each offering a different price point and contractual terms. Not only does this create suboptimal price inequity, but keeping track of hundreds of contracts also becomes impossible, and much of the spend "leaks" out in the form of unrealized price/volume rebates.

The chart in Figure 4.2 shows how vendor rationalization opportunities can be identified at the commodity level. In the example, the services category is ripe for vendor consolidation.

Demand Aggregation (or Disaggregation)

Demand aggregation works on the principle that if you increase volume by consolidating demand, you can negotiate lower costs with your suppliers. The example in Figure 4.3 shows business unit fragmentation per supplier. In the example, certain suppliers enjoy strategic relationships (on account of their large spend), but this situation is not leveraged in other geographies. Demand aggregation assumes that the supplier cost curves downward as volume increases. In some situations, this is not true. There are cases when this curve is U-shaped, i.e., the cost decreases initially with volume, but then increases at very high volumes. This may occur, for example, if the transportation costs to ship products to another city increase with volume or if capacity constraints cause fixed costs to increase at large volumes. In such cases, it may make sense to appropriately disaggregate volumes and allocate business to multiple suppliers optimally so that you "catch" the lowest point on the cost curve for each supplier.

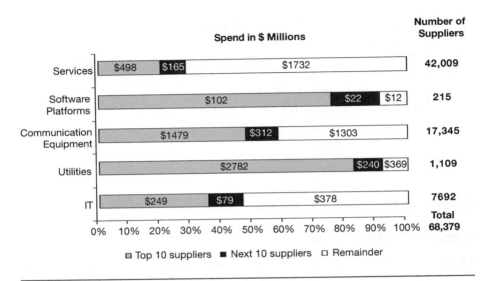

Figure 4.2. Commodity supplier rationalization.

Top 10 Global Suppliers	North America	Europe	Africa	South Asia	East Asia
M-TELECOMMUNICATIONS	8%	27%	1%	9%	7%
MULTI-TEL INC	14%	3%	1%	6%	4%
UNICOM	14%	3%	0%	12%	4%
PROXYTEL	5%	8%	5%	13%	9%
GLOBAL UNITEL	–	40%	9%	3%	18%
UNITED COMMUNICATIONS	19%	9%	4%	20%	28%
GENERAL SYSTEMS	20%	–	74%	3%	–
UNIFIED DATA	5%	3%	–	–	1%
ULTIMODE TELECOM	1%	1%	4%	7%	21%
INTL VOICE AND DATA			2%	23%	2%
Totals	**86%**	**94%**	**100%**	**96%**	**94%**

Figure 4.3. Business unit supplier rationalization—large suppliers dominating individual operating units.

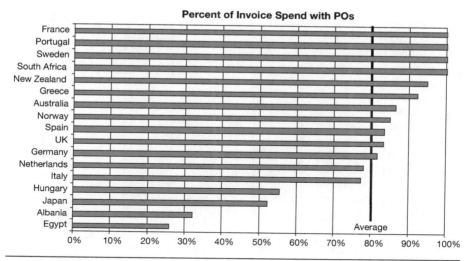

Figure 4.4. PO bypass example.

Bypass of the Preferred Purchasing Process

This category includes violations associated with the purchasing process. There are so many examples of a PO being "rushed" in order to purchase a critical part, often with a nonpreferred supplier and without obtaining all approvals. An extreme case of this is when the invoice is dated earlier than the PO. Such instances of bypassing the standard process can easily result in spend leakage in the form of higher item prices and less favorable payment terms and refund policies.

Non-PO Spend

The example in Figure 4.4 shows spend that is not tied to POs and thus is deemed to be leaking out as "maverick spend." The 80% tolerance line clearly shows which operating units are not compliant.

Off-Contract Spend

The stacked bar chart in Figure 4.5 shows the spend associated with the top seven travel and entertainment vendors for five quarters. The NC and C in the legend represent "not contracted" and "contracted," respectively. As you can see, apart from two suppliers (Groeschel Company, Inc. and Reading Bakery Systems), all other spend is off-contract, meaning there are no strict financial, operational, and legal constraints or guidelines associated with these services. This in turn means that the company is not getting favorable terms (rates, payment terms, etc.). Given

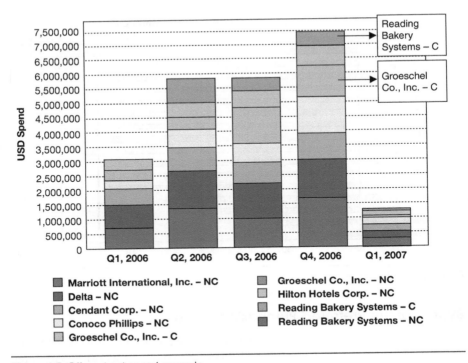

Figure 4.5. Off-contract spend example.

the amount of money involved, even a 5% savings in 2006 could have translated to savings of over $1 million.

Diversity Spend Compliance

The pie chart in Figure 4.6 shows the percentage of spend tied to diversity suppliers for the top five UNSPSC commodities. Assuming the corporate policy is that 10% of spend should be directed toward MWBEs (minority- and women-owned business enterprises), it is clear from the lower part of the figure that the commodity transportation, storage, and mail services is underrepresented and that the commodity editorial and design services is overrepresented.

Supplier Performance

Supplier performance monitoring constitutes a critical piece of supply management best practices. Even after they start tracking suppliers for performance, many companies have a poor understanding of exactly how much they spend with such suppliers. Performance itself can be measured along several dimensions—

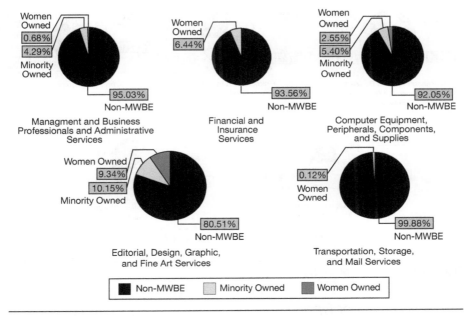

Figure 4.6. Diversity spend example.

quality of service, quality of product, delivery date compliance, price, payment terms, payment methods, etc. Below are some examples of how spend analysis can be used to monitor some of these parameters.

Spend with Poorly Performing Suppliers

The pie chart in Figure 4.7 shows the spend associated with the same top five UNSPSC commodities as in the previous example, but this time the spend is plotted against supplier ratings. As can be seen, the editorial and design services commodity has a large percentage of spend tied to poorly performing suppliers. Ironically, this same commodity has very little spend tied to MWBE, so perhaps there is a hidden message in this finding.

Approved versus Nonapproved Spend

The cross-tabular table in Figure 4.8 shows the spend for the top five commodities for the top five vendors split into approved versus nonapproved. There is a fairly big nonapproved spend tied to printing, and this must be addressed. If "Buyer" is modeled as a dimension, you can further nest this dimension into the cross-tabular table. Doing so will pinpoint the exact buyer who should be held accountable for the nonapproved spend.

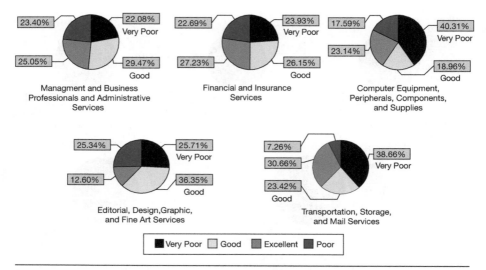

Figure 4.7. Spend with poorly performing suppliers.

Spend by Payment Type

The chart in Figure 4.9 shows the payment type (check, credit card, electronic funds transfer) used in reimbursing the top ten suppliers. Clearly, EFT (electronic funds transfer) is the most cost-optimal mechanism. In this case, less than 10% of spend is tied to EFT, whereas a whopping 70% is tied to checks, with IBM being the biggest contributor. This is an opportunity that should be addressed.

TRANSACTION-LEVEL OPPORTUNITIES

Transaction-level opportunities cannot readily be identified by examining aggregate spend or count measures. Rather, the individual transactions have to be analyzed (mined) and certain patterns need to be uncovered.

Contractual Term Opportunities

Contract violations constitute the biggest and also the most elusive portion of spend leakage. In order to identify contract violations, the contract line item detail needs to be compared with the actual transaction details, which is fairly tricky if the contract and the AP (accounts payable) systems are not integrated (which is the case with almost all companies). We will review this topic in Chapter 10 (*Spend Analysis and Compliance*) to understand how such information can be

UNSPSC Commodity	Approval	IBM Spend ($)	HP Spend ($)	KPMG Spend ($)	International Print and Design Accenture Spend ($)	Group Spend ($)
Management and business professionals; and administrative services	Yes	74,239,069		41,229,764	25,312,319	
Computer equipment and peripherals and components and supplies	Yes	57,746,737	52,896,191	197,413	710,822	
	No		6,953,162			
Financial and insurance services	No					
	Yes	3,799,319		13,121,617	9,799,180	
Editorial and design; and graphic and fine art services	No					33,068,567
Transportation and storage; and mail services	No					
Column totals ($)		135,785,126	59,849,353	54,548,794	35,822,321	33,068,567

Figure 4.8. Unapproved supplier spend.

extracted and used in spend analysis to provide visibility into the types of violations listed below.

Unrealized Discounts and Rebates

Within contract compliance, the category of unrealized discounts and rebates is arguably the biggest source of spend leakage. In the report shown in Figure 4.10, the "Discount" column shows the calculated or specified discount for each invoice. In each case, the "Invoice Total Amount" (prior to taxes) does not take into consideration the discount. For example, in the first two records, the invoice total amount has been calculated simply as price multiplied by quantity; thus

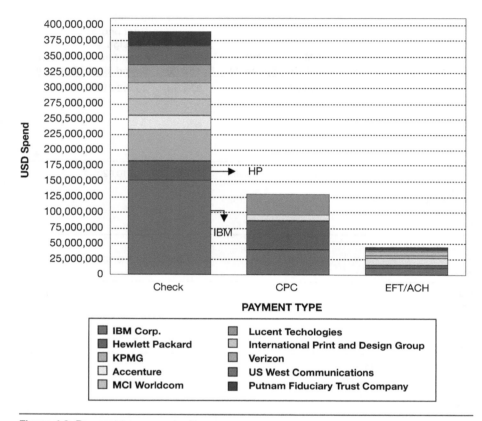

Figure 4.9. Payment type opportunities.

$8152.25 has leaked out. In the four subsequent records, 7% of the total amount has leaked out because it has not been claimed.

Quantity Violations

Oftentimes, a contract specifies a ceiling on the quantity that can be ordered. If there is no visibility into this specified quantity, purchasing can easily exceed the limit and might inadvertently pay a higher price for the units in excess of the contract. The report in Figure 4.11 shows instances in which POs have been cut for quantities that exceeded the quantities that had been specified in the contract. Fortunately, because no shipment has been received, it might be possible for the company to void these POs and issue new ones.

Contract Number	Invoice Number	Discount	Invoice Item Price ($)	Invoice Quantity	Invoice Total Amount ($)	Vendor
101	ICVR1	$8,152.25	200	542	108,400	Barbarits, Bruno
101	ICVR2	$8,152.25	200	272	54,400	Barbarits, Bruno
102	ICVR2	7%	298	542	108,400	Vendor 1164
102	ICVR2	7%	298	542	108,400	Vendor 1164
102	ICVR1	7%	298	542	108,400	Vendor 1164
102	ICVR1	7%	298	542	108,400	Vendor 1164
103	ICVR2	3%	498	542	108,400	Vendor 1163
103	ICVR1	3%	498	542	108,400	Vendor 1163
103	ICVR2	3%	498	542	108,400	Vendor 1163
103	ICVR1	3%	498	542	108,400	Vendor 1163
104	ICVR2	$24,283.50	878	542	108,400	Vendor 1162

Figure 4.10. Contractual term violations of discounts.

Contract Number	Contract Quantity	PO Quantity	Invoice Quantity	Received Quantity	Test Results
203	125	146	0	0	PO Quantity
204	331	347	0	0	PO Quantity
205	93	115	0	0	PO Quantity
206	610	625	0	0	PO Quantity
207	440	446	0	0	PO Quantity
208	642	666	0	0	PO Quantity
209	551	564	0	0	PO Quantity
210	627	643	0	0	PO Quantity
211	531	554	0	0	PO Quantity
212	139	148	0	0	PO Quantity
213	435	447	0	0	PO Quantity
214	539	541	0	0	PO Quantity
215	471	493	0	0	PO Quantity
216	30	44	0	0	PO Quantity
217	636	646	0	0	PO Quantity
218	429	433	0	0	PO Quantity
219	562	578	0	0	PO Quantity
220	409	424	0	0	PO Quantity
221	12	24	0	0	PO Quantity

Figure 4.11. Contractual term violations of quantity.

Criterion: Payments made within 15 days
Total Amount: $90,277,083.48

Vendor Name	PO Number	Invoice Date	Payment Date	Payment Amount ($)
Aaron Abbott		1/9/2006	1/12/2006	7,861.67
Aaron Abbott		1/11/2006	1/12/2006	7,861.67
Academy of Life Underwriting		12/21/2005	1/4/2006	150.00
Academy of Life Underwriting		12/21/2005	1/4/2006	115.00
Acc Telecom		1/1/2006	1/7/2006	1,035.66
Accent, Inc.		1/10/2006	1/11/2006	400.00
Access Insurance Services		1/12/2006	1/20/2006	34.04
Accudata		1/1/2006	1/12/2006	175.00
Accurate Communications		12/31/2005	1/13/2006	116.49
Accurint		12/31/2005	1/6/2006	187.50
Accurint		12/31/2005	1/11/2006	163.50
Ace Mailing		12/23/2005	1/4/2006	340.29
Actex Publications		1/4/2006	1/11/2006	568.10
Actex Publications		1/16/2006	1/25/2006	318.61
Actuarial Bookstore		1/18/2006	1/30/2006	4,197.20
Actuarial Society of Greater New York		1/19/2006	1/30/2006	25.00

Figure 4.12. Delayed payment opportunities—inefficiencies due to early payment.

Delivery Date Violations

Many contracts specify strict delivery guidelines. In industries that depend on JIT (Just In Time) delivery, violation of delivery terms can mean back orders or surplus inventory, both of which increase costs. For example, in the food business, perishability is a big concern, and delivery date violations can impact day-to-day profitability. Because delivery delays constitute violations, the company can claim penalties, if specified in the contract. At a minimum, the company can use this information to negotiate better deals when the contract is renewed.

Payment Term Opportunities

The table in Figure 4.12 is part of a report that shows payments that were made within 15 days of the invoice date, even though the payment terms were net 30. Just for the month of January, the total spend adds up to $90 million. Assuming that on an average, each payment could have been delayed by 15 days, and assuming a 4% annual interest, a savings of $1.6 million could have been obtained. This

Vendor Name	Number of Payments	Year of Payments	Month of Payments	PO Number	Payment Type
50 Corridor Transportation Management Assoc.	30	2006	June		Check
Abair Lavery, Inc.	23	2006	May		Check
ACC Telecom	42	2006	March		Check
ACC Telecom	42	2006	April		Check
Achieve Global	24	2006	March		Check
Action Label	20	2006	June	245200	Check
ADT Security Services, Inc.	23	2006	January		Check
ADT Security Services, Inc.	32	2006	February		Check
ADT Security Services, Inc.	32	2006	March		Check
Advance Sound & Electronics	30	2006	January		Check
Advanced Printing Services	37	2006	January	219645	Check

Figure 4.13. Consolidated payment opportunities.

sum also does not take into account any discounts that the company might have missed by paying early.

Invoice Processing Opportunities

The "payment" part of the P2P (procure-to-pay) process is oftentimes ignored. This area is actually a hidden gold mine of information that can reveal fairly big opportunities, some of which are listed below.

Consolidated Payments

The table in Figure 4.13 is part of a report that shows how many payments were made to suppliers each month. The cost of processing a payment (especially a check) is usually around $10. By consolidating these individual payments into a single payment, processing costs can be reduced. The full report identified around 500 suppliers and an average number of 30 payments per month. Assuming a $5 cost of payment, an annual savings of 500 $\times$ 30 $\times$ 12 = $180,000 can be achieved by consolidating these payments.

Frequent Charges and Credits

The table in Figure 4.14 is part of a report that shows frequent charges and credits for one supplier. This pattern might suggest many things—the person buying the item does not know exactly what he/she wants and after receiving the item finds that it is not the right part and hence returns it; or the person is trying to

Vendor Name	PO Number	PO Date	Payment Amount ($)	Payment Date	Approver
Compucom Systems, Inc.	223546	1/10/2006	42	1/26/2006	LAE
Compucom Systems, Inc.	3992	12/6/2005	−1,093	1/27/2006	DAE
Compucom Systems, Inc.	3992	12/6/2005	−113	1/27/2006	DAA
Compucom Systems, Inc.	3992	12/6/2005	−5	1/27/2006	DAA
Compucom Systems, Inc.	223548	1/10/2006	−2,403	1/27/2006	LAE
Compucom Systems, Inc.	225589	1/19/2006	261	1/26/2006	LAE
Compucom Systems, Inc.	225589	1/19/2006	4.3	1/26/2006	LAE
Compucom Systems, Inc.	225589	1/19/2006	4	1/26/2006	LAE
Compucom Systems, Inc.	225909	1/23/2006	22	1/26/2006	DAA
Compucom Systems, Inc.	226072	1/23/2006	224	1/26/2006	LAE
Compucom Systems, Inc.	223618	1/10/2006	−405	1/26/2006	LAE
Compucom Systems, Inc.	221830	12/28/2005	−810	1/26/2006	LAE
Compucom Systems, Inc.	4072	1/6/2006	−284	1/26/2006	LAE
Compucom Systems, Inc.	225909	1/23/2006	9	1/26/2006	DAA
Compucom Systems, Inc.	74836	1/24/2006	−320	1/26/2006	LAE
Compucom Systems, Inc.	74803	1/24/2006	304	1/26/2006	LAE
Compucom Systems, Inc.	226191	1/24/2006	−352	1/26/2006	LAE
Compucom Systems, Inc.	74686	1/20/2006	404	1/26/2006	LAE
Compucom Systems, Inc.	4120	1/24/2006	708	1/26/2006	LAE
Compucom Systems, Inc.	224374	1/13/2006	141	1/26/2006	LAE

Figure 4.14. Frequent charges and credits.

qualify for a promotion by spending a certain amount of money and then return-ing items for credits; or the supplier's parts have quality problems and therefore need to be returned. Whatever the cause, the company is bearing a cost for pro-cessing these charges and credits.

PO Approval Limits

The table in Figure 4.15 shows purchases made that are just below $500, which (in the case of this client) is the amount above which an approval is needed. In order to circumvent this approval, employees typically cut two or more POs, each below the $500 limit. Such circumventing can increase processing costs because more POs and payments now need to be processed. Furthermore, there is always a dan-ger that employees will overindulge because they are free to buy under that limit. The authors understand the necessity of introducing these kinds of "floors" or "ceilings," but the resulting payments must be analyzed at least annually to ensure

Vendor Name	PO Number	PO Amount ($)	PO Date	Approver
Advanced Mailing Solutions	219927	500.00	12/13/2005	PR
Advanced Mailing Solutions	244603	500.00	5/8/2006	PR
Advanced Mailing Solutions	219419	500.00	12/9/2005	NL
Advanced Printing Services	77956	498.58	3/29/2006	WTJ
Advanced Printing Services	78123	498.58	3/31/2006	WTJ
Advanced Printing Services	80792	499.65	5/24/2006	WTJ
Anacomp	195295	500.00	7/20/2005	NAA
Anacomp	195295	500.00	7/20/2005	NAA
Anacomp	195295	500.00	7/20/2005	NAA
Anacomp	195295	500.00	7/20/2005	NAA
Bernies	231718	500.00	2/24/2006	RS
Call One, Inc.	224515	500.00	1/13/2006	RS
Call One, Inc.	232324	499.20	2/28/2006	RS
Call One, Inc.	234379	500.00	3/13/2006	RS
Call One, Inc.	235094	500.00	3/15/2006	RS
Call One, Inc.	240587	499.20	4/13/2006	RS
Clientize.com, Inc.	74556	500.00	1/18/2006	PR
Clientize.com, Inc.	74556	500.00	1/18/2006	PR

Figure 4.15. PO approval limit violations.

that these limits are actually working and are not causing unintended consequences.

PRIORITIZING OPPORTUNITIES

In the previous sections, we have provided examples of opportunities that can be unraveled through spend analysis. Some of these might be easy to address and have a higher ROI than others. Thus, these opportunities need to be prioritized. In this section, we will provide a few guidelines for doing this. The concepts and ideas are generic enough (and well known enough!) for application to your particular industry.

Step 1—Conduct Buyer Interviews

Buyer interviews should be conducted in the following areas:

- Category history
  - Ownership

- Past success
- Sourcing strategies
- Sourcing history
- Demand management
- Compliance
- Category characteristics
  - Subcategory scope
  - Geographic scope
  - Difficulty level to optimize
  - Ease of baseline creation
  - Strategic relevance
- Supplier situation
  - Supplier performance
  - Supplier availability
  - Supplier relationship management
- Market perspective
  - Spend and pricing trends
  - Industry concentration
  - Key technical innovations
  - Savings opportunities

Step 2—Create a Segmentation Framework

The information obtained from Step 1 can be used to assign to each category a relative score for different metrics such as size of opportunity, complexity to source, strategic impact, cross-functional impact, implementation difficulty, likelihood of success, etc.

Step 3—Segment the Categories

The categories can now be segmented based on a number of frameworks. A sample framework is shown in Figure 4.16. In this figure, categories are mapped based on savings opportunity and implementation difficulty. You could create a metric called "difficulty to source" based on all of these parameters.

Step 4—Assign Category to Implementation Waves

Create category "waves" which are based on the segmentation strategy. In the above case, the four quadrants are prioritized as large opportunity, low difficulty (Wave 1); large opportunity, high difficulty (Wave 2); low opportunity, low difficulty (Wave 3); and low opportunity, high difficulty (Wave 4).

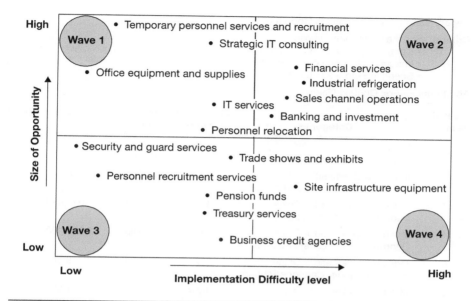

Figure 4.16. Category segmentation example.

If the segmentation metrics are modeled as dimensions in the spend cube, you could easily create a report such as the one shown in Figure 4.17 to identify Wave 1 categories. This report shows categories that were not sourced in the last year and whose complexity to source is low, impact on sourcing is high, and spend is greater than Euro 2 million. The header of the report shows the criteria used to identify the categories. The context filter shows that only categories that were not sourced within the last year were considered for the report.

SUMMARY

Chapter 4 has presented some common and some uncommon savings opportunities that can be identified by using a spend analysis application. We classified these opportunities as aggregate spend level versus transactional level. Most of the common opportunities such as vendor fragmentation and demand consolidation can be identified using aggregate spend analysis. On the other hand, contract line-level violations and invoice processing violations can be identified only at the transactional level. The capabilities of your application will determine how many opportunities you can identify. If your application can only provide aggregate spend reports, you might need to go outside your application in order to search for transaction-level opportunities. Some of the reports we presented might be

Report Name: Wave 1 Sourcing Opportunity

Criteria: Show all categories whose
- Complexity to Source contains Low
- Impact of Sourcing contains High
- Spend in Euro ≥ 2,000,000

> Date Last Sourced: Unspecified
> Date Last Sourced: Greater than 24 Months
> Date Last Sourced: 13 – 24 Months

Additional Filters: Context Filters

Level Number	Categories	Complexity to Source	Impact of Sourcing	Spend in Euro	Select All
4	Indirect > Travel > Hotel/Entertainment > Hotels	Low	High	57,212,427	❏
4	Indirect > Overhead > Office Supplies > Bags/Carriers/Boxes	Low	High	4,638,464	❏
4	Indirect > Overhead > Office Supplies > Binders/Folders	Low	High	2,043,028	❏
4	Indirect > Overhead > Office Supplies > Pads/Labels/Post-Its	Low	High	2,037,483	❏
4	Indirect > Overhead > Office Supplies > Toner/Cartridge/Ribbons	Low	High	7,789,087	❏
3	MRO > Supplies > Boilers	Low	High	10,101,564	❏
3	MRO > Supplies > Compressors	Low	High	6,259,624	❏
3	MRO > Supplies > Glue/Adhesives	Low	High	68,130,272	❏
3	MRO > Supplies > Fasteners	Low	High	27,078,056	❏
3	MRO > Supplies > Tape	Low	High	36,762,931	❏
3	MRO > Supplies > Mill Supplies and Tools	Low	High	4,798,227	❏
3	MRO > Supplies > Welding Supplies	Low	High	2,834,008	❏
3	MRO > Pipe > Valves and Fittings (Plumbing) > Stainless	Low	High	4,827,746	❏
3	MRO > Services > Insulation	Low	High	2,080,021	❏
3	MRO > Capital Equipment > Filter	Low	High	27,481,823	❏

Figure 4.17. Wave 1 identification report.

available as standard reports in your application but others might not; therefore you will need to work with your provider or your IT department to create these reports. We have also presented some techniques to prioritize these opportunities based on segmentation strategies.

PART II

THE ANATOMY OF SPEND TRANSACTIONS

In this chapter, we will take a closer look at how spend transactions are generated and the kind of data that are typically captured and available from business information systems. This information is important for two reasons:

- Understanding the data is key to understanding the type of enrichment and cleansing that needs to be performed in order to yield meaningful spend visibility.
- Understanding the purchasing process is key to understanding how spend leakages occur.

TYPES OF SPEND

At a broad level, corporate spend can be classified as belonging to direct, indirect, and MRO categories.

Direct

Direct spend encompasses all spend associated with raw materials and services that go into the actual products (or services) that the company sells. For example, for a construction company, all of the raw materials needed for construction, including custom fabricated parts, will fall under direct materials. In the case of a pharmaceutical company, all of the chemical ingredients that go into making a drug, along with the accompanying services, will be part of direct costs.

In a financial statement, direct spend can be rolled up into various accounts:

- On the balance sheet, direct spend can be assigned to various inventory accounts (e.g., finished goods, work in process, and raw materials).
- On the income statement, the COGS (cost of goods sold) account captures that portion of the cost of inventory which has been sold in that period of time.
- On the balance sheet, some purchased items may be capitalized under long-term assets and then periodically moved onto the income statement as a "depreciation expense." For example, if a construction company were to purchase a crane, they would capitalize the $500,000 cost of the crane on the balance sheet and pass on $100,000 of depreciation expense every year to the income statement.

Direct material categories have traditionally been better sourced than indirect categories. However, direct materials pose unique challenges. Their spend needs to be categorized to a higher granularity in order to identify opportunities. Parts equivalency is a big opportunity, but also tricky to identify. OEM (original equipment manufacturer) and custom parts tend to be more difficult to categorize to an appropriate commodity because they tend to be complex and their descriptions are not easily available.

Indirect

Indirect spend encompasses all of the supporting materials and services that are needed to build the core products of the company. For example, business services, travel, insurance, IT hardware and software, facilities, telecommunications, laboratory supplies and equipment, advertising, print and marketing, utilities, office supplies and equipment, and office rent are all examples of indirect spend categories.

In an income statement, this indirect spend is captured in the account SG&A (selling, general, and administrative). Similar to direct spend, there might be cases when an "indirect" equipment expense (e.g., a Cisco Systems, Inc. router) could be capitalized on the balance sheet. Most indirect materials are purchased through separate systems. For example, it is common to use P-cards for office supplies or American Express cards for travel. From a spend analysis perspective, indirect spend is viewed separately from direct because traditionally this category has not been managed centrally. There are big data and compliance issues because of decentralized management, leading to inefficiencies—large vendor fragmentation, suboptimal pricing, and maverick spend. Because this category can account for as much as 20% of the overall spend, immediate and substantial savings can be obtained by identifying "low-hanging" opportunities such as vendor consolidation.

	Direct Procurement	Indirect Procurement	
	Raw Material and Production Goods	MRO Supplies	Goods and Services
Quantity	Large	Low	Low
Frequency	High	Relatively high	Low
Value	Industry specific	Low	High
Examples	Crude oil in petroleum industry	Lubricants, spare parts	Machinery, computers

Figure 5.1. Types of spend. (Modified from Wikipedia®.)

MRO

MRO spend is a special category that includes the spare parts and supplies (such as screws, nuts and bolts) required for upkeep of the capital equipment needed in manufacturing. In financial statements, MRO cost is usually apportioned to COGS (just like capital equipment), so there is no separate account to deal with MRO. The reasons why MRO categories are treated separately include:

- In many manufacturing companies that have grown through acquisitions, each plant tends to buy from local MRO suppliers. In such cases, the percent of maverick MRO spend is high and is an immediate opportunity for supplier rationalization and P-card on-boarding.
- MRO items can easily be procured through one or two suppliers. For example, in the United States, Grainger or MSCDirect can be used for 90% of MRO purchases; therefore, implementing vendor rationalization and preferred supplier compliance is relatively straightforward.
- Most MRO purchases are through online catalogs; therefore it is quite simple to leverage these catalogs in on-boarding MRO suppliers onto e-procurement systems.
- It is relatively simple to find functional equivalents for MRO and conduct item-level rationalization.

In synopsis, direct, indirect, and MRO spend have different characteristics and opportunities. Therefore, in the selection of a commodity schema, separating these categories from each other is usually prudent. The chart in Figure 5.1 summarizes the three categories.

PROCUREMENT PROCESSES

Goods and services are procured in three ways—by the procure-to-pay process, P-cards and through travel and entertainment procurement.

Procure-to-Pay (P2P)

P2P (also known as Req-to-check) denotes the traditional process:

$$\text{Contract} \rightarrow \text{PO} \rightarrow \text{Invoice} \rightarrow \text{Payment}$$

The P2P process is used for direct materials and services, for most MRO, and for some indirect goods. The P2P process often accounts for over 80% of the spend of a company. Because this process is so critical from a price, quality, and performance perspective, most P2P purchases are based on a contract between the buyer and the seller, are carefully negotiated, and usually are long term in nature.

Purchasing Cards (P-Cards)

P-cards are a more recent phenomenon. P-cards are similar to credit cards. In fact, they are issued by some common credit card issuers such as American Express and MasterCard. Companies issue P-cards to selected employees so that these employees can make frequent low-value purchases. They are mostly used for purchasing indirect goods such as office supplies and some frequently needed MRO items. The buyer orders the products by telephone or on the Web and uses a P-card to make the purchase. The issuer of the P-card manages the payment. Payment is made to the seller as soon as the order is placed, very much like using regular credit cards. The card issuer sends a monthly statement that lists the order history. Therefore, typically, there is a single file that captures all of the transaction information. Most P-cards have an upper limit on the amount of purchases that can be made in a billing cycle. Because P-cards are used for purchasing low-cost items, the limits tend to be small—$500 is common.

Travel and Entertainment (T&E)

This type of procurement covers the travel expenses of employees. The process is similar to the P-card process, wherein each employee is issued a corporate credit card (such as from American Express). The employee uses this card to make purchases. At the end of the month, the employee files for reimbursement. The company reimburses the employee based on receipts and allowable per diems. The corporate credit card issuer sends a statement every month that lists all of the transactions. Therefore, as with P-cards, there is usually a single file that captures all of the T&E information. However, usually there are some anomalies. For example, many companies do not issue separate corporate cards, but instead ask employees to use their personal credit cards for making purchases and then to file for reimbursements later.

Both P-cards and T&E procurement could be based on contracts. In fact, companies might use P2P and P-cards to purchase from the same vendor (e.g., Office Depot). The reasons why these three processes are listed (and handled separately) are the following:

1. The processes and "touch points" for P2P, P-cards, and T&E are quite different. For example, T&E reimbursement policies are typically managed centrally; P-card purchases are handled by individual departments; and P2P processes are handled by the purchasing departments.
2. The IT systems that handle these processes are usually separate. For example, SAP R3 might be used for P2P, but P-cards might be implemented in conjunction with e-procurement using Ariba Buyer, and T&E might be outsourced to American Express.
3. The data feeds required to analyze the spend associated with each of these processes are quite different. For example, P-card purchases are highly automated, and most transaction information is available digitally. For P2P, some information (transaction description) might not be available digitally. For T&E, the receipts submitted by employees might not be digital and therefore reconciliation is a highly manual process.

INFORMATION AND APPROVAL FLOW IN P2P PROCESSES

Let us look at the P2P process in Figure 5.2 because this process is used for direct materials and accounts for 80% of the typical corporate spend:

1. The starting point of the relationship between a buyer and a supplier is the contract agreement that lays out the terms of the engagement—including price, quantity, delivery terms, payment terms, warranty, etc. The *contract agreement* is typically a text document; therefore the information is not structured, but it might be part of some section of the contract. If the contract is created within a contract management application, then these parameters are stored in a relational database and can be accessed easily.

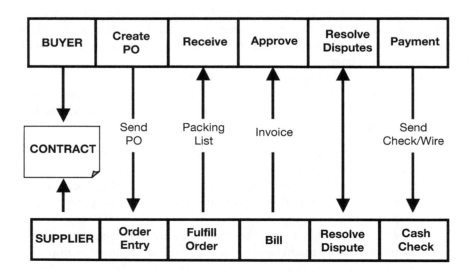

Figure 5.2. A typical P2P or "Req-to-check" process.

The following parameters should be available from a contract module:

Contract number (ID)	Volume threshold(s)
Contract name	Cumulative volume purchased to date
Contract start date	Price spend discount
Contract expiration date	Spend threshold(s)
Unit price	Cumulative spend to date
Quantity	Spend rebate
Price volume discount	Spend rebate threshold(s)

In reality, very few companies have implemented high-quality contract modules. Their contracts sit as paper copies in various filing cabinets or, in some cases, contracts are scanned into a database and some amount of header information on the contracts is entered for purposes of retrieval. This information rarely includes the line item contract terms and provisions that are listed above. Also, many items and services are procured without an official contract. For example, many companies still purchase office supplies directly from distributor catalogs at list prices.

2. The buyer creates a PO within his purchasing system and sends it to the supplier. The purchasing system will maintain PO records which typically have the following minimum fields:

Supplier (vendor) name	Price
PO number	Payment terms
General ledger (GL) code	Total purchase amount
Cost center	Creation date
Item description	Approval date
Quantity	

Ideally a PO should be based on a contract. In fact, it should be autogenerated from the contract; or, if autogeneration is not possible, then, at a minimum, a PO needs to be tallied with the contract parameters. However, because POs are maintained in separate systems and because the contract parameters are part of an unstructured document, this is almost never done at the time a PO is created. Thus, the PO terms and contract terms may not match.

3. The supplier will fulfill the PO by shipping goods or rendering a service. In the case of goods, there will be a packing slip enclosed which lists the items shipped. The receiving department will enter the shipment into their system. A receiving clerk can very easily incorrectly type the item or the quantity; also it is not uncommon for the receiving information to not tally with what was ordered. A receiving file typically has the following minimum fields:

PO number	Quantity received
Vendor name	Destination dept
Date received	Ship-to name

4. The supplier will then send an invoice to the company which will detail the total amount billed. A typical invoice file will have the following minimum fields:

Supplier name	Item price	Invoice amount
PO number	Discounts	Payment terms
Invoice number	Surcharges	Invoice date
Item description	Total amount billed	Due date
Quantity	Taxes	

Today, in a vast majority of companies, invoices are faxed, sent by a postal service, or scan-emailed to the company. Some companies have implemented an e-invoicing system, wherein the supplier must access (typically over the Web) this e-invoicing system and fill out all of the fields to submit the invoice. In certain commodities, such as transportation services, invoice information may be sent via EDI (electronic data exchange).

The invoice is then approved. This approval is usually made by the individual department manager to whom the products were shipped. For example, if laptops were shipped to a specific R&D group, then the group manager who initiated the PO would approve the invoice (typically, once he has received the laptops). In some cases, the manager might approve the invoice after he calls the receiving department and confirms that the shipment has been received. The approval can be sent by telephone or email. In the case of e-invoices, approval can be done online.

If the invoice is sent as an e-invoice, the PO number, supplier name, price, etc. might be autofilled based on the original PO information. However, if the invoice is faxed (which is usually the case), the approval process is largely manual and can be error prone. For example, the approval clerk might easily misread a number or not check into whether the PO number on the invoice is correct. Entering duplicate invoices is common even today. Thus, the systems might show invoice information that does not tally with the PO information or the receiving information.

The approved invoice is then sent to the AP department. In the case of e-invoices, this routing might be automated, meaning that once approved, the invoice can be automatically forwarded to the AP department within the ERP system or if the systems are integrated. However, if the invoice is sent via fax, then the AP department has to manually enter the invoice information into the AP system, including entering the billed amount, the quantity received, etc., which can be error prone.

The AP department will then cut and send the payment check to the supplier. The PO file will then contain payment information and will have the following additional fields:

Billed quantity	Invoice date	Approver
Billed amount	Approval date	

Note: The PO file might not have item description, invoice number, unit price, or some other fields.

Finally, it is important to note that a contract might consist of multiple POs and each PO might have multiple invoices and each invoice might have multiple payments made. For example, the contract might be for 2 years, with a maximum ceiling of $2 million, on which there might be multiple (open) POs issued, each for $100,000, and for each PO, there might be multiple shipments. For each shipment, there might be an invoice. Finally, if the payment terms are 50% upfront, 50% net 30, then two payments will be made on the same invoice. This one-to-many relationship between contracts, POs, invoices, and payments adds a layer of complexity in the reconciliation process in spend analysis, in which matching individual transactions to appropriate invoices, POs, and contracts is required.

DATA REQUIREMENTS FOR P-CARDS

The issuer of P-cards typically sends a transactions history log to the company at the end of the billing cycle. This P-card file has the following fields:

Account number/P-card number	Merchant
User (purchaser)	Cost center
Transaction ID	GL account
Transaction date	Item description
Transaction amount	

In order to do a full reconciliation, it may be necessary to tally the transactions history log of the P-cards with the receiving dock file to see if the correct quantity has in fact been received. However, in many instances, the merchant ships the items directly to the end user without going through the receiving dock; in these cases, it becomes impossible to verify the transactions history log of P-cards. Direct shipping to the end user is especially common with items purchased through P-cards.

DATA REQUIREMENTS FOR T&E

Similar to the process with P-cards, the issuer of corporate cards sends a monthly statement that lists all the transactions that occurred. Therefore, all of the information can be available digitally in a structured format. However, in cases in which some employees do not have corporate cards and are using their personal credit cards, such information is obtained through expense reports filed by employees. For verification, employees need to submit receipts. It is assumed that approved expense reports have all of the required supporting receipts. Therefore, for compliance, it might only be necessary to verify that payments are consistent with the approved expense reports. From a fraud-monitoring perspective, however, it might be necessary to look for patterns in individual expense reimbursements that might denote abuse of privileges.

Typical T&E Expense Data

Reservation_id	Hotel name	Destination city
Customer_id	Car rental name	Travel code
Cost center	Start date	Miles
Account number	End date	Airfare
Trip_id	Book date	Hotel fare
Vendor	Origin city	Car rental fare

SOURCE SYSTEMS AND DATA EXTRACTS

The previous section has described a process-centric view of the information that is generated in the procurement process and some of the systems that enable this process. In real life, this end-to-end process is not handled by one system, but by multiple systems in multiple divisions or plants. In addition, depending on the scope of spend visibility that is required, you might need data from several other systems. In this section, we will list some of the typical source systems and what kinds of data to expect from them.

Accounts Payable

AP data typically contains invoice information (invoice date, invoice creation date, invoice amount, vendor) and payment information (paid amount, payment date). A description might be present, but oftentimes this description is not the same as the description in the invoice because AP personnel might not enter the full description into the system or they might use abbreviations.

AP systems also contain the master files for cost centers, GL codes, source systems, and vendors. These are important files because you would typically want to model these as dimensions for purposes of spend analysis.

Purchasing/e-Procurement

Purchasing/e-procurement systems manage the requisition/invoice/payment process. This is where POs are created and approved, invoices are entered and approved, and approved invoices are submitted to AP.

All PO-related information, such as PO number, PO creation date, PO approval date, PO amount limit, ordered quantity, unit price, vendor, etc., are available in this system. Usually (but not always), the PO number (or a key based on PO number) links the PO data to the AP data.

A distinction needs to be made between traditional purchasing systems and e-procurement systems. The latter typically denotes systems for indirect purchasing, such as Ariba Buyer (more and more often, direct material spend is now being channeled through such systems).

Note that the purchasing system might have its own vendor master file, which might not be the same as the vendor file in AP. Also note that these systems provide the PO data only. These POs can be in various WIP (work-in-process) stages. Some of these POs have been fulfilled and the suppliers have been paid. Others might be fulfilled and the invoices received, but the invoices have not been paid. Then there might be POs that are fulfilled, but the invoices have not been received. Finally, POs might exist that are approved, but not fulfilled. By capturing all of this information, the spend cube can show not only "actual spend" information, but also "immediately forecasted spend." After incorporating the MRP data (to be discussed shortly), the spend cube can also show "mid- and long-term forecasted spend."

Receiving

Most companies have a system at their receiving docks. When a shipment is delivered, the receiving person examines the contents and scans the packing slip, which usually has the PO number on it. This type of receiving system provides information on the date of receipt and the delivered quantity.

Materials Management

Materials management systems manage the product information on direct materials and MRO items. A materials management system has an "item master" file which typically provides a much better description of the parts than is available in the invoices or POs. This system also has a commodity schema to which these items are mapped. The system provides information such as material number, material group (or commodity number), manufacturer name, manufacturer part number, description, etc. It also provides details on the commodity schema. Note that the PO data might or might not be directly linked with the materials management data. In some cases, the material number might be specified in the PO, in which case a link can be established. In other cases, "fuzzy mapping" techniques need to be used to compare vendor and part description information to map the PO item to a materials master item.

Freight Transactions

If a third party transportation provider is used to manage logistics, then usually it is possible to get freight transaction details from the provider. Freight transaction details include mode of transport, start date and location, end date and location, LTL (less than truckload) status, etc.

Corporate P-Cards

P-cards have been explained in a previous section in some detail. Because P-cards account for the bulk of indirect spend, these systems are therefore very useful for the purposes of spend analysis.

Travel and Entertainment

T&E have been covered in a previous section in some detail.

Contract Management

Contract management systems typically provide contract details—vendor, contract start and expiration dates, and other items which have been detailed in previous sections.

Material Requirements Planning or Manufacturing Resource Planning Systems

MRP systems develop material and manufacturing plans based on forecasted demand. These material and manufacturing plans can be exported and used in spend analysis for forecasted spend. Typically, MRP plans provide order quantities, order dates, and other replenishment-related information for each SKU (stock keeping units). They may also provide other useful information such as date effectivity (when to substitute one part with another) and use effectivity (after using one part, substitute with another). Note that organizations might have multiple MRP systems for each facility and/or a central "master" MRP system that creates a master procurement plan across the organization. In general, very few companies use MRP data to forecast spend in their spend cubes, although doing so is an important future area of expansion.

Contract Manufacturer Data

If a supplier is a contract manufacturer, then the BOMs (bills of materials) or parts lists and the component approved vendor list can also be used. For example, in the high-tech industry, it is common to use contract manufacturers (such as Flextronics) to do all of the procurement and assembly work. In such cases, all of the detailed part- and PO-level information is needed from the contract manufacturer in order to construct the item-level costing and spend details.

Other (External Sources)

Many third party content and research companies provide market research data which can be incorporated into the spend cube for visibility into opportunities:

- Competitive intelligence and benchmarking data
- Supplier intelligence data (geographies, diversity status, past performance)

QUALITY OF DATA

Once you extract all of the transactions from your source systems, and all of the associated data that may come from other business systems, you are ready to start normalizing the data and building the spend cube.

The two default properties you will need for each transaction are the paid amount and the payment date. Unless you have these two basic fields populated with accurate data, no spend analysis is possible. It is very common to have the dates formatted differently in the various systems. You will also be dealing with different currencies if your company has a global presence. These two fields will need to be normalized to a single format and currency.

Above and beyond these two fields, you will need a number of other data elements for each transaction. These data elements correspond to the various dimensions you want to use in your spend cube. For example, if you want cost center, GL, geography, and commodity as the dimensions, you will need this information for each transaction.

Of all these data elements, all but the commodity code are generally available in the transaction files. In some cases, the commodity codes are also assigned. However, in many companies, these internal commodity codes have been historically created by the material master group and do not have sufficient granularity for spend analysis. Thus, a new commodity structure may need to be used, preferably an industry standard schema such as UNSPSC. We will discuss commodity schema selection at length in Chapter 6 (*Spend Analysis Components*) and Chapter 7 (*Taxonomy Considerations*). Once you standardize on a commodity schema, you are ready to begin classifying the transactions to these commodities.

We will review the theory of classification in Chapter 8 (*Technology Considerations*), but let us take a quick look at how you can classify transactions to commodities. Figure 5.3 shows some of the common transaction fields that can be used for this purpose. The lower part of the figure shows transactions that can be classified if a high-quality description is available. The upper part of the figure shows fields that can be used for classification in the event that the item description is not available. Clearly, the precision or granularity of classification is better if the item description is available.

We will now review each of these elements.

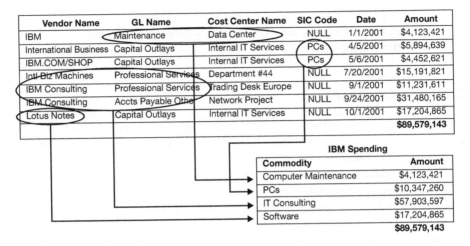

Vendor Name	GL Name	Cost Center Name	SIC Code	Date	Amount
IBM	Maintenance	Data Center	NULL	1/1/2001	$4,123,421
International Business	Capital Outlays	Internal IT Services	PCs	4/5/2001	$5,894,639
IBM.COM/SHOP	Capital Outlays	Internal IT Services	PCs	5/6/2001	$4,452,621
Intl Biz Machines	Professional Services	Department #44	NULL	7/20/2001	$15,191,821
IBM Consulting	Professional Services	Trading Desk Europe	NULL	9/1/2001	$11,231,611
IBM Consulting	Accts Payable Other	Network Project	NULL	9/24/2001	$31,480,165
Lotus Notes	Capital Outlays	Internal IT Services	NULL	10/1/2001	$17,204,865
					$89,579,143

IBM Spending

Commodity	Amount
Computer Maintenance	$4,123,421
PCs	$10,347,260
IT Consulting	$57,903,597
Software	$17,204,865
	$89,579,143

ID	Item Description	Commodity
23	BEARING 135658 STEER AXLE CUP	Bearing cups
14	BEARING 193088 DR AXLE CUP	Bearing cups
115	BELT V A-42	V belts
253	CONTACTOR, DEFINITE PURPOSE MAGNETIC, DC CRANE	Contactors
68	GASKET 112632 STARTER MTR	Gaskets
226	DRILL TWIST A SS	Twist drills

Figure 5.3. Transaction fields that can be used to assign commodity codes.

Item Description

Item description is perhaps the most important field available for classification, especially in direct materials and MRO. The accuracy and granularity to which the transaction can be classified depends on the quality of the description. The descriptions in Figure 5.3 are of the average quality that you will encounter in 90% of companies. High-quality item descriptions are hard to come by. Below is an example:

DUAL RANGE PRESSURE CONTROLLER, PCS400M-12
RANGE: 20/5 PSIA, .01%, FS ACCURACY

Transforming poor-quality descriptions to high-quality descriptions is possible by leveraging product data sheets. Figure 5.4 shows examples of such enriched descriptions. Such enrichment is usually manual in nature (or at best semi-automated) because it involves searching for data sheets in online catalogs, then parsing description attributes, and then constructing a structured, well-formatted description.

Vendor	Original Description	Cleansed Description
AMCO ENGINEERING	CLV412A1010 SCANNER REPAIR S/N:00238134	Stationary Bar Code Scanner; Application Type: High Density; Height: 35.2 MM; Length: 59 MM; Range: 50 – 380 MM; Scan Technology: Rastor; Weight: 250 GR; Width: 62.5 MM
DIGI KEY CORP.	CAX2S	Caster; Load Capacity: 275 LB; Mounting Type: Swivel; Wheel Diameter: 3.5 IN
VISHAY INTERTECHNOLOGY, INC.	HM365-ND .2 X 1.5 X 1.2" DIE CAST ENCLOSURE	Electrical Box; Conduit Size: 2 X 1.5 X 1.2 IN; Depth:1.5 IN; Height: 1.2 IN; Material: Aluminum; Width: 2 IN; Color: Natural

Figure 5.4. Example of enriched item descriptions. MM, millimeters; GR, gram; LB, pounds; IN, inches.

Vendor Name

The next important data element that is used for classifications is the vendor name. There are usually quality problems associated with vendor names. The list in Figure 5.5 shows the many ways in which a vendor's name (and its divisions) might be entered into a business system. The situation illustrated in Figure 5.5 is an extremely common occurrence. Two steps need to be performed:

- Vendor normalization—All vendor names need to be associated with their correct names. For example, ADM Milling G P should be associated with ADM Milling Company which is the official name of the subsidiary.
- Vendor enrichment—A parent/child relationship needs to be established to create a hierarchy.

Cost Center and GL Code

Similar to vendor names, cost centers and GL codes can have many variances. These variances typically come from accounting systems. If there are multiple accounting systems that have not been standardized, having variations of the same GL code, such as computer hardware, IT hardware, IT equipment, etc., is very easily possible. It is important to normalize these to one standard name.

Once these data fields are cleansed and normalized as shown above, you are ready to start assigning commodities to the transactions, either on the basis of item descriptions or from a combination of the other dimensions. The reader

-------- ARCHER DANIELS MIDLAND CO
-------- ARCHER DANIEL MIDLAND CO
-------- ADM COCOA PRODUCTS INC
-------- ARCHER DANIELS MIDLAND
-------- ARCHER DANIELS MIDLAND CO
-------- ADM MILLING G P
-------- ARCHER DANIELS MIDLAND
-------- ARCHER DANIELS MIDLAND ARKADY
-------- ADM COCOA
-------- ARCHER DANIELS – ARKADY

Figure 5.5. Vendor name variations.

must note that classifying millions of transactions is a task that should be done by using autoclassification and rules-based classification technology. We will describe these in Chapter 8 (*Technology Considerations*). Once your transactions are classified, your data set is ready to be cast as a dimensional model (as explained in Chapter 1), which will group the transactions with respect to each dimension and show aggregate spend levels.

SUMMARY

Chapter 5 has taken a closer look at the types of spend—direct, indirect, and MRO. We have also examined the three common purchasing processes—procure-to-pay (P2P), purchasing cards (P-cards), and travel and entertainment procurement (T&E). We have also reviewed how purchasing transactions are generated, the source systems that generate these transactions, and the data fields that one can expect to find in these transactions. The AP system is perhaps the most important source system, without which no spend analysis is possible. However, the AP system might not account for all of the spend; therefore it is important to tap P-cards and other systems. It might also be important to feed in data from other systems—MRP, e-procurement, and others, depending on the requirements. We have also shown which data elements are important for the purposes of classifying the spend—item description, vendor name, and cost center/GL name.

SPEND ANALYSIS
COMPONENTS

INTRODUCTION

In Chapter 1, we discussed the components that make up a spend analysis application. We also saw how a simple spend cube is constructed. In this chapter, we will examine these components in depth. We will focus on the design challenges, but our presentation will not require specialized technical skills; all of the prerequisite information will be introduced in a way that will make the topics easily understood by nonexperts. Whether you want to license or build your own solution, the following sections contain useful information that you should familiarize yourself with.

The main thesis of this book is that a complete and successful spend analysis implementation requires four modules:

- Data definition and loading (DDL)
- Data enrichment (DE)
- Knowledgebase (KB)
- Spend analytics (SA)

We will briefly revisit each of these modules and then examine each one of them in detail.

The *data definition and loading module* is responsible for the definition of the desired schema and the import of the transactional data into the spend analysis platform. In addition, the DDL module should facilitate the analysis of the transactional data by identifying spurious entries and violations of the schema definitions. The analysis should also include statistical information that can be leveraged at later stages of processing or during the loading of new transactional data; the latter phase is typically referred to as the *refresh cycle*.

The *data enrichment module* is a critical piece of the spend analysis implementation. It is the module that facilitates the assignment of transactions from one category to another based on user defined rules; the classification of the transactions based on their attribute values; the structuring of the dimensional information; the enrichment of attribute values based on knowledge that can be considered as authoritative; and so on.

It is very important to execute the DE phase in well-defined stages. The reason for this is twofold. Firstly, you want to ensure that there are well-defined checkpoints so that the processing can be monitored at these checkpoints. Having well-defined checkpoints is extremely valuable during the first time that you load data. Well-defined checkpoints are equally valuable at a later time, if significant changes in the processing steps are involved or if the authoritative knowledge that is used as a reference has changed significantly. Secondly, you want to be able to combine the processing that happens in the various stages in a different order, or you might want to eliminate a certain part of the processing during a specific refresh cycle and observe the differences of the various outcomes. In order to do that, the processing itself should consist of stages that have a well-defined scope, with respect to the data changes that result from their execution. This enhances the overall quality of the data and facilitates the monitoring process.

The *knowledgebase module* is responsible for the maintenance of the authoritative information that is used as a reference during the DE phase. Maintaining a repository of knowledge can be as simple as storing the data in a relational database or a plain ASCII file. However, in the latter case there is very little business value added in the whole process. The KB module should provide tools that:

- Facilitate the life cycle of the KB data entries, e.g., the import of new information, the structural modification of a hierarchy, and the enrichment of the attribute values
- Facilitate the semantic, syntactic, and grammatical analysis of the information
- Provide a versioning infrastructure for keeping track of the KB evolution

Lastly, the *analytics module* is the platform that facilitates the consumption of the information that was created during the DE phase and extracts the knowledge that is required for decision making. The functionality that can be provided in an analytics module is limited only by the creativity of the user and the innovation

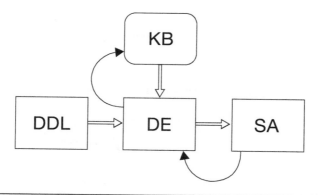

Figure 6.1. The four essential modules of a spend analysis implementation.

level of the platform vendor. Nevertheless, you should require, as a minimum, the following:

- An OLAP (online analytical processing) tool, capable of answering questions with respect to several, if not all, of the dimensions of your data—The ability to "slice and dice" across various dimensions in an efficient manner is critical to the success of your project. However, you should be aware that response times of 8 to 10 seconds are typical in OLAP cubes with tens of millions of transactions and a dozen dimensions.

- A reporting tool that allows the creation of reports in various formats (e.g., CSV, PDF, Excel)—The ability to support cross-tabulation is very important in the context of reporting. For example, it is customary to create cross-tabulations across commodities for vendors over a certain time period.

- A search-enabled interface that allows the quick retrieval of information based on the values of the transactional or dimensional attributes.

The four modules are shown schematically in Figure 6.1. The double-line arrows indicate the flow of the transactional data. The two single-line arrows indicate the feedback from the end users of spend analysis.

DATA DEFINITION AND LOADING (DDL)

As mentioned in the first part of this book, the analysis of corporate spend begins with the identification and extraction of all relevant information from disparate sources. So, before you begin a "build or buy" process for your spend analysis

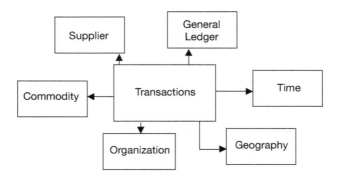

Figure 6.2. A star schema.

needs, you should collect adequate information about your data. You should assess the availability, extraction efficiency, and accuracy of your operational sources and processes. You should create a list of your file structures and a list of attributes about them, such as their origin, the contact person responsible for them, etc. You should also take notes concerning the operational life cycle of the data.

The end result of the data definition phase is typically a star schema, i.e., a set of files that corresponds to the dimensional aspects of the transactions and a single file that contains the transactions themselves (Figure 6.2). Dimensions are typically hierarchical, so we often refer to their records as "nodes" (discussed in Chapter 1 in the context of a small cube with three dimensions). The dimensional nodes have, at least, three fields—an ID number, a parent ID, and a name. Of course, the dimensional nodes can have other attributes. In fact, there are dimensions that have up to hundreds of attributes in the dimensional nodes. Having dimensions with hundreds of attributes is not recommended, but it does occur in practice because the data have not been through an attribute selection phase.

The transactional table is flat and contains its own ID number, the foreign keys to the dimensional tables, the measure fields, and optionally other attributes of the transactions. More complicated schemas do exist and should be considered if there are specific business requirements or if there are technical constraints that impose a normalization of the schema. For example, the snowflake schema uses a single fact table as does the star schema, but it normalizes the dimensional tables. In general, more complicated schemas result in slower response times. Without loss of generality, hereafter, we will assume that our target schema is a star schema. The interested reader can find more details on the various schemas in the data warehousing literature.[1]

The top priority during the aggregation of the data from the various heterogeneous systems and their loading in the spend analysis system should be the achievement of a high information quality index (IQI):

In order to define an *information quality index* (IQI), we need to have metrics that define the quality of information in our data. In general, there is a direct relationship between the "richness" of the data and the degree of difficulty in processing the data for the purpose of analysis. This is true for spend data as well as any other kind of data. Let us define the *lexicographic entropy* (λ) of a data set as follows:

$$\lambda = -\sum_i p(i)\log p(i)$$

where *p(i)* is the probability of occurrence for the *i*-th word in our data and the summation is taken over the set of all the distinct words. If we only had a single word in our data set, even if that same word were repeated millions of times, then the lexicographic entropy would be exactly zero and the cost of enriching the data would be minimal, at least as far as their lexicographic and semantic attribution of their content is concerned. On the other hand, if each word in our data set were unique (in the sense of being a different string of characters), then the lexicographic entropy would attain its maximum value and so would the cost of enriching the data. This is a general rule and it is actually far reaching. It is not important if your transactional data come from credit card systems, payrolls, clearing houses, or whatever else. Thus, it is often useful to define the lexicographic entropy and use it as a metric of the effort that will be involved in achieving a certain enrichment quality level. Of course, you should never rely on a single number for assessing something that can only be described by a multidimensional distribution. Nevertheless, this quantity is easy to compute and comes in very handy for "back of the envelope" estimates.

The business value obtained from the subsequent analysis of the data is proportional to the IQI that we achieve during the DDL and DE phases.

There are many ways to execute the ETL (extraction, transformation, and loading) of the data from the source systems into a star schema for implementing a spend analysis solution, and many vendors provide excellent ETL facilities. The ETL processes involved are not technically different from what is currently applied in the construction of many data warehouses. Similarly to the case of data warehousing, the cost of failing to produce a "good" set of data during the ETL phase is fairly high.

Data Cleansing

There is a special phase of ETL that is particularly important, namely, data cleansing, also known as data cleaning or scrubbing. During this phase we identify and eliminate errors from the data in order to improve their quality. There are many types of data errors, e.g., errors due to misspellings, missing information, inconsistent attribute values, etc. Eliminating these errors requires an understanding of their nature. In this book, we will adopt the classification of data errors that was given by Rahm and Do.[2] In particular, data errors belong into two broad categories:

- Single-source errors
- Multisource errors

Within each category, we can further differentiate the errors based on whether they are schema- or instance-related errors. For both schema- and instance-level problems there are four different problem scopes: attribute (field), record, record type, and source. The top four categories of errors and some representative examples include:

Single source, schema level:
- Self-integrity (uniqueness) errors, e.g., duplicate transaction IDs
- Self-referential errors, e.g., hierarchical reference mistakes (missing parent IDs)

Single source, instance level:
- Misspellings, e.g., "Analysis" versus "Anaylsis"
- Redundancy of terms (meaning overloading), e.g., the terms "done," "completed," and "100%" might all refer to the same status of a project
- Attribute values that are inconsistent with the schema definition, e.g., a column might be holding the invoice date and some values might not be valid date formats

Multisource, schema level:
- One-to-many field mappings, e.g., if there are two sources of data for "employee," the first source's schema might have a "name" field whereas the second source's schema might have two or three fields, e.g., for the first, middle, and last name, respectively
- Different field labels, but semantically identical fields, e.g., "sex" versus "gender"

Multisource, instance level:
- Different representations for the values of the fields, e.g., Boolean versus numeric (0,1)
- Different units for the values of the fields, e.g., meters versus feet
- Different formats for the values of the fields, e.g., "2007-04-02" versus "April 2, 2007" or "John, Smith" versus "Smith, John"

DDL Considerations

In the DDL phase, you will almost certainly encounter the following business and technical ailments (directly or indirectly):

- The processes and tools typically depend heavily on manual effort and expertise. If you would like to visualize your spend data based on the UNSPSC structure, but you only have the assignment of the transactions to your own custom taxonomy, then typically a human will create a mapping—also known as a "crosswalk"—that will assign the spend associated with a given custom taxonomy to the UNSPSC structure. Examples in this category abound. The degree of manual effort depends heavily on the nature of your data and the ETL capabilities of the various systems that are involved during the extraction process. You should bear in mind that the IT time that is allocated to your project, and the degree of cooperation between the various departments that are involved, are crucial because nobody gets it right the first time. Thus, it is always necessary to allow for sufficient time and resource capacity in your plan for the iterations that are required in order to meet your quality metrics.

- The processes and tools involved are not scalable with respect to client volume. A typical example would be an Excel macro that you have written to cleanse the data or collect preliminary information about your data. Excel cannot handle a file with more than 65,536 rows or 256 columns. Thus, your macro which performed well on your small test data set, or the data set of a single system, will not work at all for the data from other systems whose size exceeds these limitations. Workarounds that involve command line or other "glue" scripting are often employed, but they are difficult to maintain and hard to debug.

- The processes and tools involved do not guarantee repeatability with respect to a specific data set nor uniformity within a business domain. Let us consider, for example, a case in which you are lacking the PO description from your spend data—that is not encouraged, but it does happen in practice—and let us further assume that you plan to assign commodities based on the vendor information. You assign the task to four good analysts and they begin, feverishly assigning commodities to transactions based on the vendor information. Two weeks later, you have assigned your spend data, you commend your people for a job well done, and you start analyzing the data. Six months later you are ready to integrate the new transactions on your system. Two of the four people who were responsible for the mapping are now at another company. The new people make assignments that are different from the assignments of their predecessors (that can happen for many reasons). Moreover, the two veterans on the project might also assign new transactions to the UNSPSC in an inconsistent manner because all of the work was conducted manually and the criteria for their selections were not captured at the time of the selection.

State-of-the-art DDL modules are able to address these ailments more or less satisfactorily. It should be noted that the ability to streamline the processing of the data can yield high payoffs in terms of efficiency. The first time that the DDL module is used to process the totality of the data sources is the first time that you can have a first good estimate of the complexity that is involved in processing your data and performing a successful spend analysis program. It is imperative that you set two concrete and clear goals during that phase. Your first goal is to establish a comprehensive assessment of the data content. The second is to set a clear set of success criteria for the enrichment process that will follow.

Data Assessment

Let us define the assessment of the data content on the basis of the following factors:

1. The categorization of errors as described above in this section
2. The size of the data
3. The quality of the data as measured by quantities such as the lexicographic entropy

The categorization of errors is critical because not all errors are equally costly to fix. If your organization is a large corporation and your data are collected from various sources, as it is often the case, then the possibility of facing business process management constraints will extend the timeline of your program in unexpected ways. Aside from the fact that the various errors in the data require iteration between your spend analysts and the IT infrastructure groups, some of the errors are technically difficult, although not impossible, to correct. For example, the meaning of certain codes in the schema of one system might be undocumented and therefore a correspondence with another schema, from another system, might have to be inferred.

We should note that the "size of the data" does not refer to a single number, but rather to a set of numbers that characterize the various data sets. Typically, we use the following quantities to describe the size of a data set:

- Number of transactional records (N_t)
- Number of dimensions (N_d)

- Number of dimensional nodes per dimension (D_n^i; i-th dimension has n nodes)
- Maximum depth (level) per dimension (L_n^i; i-th dimension has n levels)

For example, let us consider two sets—set A is characterized by ($N_t = 2M$, $N_d = 10$, max $\{D_n^i\} = 10K$, max $\{L_n^i\} = 4$) and set B is characterized by ($N_t = 2M$, $N_d = 12$, max $\{D_n^i\} = 80K$, max $\{L_n^i\} = 7$). In this case, even though both sets have two million transactions, set B is larger than set A.

It is important to realize that every "fix" introduces a risk of "polluting" the data, i.e., it increases the probability of spurious entries in the data. In addition, the DDL cleansing is often done across entire dimensions or across the entire transactional (fact) table. Thus, we should identify both the errors in our data and the risk that we would take to correct them. Here is a simple solution that you can employ:

1. Evaluate the coverage of the error, i.e., the amount of data that has to be altered in order to fix the problem. You can simply use the count of row updates for this purpose.
2. Attribute the risk of your error-correcting task to one of the following categories based on the information that is available to you and your group:
   i. The root cause is perfectly understood and well documented.
   ii. The root cause is not documented, but it has been inferred. There are no other inferences available that would explain the data. There is not a single objection in the interpretation of the data. It is a single-source error.
   iii. The root cause is not documented, but it has been inferred. There are no other inferences available that would explain the data. There are objections to the interpretation of the data. It is a multisource error.
   iv. The root cause is not documented and cannot be inferred. There is no agreement as to what may be a final resolution for this error.
3. If you have errors in category iv, then you have two alternatives. The first alternative, if possible, is to exclude these data from your sources. The second alternative is to look for additional information that will allow you to classify the error in a less risky category. In other words, errors of category iv are unacceptable and could jeopardize your entire analysis, so they should be eliminated completely.
4. If you do not have errors in category iv, then you can evaluate a measure of risk as follows:

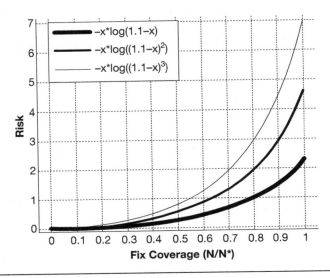

Figure 6.3. Operation risk as a function of coverage.

$$\rho = -\sum_i (\frac{N}{N*})\log(1.1 - \frac{N}{N*})^m,$$

where N is the coverage of the error; $N*$ is the total number of records within the context of the error; m is equal to 1, 2, or 3, depending on whether the error belongs in category i, ii, or iii, respectively; and the sum is taken over all errors that need to be fixed. The numeric value 1.1 is an *ad hoc* value and should be calibrated to your tolerance for an error that affects all the records. Mathematically, this constant eliminates the infinite value of risk when $N/N*$ is equal to one.

The cost for the DDL processing of the original data will be proportional to the risk as defined above. You can get a sharper estimate of the cost if you multiply each term of risk in the above formula with weights that depend on the actual operation that is performed, which in turn depends entirely on your implementation. A graph of the above formula is given in Figure 6.3.

DATA ENRICHMENT (DE)

Overview

A good IQI, the index that we discussed in the previous section, sets the stage for the DE-related processing. However, much more remains to be done in order to accomplish the primary and most important goal of a DE module, which is a *complete, accurate, precise, consistent, and coherent* representation of the transactional and dimensional data. The adjectives have been chosen carefully, so the reader should be alert to the implications that each one of these data properties can have in the final outcome of a spend analysis program.

It all starts with the data. If your data representation is deficient in any one of the ways that was just mentioned, you are running the risk of immaterializing the entire spend analysis program. If your data are incomplete, you will not have the full picture of your corporate spend. Of course, the magnitude of incompleteness will determine the severity of your deficiency during analysis. The outcome is obviously worse if you do not know that your data are incomplete. If your data are inaccurate, there is no point to proceed any further. It will be impossible to draw any conclusions from inaccurate data. Once again, the degree of the ignorance involved is important. If you know that your data are inaccurate and you also know the extent, the origin, and magnitude of the inaccuracies, you can probably compensate for this situation later on, but you probably want to eliminate these inaccuracies before doing anything else.

People often confuse precision with accuracy. Let us clarify these two concepts in the context of a spend analysis program. If you purchased a "Dell D620 Latitude" computer, then an assignment of that transaction to the commodity that corresponds to "Computers" is accurate, but it is not precise. An assignment that corresponds to "Laptop Computers" is equally accurate, but it is more precise than our previous assignment. The conceptual difference between accuracy and precision is important for entities that are characterized by many scales, e.g., a hierarchical structure, the measurement of a continuous or semicontinuous quantity in different units, etc.

Consistency of the data has two aspects. The first is the schema and attribute level consistency, which we examined earlier in the DDL module. The second aspect of consistency is semantic. If a transaction refers to a commodity, say, "Computers" and its vendor refers to a vendor that is well known to produce only coffee, and nothing remotely considered to be a "Computer," then these data contain semantic inconsistencies.

Finally, the data are coherent if their internal structure is sufficient to contain all of the information that is available without excess or duplications. It is also possible to have semantically incoherent data. For example, consider the case of a dimensional hierarchy that represents vendors and contains in its first level four continents and three janitorial services vendors—such a structure is clearly incoherent. Therefore, the DE module should support a variety of enrichment functions that ensure all of the fundamental properties that we have discussed above.

The fundamental idea that underlies all data enrichment-related work can be understood in terms of the following simple example. Let us consider some data

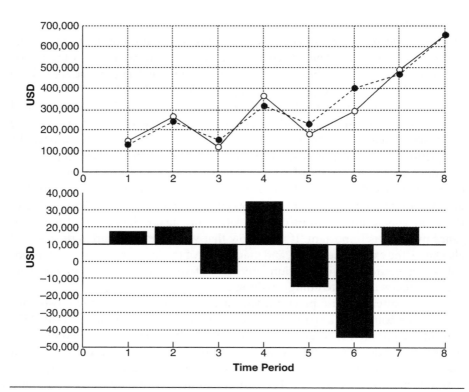

Figure 6.4. The amount of spend (in USD) for some commodity as a function of time.

that represent the amount of spend (in USD) for some commodity as a function of time, as shown in Figure 6.4. In the top of the figure, the solid line indicates the true amount spent during a period, whereas the dashed line indicates the amount recorded in our data. In the bottom of the figure, the bars denote the variance between true and actual values.

> The goal of all data enrichment activity is the alignment between the true distribution of the amount spent and the distribution recorded in our data.

Implicitly the same principle applies for the DDL module. This would have been a trivial problem to solve, if you knew both lines; however, notice that you do not know the solid line explicitly! In real data, there are many more dimensions to consider. The lines are substituted by hyper-surfaces and the detailed analysis can be a scientific challenge, but the main idea remains the same. The goal of the DE module is to "interpolate" the values of the recorded spend as accurately as is possible with the information that is available to us. Interpolation in this context does not refer to numeric interpolation, but rather to *information content interpolation*.

You should be aware of two important conceptual distinctions. The first is a distinction about the type of data that we enrich. Do we enrich the transactional information or do we enrich the dimensional information? The second distinction is related to our principle of executing the data enrichment phase in well-defined stages and identifies the kind of operation that we want to perform on the data.

The distinction on the type of data divides enrichment into two broad areas, namely, *transactional enrichment* and *dimensional enrichment*. Notice that in the context of spend analysis, the terms "transaction" and "fact" are used interchangeably. This categorization is true regardless of the underlying OLAP schema. For example, the process of assigning a commodity code on the basis of its description belongs to the class of transactional enrichment because the end effect is a new commodity code assigned to a set of transactions. In other words, at the end of that process every value of every dimension remains unchanged, but the value that corresponds to the commodity code key in the transactional record has changed. On the other hand, embedding your custom taxonomy into the UNSPSC taxonomy is a process that belongs to the class of dimensional enrichment because the end result is an enriched commodity structure. However, the assignments of the transactions with respect to your commodity dimension have not been altered at all.

The second distinction, which identifies the kind of operation that we want to perform on the data, results in a finer partitioning of the data enrichment universe. This is natural because we have only two kinds of data conceptually, i.e., transactional and dimensional data, whereas we have practically an infinite number of ways to alter these data. It is exactly this large number of ways that we can change the data that results in a plethora of errors when either the processing is entirely manual or whatever automation is used does not take into account the conceptual distinction between the changes in the data. Let us consider this point more carefully because it is very important.

In general, we can change our data solely by manual effort, solely by automation, and in any other way that is between these two extremes. From the set of all operations that are available, we need to consider only the following three categories:

- Manual
- Fully automated
- Man-in-the-loop or hybrid

We will discuss all of these operational categories in more detail in the sections that follow. Nevertheless, it is worthwhile to provide a quick summary of their characteristics now.

Manual operations should be available to the user of the DE module, but they should be reserved for surgical changes of the data or changes that would be inefficient, or impractical, to perform in any other way. The reasons for this are quite simple. Manual operations require the expertise of the operator. They are less efficient because they are usually very granular, which implies high effort, but low impact—notice that if that is not the case for some operations, then they could be fully automated and therefore they should not be manual. Lastly, manual operations typically have higher maintenance cost.

Fully automated operations are the most efficient and the easiest to maintain, but if they are not chosen cautiously, they can lead to gross errors. A case of fully automated operation for the DE module is the application of a set of rules that were defined by the users and have undergone an approval workflow as to their legitimacy. For example, if you know, *a priori* that your company purchases only "valves" from vendor "XYZ," it makes perfect sense to include a rule in your system that automatically assigns all of the spend associated with vendor "XYZ" to the UNSPSC commodity code "42192210," which corresponds to "valves."

Man-in-the-loop, or hybrid, operations are a nice compromise between the efficiency of a fully automated operation, on the one hand, and the precision and accuracy of the manual operations, on the other hand. Man-in-the-loop operations will typically have an automated component that acts on the entire dataset and a human review process that acts as a quality assurance step for the whole operation. For example, a man-in-the-loop case is the automated transactional classification of spend with respect to the UNSPSC, followed by a review process that qualifies the results of the classification. As we will see, the last step is extremely important in cases in which the classifier is asked to classify data for which the classifier knows very little and can infer nothing about them. Notice that man-in-the-loop operators do not consist of some arbitrary mixture of manual and automated operations. They only refer to operations that form a synergy between the machine component and the human component. The machine is doing most of the work while the human, with minimum effort, is validating the results and occasionally augmenting the knowledge that is available to the machine.

Now, we are ready to discuss in more detail the abstract concept of "operation" that we have used so far. If there are an infinite number of operations that we can perform, how do we build a complete and successful spend analysis program? It is clear to everyone that the transactional data of company X will be different from the transactional data of company Y. It is also clear that the content and the structure of commodity codes, general ledger codes, cost centers, and so on, will be different as well. It turns out that a handful of well-defined operations suffice for the complete and successful enrichment and classification of spend data. These operations are the following:

- Classification
- Clustering
- Application of business rules
- Manual editing

Classification

Classification in this context refers to machine learning algorithms that can identify missing information in your current data set based on information that you have collected in the past. That prior knowledge could be based on data that you or others (third party vendors) have accumulated and whose quality meets fairly high standards, so that it can be used effectively as a reference frame. It is worth making these concepts a bit more concrete by providing a few examples.

Consider the following scenario. We have obtained our transactions from a number of different operational systems. In each system, a transaction refers to a commodity code, but there are three different commodity codes across all of the systems. Thus, when we aggregate the data, there is no consistent spend visibility across the systems. Nevertheless, all systems include a description field in every transaction. Naturally, you would like to leverage that information in order to provide a commodity view of spend that is consistent across the entirety of your data. Classification enables you to do this by assigning every transaction to the commodity code of your choice—it could be one of your existing commodity codes or a universal code such as the UNSPSC—on the basis of its description. This is an instance of transactional classification because you are classifying the transactions with respect to some reference commodity code. The end result is a redistribution of the money allocation.

A different example of classification would be the case of dimensional classification. Consider the following case. We have obtained our transactions from a number of different operational systems. In each system, a transaction refers to a location code that you would like to use as one of your dimensions. However, the location code has no structure, but is rather a flat description of the location such as "New York City, NY," "Boston, MA," "Toulouse, France," and so on. Thus, when we aggregate the data, your spend view across the systems in terms of location will be a long list of locations without any structure. Hence, your visibility about the geographic distribution of your spend will be significantly hindered by that fact. Ideally, you would like to have a hierarchical structure that has, say, four levels and shows continents, countries, regions, and cities. That way, if you asked a question, such as "How much money do we spend on 'Computers' in 'North America?,'" the answers would be readily available to you. Dimensional classification can help you do just that. It helps you imprint a structure to a structureless list of dimensional nodes and it helps you correct the structure of an already hierarchical dimension with respect to some other structure that is considered authoritative.

Clustering

Clustering refers to a process that examines a large set of entities and identifies subsets of entities that are "alike," in some specific sense. Typically, a set of dimensional nodes would be clustered based on the dimensional node name, but any other attribute or combination of attribute values can be used in the metric that defines the distance between the various records.

Business Rules and Manual Editing

Application of business rules is a straightforward operation that implies the presence of a rules engine, which executes the rules that end users of your spend analysis platform have captured. Finally, manual editing is literally a set of manual operations on the data which allows pinpoint precision and highly accurate changes to be performed.

It should be noted that a pure "reductionist" would probably argue that a single operation is sufficient, i.e., manual editing. This is correct. Manual editing is sufficient, but it is also extremely inefficient. It is significantly more expensive; it is not scalable with respect to the size of the data; and its data processing throughput speed can be several orders of magnitude smaller than automated or semiautomated processing. Thus, our reduction to the basic four operation forms listed above is aimed not only at the conceptual simplification of our problem, but also at the financial aspects of our spend analysis program, specifically its ROI.

Figure 6.5 summarizes the categorization of the DE processing on the basis of the data and the four forms of operations that we need to consider. What do these operations mean? How is a classification of transactional data different from the classification of dimensional data? In what order should these operations be applied? Does order matter? Which operations are more "valuable" for my program? We will answer these and many more questions in the following sections.

Dimensional Enrichment

The purpose of dimensional enrichment is the enhancement of either the structure or the content of our dimensions. Dimensions may be readily available to you either internally, e.g., a master items list, or externally, e.g., the UNSPSC. Alternatively, we may need to extract that aspect of the transactions from the

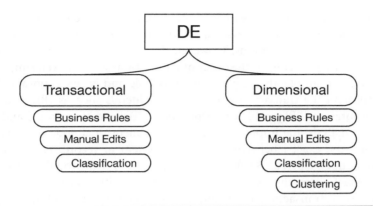

Figure 6.5. Major distinction of functions for a DE module.

transactions themselves. A standard case in this category is the transaction time; the transaction date is typically a field (attribute) of the transactional table. Dimensions may be structured or unstructured. They may have a dozen nodes or a few hundred thousands of nodes. So, what are the elements that make a certain dimension valuable and easily usable? There are a few rules of thumb for forming useful dimensions that lead to a powerful analysis:

- In terms of size (number of dimensional nodes), a dimension should follow a minmax principle. It should have as many nodes as required for analysis, but no more than that.
- In terms of hierarchical depth (number of levels in the dimensional hierarchy), a dimension should also follow a minmax principle. It should have as many levels as required for analysis, but no more than that.
- In terms of size and hierarchical depth, a dimension should grow in depth as the number of nodes increases, so that the distribution of nodes in the hierarchy remains as balanced as possible.
- In terms of content, a dimension should contain all the attributes that describe a dimensional node accurately. It should also contain as attributes all the fields that you intend to use for searching through the dimensional nodes.

The above rules are fairly abstract and generic. You should be able to implement them regardless of the specific vendor that you employ for your spend analysis needs. We will now review these rules one by one by providing a few examples.

Consider a case which has millions of transactions. The number of unique vendor names (also suppliers) associated with these transactions will be on the order of hundreds of thousands. However, the number of semantically unique vendor names may be only on the order of tens of thousands or even simply a few thousands. For example, the single legal entity "Big and Nice Corporation, Inc." might appear in the transactions under several literals such as "Big and Nice," "B&N Corporation," "Big and Nice Corporation," "Big and Nice Corp.," and so on. In terms of analysis, the important aspect of a dimensional node is its semantic content, not the exact label that is used per system of record. Hence, a single dimensional node labeled "Big and Nice Corporation, Inc." would suffice in this case. The exact name that was associated with a specific transaction should be accessible as a transactional attribute, if needed for verification purposes. Retaining all of the name values as dimensional nodes is a waste of resources without analytical value.

A well-known anti-pattern in a dimensional structure is related to the second rule, which refers to the optimal depth of our hierarchy. For example, consider the following structure:

- Computers
  - Computers
    - Laptop
    - Desktop

The second level in this structure adds absolutely no value to our analysis. It is possible that the intention was to allow extension or that this structure is simply the residual of another superset structure that has been truncated. There are many reasons why these anti-patterns might occur, nevertheless, they should be avoided. Another example, in this category, is the following:

- General Services
  - IT
    - Services

This structure is not optimal. A better structure would have the following:

- General Services
  - IT Services

There is no reason for a third level because there are no other children nodes for node "IT."

The third rule is also simple to understand in terms of an example. Consider a dimension that captures the duration of a service. Entering every value that we encounter in the transactions as a dimensional node is far from optimal. It can result in thousands or even tens of thousands of nodes, depending on the granularity of the time unit. A structure that contains ranges would be much better:

- Duration > 2 months
- 1 month < Duration < 2 months
- 3 weeks < Duration < 1 month
- 2 weeks < Duration < 3 weeks

The fourth, and last, general rule is almost trite. The more information we have about a dimensional node, the more we know about the transactional context, e.g., if we enrich our vendor dimensional nodes with the DUNS number; or with an attribute that denotes whether the vendor is a minority vendor or not; or with an attribute that denotes whether our company has a contract with a vendor or not. All of these bits of information make our analysis more valuable and lead to better decisions.

These are the general principles that should guide our dimensional enrichment. We will now show how we can use the four fundamental operations that we described earlier in order to achieve our goals. We do not need to cover the manual editing operations because these, as already mentioned, should be surgical, context and content specific. The application of business rules is fully automated and it can be recurrent—in case we want to enforce certain constraints in the structure or the content. The two most important operations are *clustering* and *classification*.

Classification

Let us first consider the classification operation. The classification of a dimensional node always happens with respect to a reference schema. The reference schema could be some internal dimensional structure (e.g., a master items list) or an external schema (e.g., the UNSPSC). When we say that a dimensional node is classified with respect to schema X, we mean that we have identified one, or more, element of X whose "distance" from the node under consideration is as small as possible. The elements of X are typically called "classes," hence the name classification. The notion of distance here is very precise, but it is implementation dependent. Generally speaking, the attribute values of the dimensional node must be the same or very similar to the attribute values that correspond to the assigned classes. Once a class has been assigned to a dimensional node and if the assignment is accepted by the approval process (man-in-the-loop), we can leverage the information that is contained in the reference schema in order to enrich our dimension. The information can be at the instance level (e.g., the class has attribute values for attributes that the dimensional node does not have values for) or it can be relational (e.g., the class belongs to a refined hierarchy, whereas the node belongs to a flat list). Thus, at the end of the classification operation our dimension can have both a richer structure and a richer content.

Clustering

Clustering is the operation of choice for creating an initial structure in a structureless dimension, primarily when there is no internal or external reference schema. Even when a reference schema exists, it can be prudent to cluster the dimensional nodes before we classify them with respect to our reference schema. The execution of the clustering operation can result in a single-level or a multi-level grouping of the dimensional nodes. Our choice will depend on the nature of the data and the final objective of enrichment that we are performing. For example, if the dimension contains a list of vendors which is typically very large, then we may want to first cluster the dimensional nodes, at a single level, and then classify the first level nodes with respect to our knowledgebase of vendors. Another example is the clustering item descriptions. The size of the set of item descriptions is roughly equal to the number of transactions. If an "Item Description" dimension is desirable, it would be prudent to cluster the item descriptions into groups of similar items and retain only a representative from each group in our dimension. In clustering, the notion of similarity, or distance, between two dimensional nodes is usually based on the lexicographic edit distance of the names that correspond to these two nodes. When we speak of distance, we mean a number that indicates how similar two terms are—that number is typically between zero and one, inclusive. More general notions of distance can be defined and, in fact, are required in certain cases.

Transactional Enrichment

Transactional enrichment is responsible for assigning a set of transactions to its rightful position in the dimensional cube. The total amount of spend always remains the same (if it does not, something is awfully wrong!)—it is a redistribution of the amount that transactional enrichment addresses. Aside from the trivial case of manual assignment, there are two essential operations that we can use. The first is the application of business rules and is fully automated. The second is a classification of our transactions on the basis of some attribute values and belongs to the man-in-the-loop category of operations.

Business Rules

Let us first consider the case of business rules. Figure 6.1 depicts the four essential modules of a spend analysis implementation and the single-line arrow between the DE and the spend analytics (SA) modules indicates the flow of information (feedback) from the end users of our spend analysis solutions. A natural question to ask is the following: "Why don't we create the business rules in the DE module itself?" The answer lies in the definitions of the data life cycle and our business workflow. We actually do create business rules during the processing of the data in the DE module. For example, the data enrichment team may construct a simple rule:

If Vendor is Dell Computers, then classify all transactions to the commodity "Computer Hardware."

Such rules are either captured during the inception and elaboration of the project, via verbal or email communications, or they are universal facts that are known *a priori*. However, most of the interesting rules come from the end users of the SA module. The end users are the ones who have the detailed knowledge about the transactions and therefore they are the ones with the information about the most appropriate location of the transactions in the dimensional cube. For example, in the above example, the commodity manager for IT hardware might examine the underlying transactions and suggest a modified version of the rule as follows:

**If Vendor is Dell Computers, then
If GL code is IT, classify all transactions to "Computer Hardware."
Else if GL code is Marketing, classify all transactions to
"Marketing Equipment."**

Thus, the ability of the SA module to capture these rules and transfer them seamlessly to the DE module is paramount to the efficiency of the spend analysis program.

The creation of business rules should be complemented by an approval workflow in the SA module. When an end user realizes that a set of transactions is misplaced, he/she should create a request for a business rule, which captures the new assignment as well as the justification for it. Subsequently, a user with feedback request approval permissions should review each request and allow, or reject, the submission of that feedback request to the DE module. Upon receipt by the DE module, the feedback request becomes a business (transactional) rule. The fact that a rule exists, however, does not imply that the rule will be applied. It should be noted that in a multiuser system there will be conflicts between candidate rules. Thus, if rule A assigns a certain set of transactions, say T, to a commodity X, and rule B assigns the same set T to commodity Y (referring to the same dimension, of course), then the two rules are in conflict. In order to determine the outcome of that conflict, a conflict resolution strategy is required. It is extremely important to understand that the same rules applied to the same data with different conflict resolution strategies can result in different outcomes. A conflict resolution strategy assigns a weight to each rule based on a number of factors. A few factors to choose from include:

User weight definition. This number will express the weight that an individual user, typically the creator of the rule, assigns to the rule based on his/her assessment.

Rule type. This is a number that is assigned *a priori* to a rule based on which dimensions participate in the conditional clause of the rule. For example, we may want to assign more weight to a rule that is based on the vendor and the GL information than to a rule that is based solely on the vendor information. These numbers are typically assigned during the construction of the dimensional cube before the first publication to the SA module.

Specificity. This is a number that can be determined by the rule definition in two ways. We may want to attribute more weight, or less weight, to rules that are more specific. For example, if two rules are in conflict and one of them has conditions on two dimensions, whereas another has conditions on three dimensions, we may want to give more importance to the rule that involves two dimensions or to the rule that involves three dimensions, as the case may be.

User role. This is a factor that pertains to the user's privileges in the system. We can attribute a weight based on the role of the user or we can attribute a weight based on the position of the user in the organization's hierarchy. We could also use both of these characteristics in a certain proportion. Similarly to the specificity factor, we may want to attribute more or less weight to rules that were authored by users higher in the hierarchy.

Time. Time is typically used as a tie breaker, i.e., other things being equal we want to impose that the most, or least, recent rule should prevail.

It is important to be able to define default conflict resolution strategies, but it is also important to be able to maintain and experiment with new strategies, especially as the number of rules increases.

In addition to our ability to execute the business rules, the DE module should provide the means for managing these rules. The rules are created over the period of the program, which typically spans several years. Some rules may become obsolete and should be purged and some others may have slipped through the approval workflow and should be deactivated pending further approval.

Feedback requests are submitted as a set that corresponds to the end stage of the approval workflow. Thus, they are grouped naturally by their submission time stamp. Administration of the rules should be possible at two different levels of granularity. The coarse level corresponds to their submission time stamp and the fine level corresponds to the individual rules. In this manner it is possible to have complete and efficient control over the set of rules that participate during the "application of rules" operation.

A last observation on the feedback requests deserves our attention. For a spend analysis program that spans several years and covers billions of dollars in spend, it is possible to accumulate hundreds of thousands of individual rules. The DE module should be endowed with the capability of distilling these rules into a more efficient, in terms of execution, form of knowledge representation, e.g., a Bayesian network classifier.

Transactional Classification

The second major operation of transactional enrichment is transactional classification. Here the goal is to move the money spent to new points based on information that is provided in the transactional attributes. For example, we may have a transactional attribute called "Item Description" and wish to classify our transactions, based on the various item descriptions, with respect to the UNSPSC or with respect to our own master item list. We should have the ability to execute the transactional classification on the entire transaction set or on a subset of it. This is important because frequently we do not want to reassign amounts of spend that have been already qualified. A typical example of these cases occurs in the refresh cycle. During the refresh cycle we will obtain new transactional information that must be enriched. However, if the dimensional structures remain largely unaffected and our standard schemas do not change, processing the entire data set would be inefficient and undesirable. Instead, we should be able to identify the new transactions, e.g., by their creation date, and classify only the new transactions in the data.

Transactional classification, like dimensional classification, employs machine learning algorithms that are trained on your data or on data that are very similar to yours. *It is extremely important to know that the classification is most accurate when the machine learning algorithms are trained on your own data.* Many vendors that offer transactional classification services request that they do the first enrichment themselves. During that time the algorithms are trained on your own data and the accuracy of the classification increases significantly. There is no algorithm that can be trained once and then classify all possible data efficiently. This corollary is important because it implies that:

> A single type of operation alone, even one that is based on the most sophisticated machine algorithms, is not sufficient for conducting a state-of-the-art spend analysis program.

Transactional classification differs from its sibling, dimensional classification, by the fact that the data involved in the classification process are orders of magnitude larger. For example, classifying your commodity codes with respect to the UNSPSC typically involves classifying a few thousand or tens of thousands of nodes with respect to the 22,000 nodes of the UNSPSC—the exact number differs from version to version, but we are concerned with orders of magnitude here. The classification of your transactions, typically, involves classifying millions of transactions with respect to the same UNSPSC schema. This implies that if your transactions are already classified with respect to your commodity codes, or if classifying them is fairly straightforward and efficiently done by other means, e.g., the application of business rules, then you could introduce a replica of your commodity codes dimension and perform a dimensional classification with respect to the UNSPSC. This operation would result in a cube in which the transactions are reflected in the proper UNSPSC locations without ever performing a transactional classification with respect to the UNSPSC.

The implementation of your transactional classification should be able to leverage the information that is gathered during the review of the results. There are, at least, three approaches for reviewing the results of transactional classification. The first approach is to sort the results with respect to the amount of spend that corresponds to each classification match. This ensures that even if your analyst does not review all of the results, the results that affect most of the spending are, as a minimum, reviewed and thereby leveraged in subsequent classifications. The second approach is to present the results inversely sorted by the accuracy of the match. In the second approach we are trying to focus our attention on the low-quality matches. If some low-quality matches are true matches, then the score for these matches will be higher the next time that we perform the classification. We assume here that the results of the reviews are included in the training process. The third approach is to sort the results based on the number of matches that correspond to the reference classes, which can be combined by a secondary sorting based on the inverse of the match's accuracy.

As you might suspect, each approach has its advantages and disadvantages. The first approach will give you a quick turnaround for a given effort, especially when the classification has not been trained sufficiently on your data. The second approach would be more appropriate when we want to increase the generalization power of the classifier and improve the performance of the classifier across our reference classes. The third approach is most appropriate when we know that certain reference classes are not trained sufficiently. This could happen, for example, because a new commodity or service has been introduced into your spending patterns and the classifier did not encounter similar entries previously in the training data.

KNOWLEDGE ACQUISITION AND MANAGEMENT

In the introduction of this chapter, we stated that four modules are essential for a successful implementation of spend analysis. The knowledgebase (KB) module is one of these four modules. Actionable information, which can be taken as the definition of knowledge in our context, is captured in several stages during the data life cycle. Thus, it is imperative that all the actionable information is collected in a single location for validation and further processing. The acquisition and management of that knowledge is the *raison d'être* of the KB module.

The usefulness of a KB module should not be underestimated. Since the early 1980s, scientists realized that a shared view of the world—a common KB in our terms—was paramount to the success of making machines more intelligent or, at least, to create the perception of intelligence. In spend analysis, an authoritative source of knowledge can help us to both disambiguate the meaning of our data entries and to enrich them; however, the authority of that reference frame has clearly two parts in our context. The first part is our universal knowledge about the world. For example, the meanings of "office chair" and "software development services" are fairly clear and, with a high degree of confidence, their meanings would not depend on whether we classify your transactional data, my transactional data, or someone else's data. The second part, however, is the custom knowledge. Custom knowledge represents the specific knowledge that is captured in your own data. For example, let us assume that you work for a mining company. The term "Butterfly V" in your data may mean "butterfly valve." However, if you work for an advertising company, then the term in your data may refer to photographs of the V-shape of the wings of an actual butterfly, i.e., an insect that belongs in the Animal Kingdom, the phylum Arthropoda, the class Insecta, and the order Lepidoptera. The custom part of your knowledge is important mainly for two reasons:

- Universal knowledge is typically void of custom semantics, as our previous example amply illustrates. Technically speaking, this situation refers to the knowledge (or understanding) of the relationship of the meaning, in the context of the discourse under consideration, and the term that is commonly used for describing it (i.e., *pragmatics*).
- Pieces of information that are very important to you might not occur frequently at a universal scale and therefore might not be captured by the universal part of your knowledge representation.

It is important to understand that there is always a trade-off between expressiveness and efficiency—accumulating knowledge and leveraging that knowledge efficiently can be challenging.

Typically a KB module for spend analysis contains information about suppliers and commodities (e.g., the UNSPSC). However, it could be used for any other aspect of your business whose structure and content is critical to the success of your spend analysis program. The KB module is essentially a CRUD application (i.e., create, read, update, and delete), but the usually large size of its contents make it special in comparison to, for example, a user management application or a typical catalog management application. Other terms for the content of the knowledge base are "knowledge library" and "knowledge dictionary." We prefer the term "ontology" because this term depicts more accurately our intention to use that knowledge for certain actions that will be performed on the data.

Generally speaking, "ontologies" are repositories of structured content. If a piece of information is not a tautology (a needless repetition), and if it accurately describes a domain of discourse, then this piece of information is a good candidate for inclusion in the ontology about this domain of discourse. If that sounds too mathematical, that is because ontologies originated from formal declarative knowledge representations for artificial intelligence (AI) purposes. Since the late 1990s there has been a growing interest in the design, use, and sharing of ontologies. However, in the area of spend analysis, the emergence of ontological engineering as a science or an engineering branch with merit of its own has not been fully realized. A possible explanation for this is that there is not a single generally accepted definition of the main concepts and methodologies that govern the development of ontologies. Even the very definition of what ontology is has been somewhat controversial (see Guarino et al. 1995).[3] Chapter 7 (*Taxonomy Considerations*) will be devoted entirely to knowledge representations that are appropriate and are currently in use for spend analysis.

Let us now look closer at the structure of the data in the KB module (KB data elements). For the purpose of our discussion, an ontology consists of the following three elements:

- Concepts
- Instances
- Attributes

Concepts

Concepts are abstract notions that encapsulate the essential elements of the spend information. Concepts do not exist in the real world—they are merely representations that help us classify the elements of the real world. Concepts are characterized by attributes, but concepts do not have specific attribute values, unless the latter are universal values. They can, however, admit value ranges, lists of values, types of values (units of measure), and so on. For example, in the context of commodities, a "computer" is a concept and so is a "telephone."

Attributes

Attributes of a "computer" could be the kind of its motherboard, the kind of its hard drive, the kind of its CPU, the number of its CPUs, the size of its RAM, and so on.

Instances

Instances are specific manifestations of a concept. An instance is what we can observe in the real world. Instances are not merely representations. They refer to unique objects with specific attribute values. For example, a "Dell Precision Workstation 470, with x86 Family 15 Stepping 1 Intel Pentium 4 at 3GHz" is a specific instance of a "computer." It is not a complete specification of that computer, but only a partial one. More often than not, item descriptions are not only incomplete, but they are also inaccurate. That is exactly the reason that renders a spend analysis program extremely valuable.

The concepts of a KB should form a hierarchy that divides the "known world," our domain of discourse, into subspaces with some common properties—which allows us to reach decisions much faster and elucidates the nature of our problems. The hierarchy, as well as the content of the nodes that it consists of, is dynamic. For example, a particular supplier might be acquired by another supplier. As a result, our ontology should change to reflect that structural change. Moreover, new attributes might be added to our concepts. For example, a computer might be characterized by its ability to connect wirelessly or not, by whether it supports PCI cards, and so on. The dynamic nature of the KB content and its structure is something that should be embraced by the KB module and by our spend analysis processes.

Chapter 7 will present taxonomies for classification of goods and services that range from rough schemas such as NAICS (North American Industry Classification System), which was meant to capture and analyze economic and customs data, to newer, more complete, internationalized schemas such as the UNSPSC, eClass, eOTD, and RUS.

Knowledgebase Essential Functionality

Browsing

The most basic functionality that should be available to the user of the KB module is browsing. The user should be able to navigate the KB hierarchy efficiently, but without loss of information. We believe that the most appropriate method to achieve this goal is the method of *hyperbolic projection*. This method allows the user to view local details of the KB hierarchy, while simultaneously retaining the context of the entire structure. Starting from the root concept, the user can navigate to any concept, attribute, or instance in the KB and view its details.

Given the large amount of knowledge that is typically contained in a KB, navigation can be greatly facilitated by a search function. The user should be able to search the database regardless of his/her position in the KB. The ability to search allows the user to quickly move around the KB and position the hyperbolic focus wherever he/she wants. The ability to search should be available at all levels of concepts, but it is often useful to be able to restrict the search space on the basis of certain search criteria.

Editing

Once the user has navigated to a particular concept, the next natural action is the addition or modification of information. We should be able to create new concepts, delete old ones, add and remove instances of a given concept, add and remove attributes, change their values, and so on. If the KB that you build is semantically rich, then it is possible to define relevance graphs and apply algorithms such as the PageRank.[4] Relevance graphs are valuable for searching, but they are also valuable in depicting the structure of the interconnected concepts.

Knowledge Assimilation

If you are offering spend analysis solutions as a service, then you are in a unique position to leverage the simultaneous changes that happen in data across your customers. This ability to leverage knowledge on average, across a business domain, has additional business value and can benefit greatly your customers. Depending on the specific DE modules that you employ, there will be a variety of places from which you can collect information that is relevant to your KB. In the context of this book, there are two major contributors to the KB—the process of classification and the collection of business rules. Let us consider each one of these contributors in turn.

Classification. During the classification process, the machine learning algorithms identify candidate matches between transactions and a reference structure or between dimensional nodes and a reference structure. The man-in-the-loop approach that we are advocating implies a review process, which allows the user to determine whether the match should be accepted or rejected. If the match is accepted, then your reference structure and your machine learning algorithm contain the required knowledge for your classification. Otherwise, the match should be either rejected or be characterized as ambivalent. In the latter case, we imply that we do not have sufficient knowledge to determine our assignment with certainty. In the former case, however, we are capturing new knowledge by the fact that we reject the match. One way to leverage the knowledge of rejected matches is the assignment of the nodes to a dummy dimensional node that we can call, for example, "uncategorized (due to rejection)." Subsequently, we should include the rejected matches in our training set, so that the algorithm can be tuned based on that information. This happens at the level of a particular cube and a particular client—recall that we are discussing the case in which you offer spend analysis as a service—and it might or might not be appropriate to elevate that knowledge at the level of the KB. Instead, the deviations from the KB, as identified by the rejected matches, should be propagated in the KB for review if certain criteria are met. Relevant criteria are subjective, but the following metrics are often sufficient:

1. Number of transactions that would be affected across your client base
2. Amount of spend (normalized on currency) that would be affected across your client base
3. Percentage of transactions that would be affected across your client base
4. Amount of spend (normalized on currency), as a percentage, that would be affected across your client base

Rules. The collection of business rules is a powerful means of accumulating knowledge. Rules should be viewed as exceptions themselves because they are the last part in a series of steps that are taken to create an OLAP cube for spend analysis. If you find yourself handling hundreds of thousands of rules, then stop and review your rules. You will realize that a great number of them can either be generalized or be absorbed in the training sets of your machine learning algorithms. Hence, it follows that the way of leveraging the rules should be similar to the way that we ought to leverage the rejected matches. The incorporation of the rules into the machine algorithms results in more efficient data processing regardless of the specific implementations that you use. Once again, the various rules that are collected across your customer base should be reviewed and meet certain criteria of wide applicability before they are incorporated in your KB.

SPEND REPORTING AND ANALYTICS

Spend analysis is a business application, and the extent to which it can deliver value depends on how easily it can deliver business intelligence data to the various stakeholders who need it. (Note: Chapter 6 provides basic functional requirements of reporting for spend analysis. Chapter 7 will review other technical considerations that affect performance of reporting and analytics.) As with most business applications, users have the following expectations:

- Their requests for specific pieces of information must be achieved as quickly as possible. The modern online experience on the Internet sets the benchmark of the request/response cycle to a few seconds. Several studies have shown that response times that exceed 10 seconds in Web applications create the perception of an unresponsive system, whereas response times that exceed 5 seconds create the perception of an extremely slow system. In the context of spend analysis, these expectations should be discussed with your vendor—for certain data sets, an OLAP response time of between 5 and 10 seconds can be characterized as an extremely fast response time.
- They want actionable information, i.e., data that they can use without having to perform additional analysis.
- In the context of retrieving information for the purpose of simply viewing or printing that information, they typically want the option of HTML- or PDF-based reports.
- In the event that they need to perform some type of "last mile" analysis, they want the retrieved, viewed, or printed data to be available in MS Excel, a program which they are familiar with.
- They want to be able to integrate and combine different reports in order to "synthesize" a bigger message and show that as a dashboard.
- As adoption increases, and the numbers of users increase, they expect that the analytical system can scale reasonably well with the increased demand. If sufficient hardware resources are provided, in proportion to the growth, then the system's performance should not degrade.
- Because of security implications governing certain data/reports, the system should be able to limit the access of certain users, or group of users, only to a predefined set of certain data/reports.

Delivering business intelligence is challenging because delivery has to satisfy the information needs of multiple stakeholders throughout the global organization. These stakeholders can be grouped together along various dimensions:

- Level of expertise in using software applications—A CPO would not want to be an expert in using the application, but an analyst would.
- Level of interest in using software applications—The director of sourcing might have different interests than commodity managers.

- Level of abstraction or visibility—Commodity managers want visibility down to the transaction level, whereas a CPO would want to merely view performance dashboards.
- Level of familiarity with specific details—Users are accustomed to specific types of reports (e.g., someone using pie charts might not immediately understand stacked bar charts).
- Multilingual requirements

Business Intelligence Key Capabilities

Reporting

Good reporting engines usually have the following capabilities:

- They cover a complete range of reports—ad hoc, managed, production, personalized, collaborative.
- They can display reports in different formats—HTML, Excel, CSV, PDF, Word.
- They permit different report types (tables, cross-tabular reports, pivot tables, different graph types).
- They enable self-service authoring with a template library.
- They allow drill-through and drill-down via interactive (not static) data and charts.
- They allow the user to build a report once and deploy the same report in multiple languages.
- They have user-friendly printing, sharing, and security (approval) workflows.
- They allow the creation of compound reports (i.e., multiple reports in one view).

Analytics

Analytic functions enable users to analyze large volumes of data (structured and unstructured) through ad hoc queries. Typical requirements include:

- The graphical user interfaces (GUIs) should support the creation of user-friendly queries.
- The system should be able to execute complex queries and quickly retrieve accurate and meaningful results.
- The system should support various, common and useful, statistics such as the identification of trends, the calculation of variance, the drawing of histograms and Pareto charts, as well as other common business analysis elements.

- The system should allow the user to perform outlier analysis, or cluster analysis, and present the results of the analysis in a visually appealing and informative manner that supports decision making.

Scorecarding

Scorecarding enables the reporting of performance metrics through KPIs (key performance indicators) and comparison with benchmarks and targets. The following are some of the elements that a scorecarding module should include:

- Drag and drop functionality to assemble scorecard templates
- KPIs linked to underlying reports through sharing of same metadata
- Linking of KPIs to projects, owners, and programs
- Support of balanced scorecarding and other approaches

Dashboards

Dashboards pull together information from various sources to provide a snapshot of business performance. Usually, the purpose of dashboards is to display complex information in simple, easy-to-understand, graphs and charts. The following are some of the elements that a dashboard module should include:

- The system should permit the creation of multi-object performance reports that include treetables, maps, charts, scorecards, analytics, and other information elements.
- The system should enable the personalization of the views based on user preferences.
- The system should enable the linking of dashboard elements to underlying reports and data.

Business Event Management

Good event management goes beyond notification via emails and pop-ups. It permits entire workflows, through approval management and automation of decision making, by:

- Tracking and monitoring of critical events, e.g., you might want email alerts if the spend for a critical commodity or contract exceeds the budget
- Notification of events to stakeholders through pop-ups and emails, e.g., if two feedbacks suggesting remapping of spend conflict with each other, then notifications need to be sent to the users informing them or if a user tries to modify the commodity structure, the commodity managers need to be informed via emails or pop-ups
- Providing in-context event management
- Providing integration into other workflow and event management systems.

Now having a general understanding of capability requirements, we will turn our attention to spend analysis and the specific types of reports and analytics that will satisfy these requirements in spend analysis. Reports typically include tables and/or charts. There are many types of tables and charts that can be used, depending on the information that needs to be presented. There are several good books that discuss how to visually present quantitative information using tables and charts;[5,6] therefore, we will not reproduce those recommendations here. The purpose of this section is to highlight some common tables and charts that are useful in spend analysis. (Note: Pie charts are in common use today, even though some visualization experts do not recommend using them.[6] Nevertheless, despite their limitations, we will mention pie charts simply because most business people are extremely comfortable using and interpreting them.)

Basic OLAP Reports

Probably the two most common reports are pivot tables and cross-tabular reports.

Pivot Tables

Pivot tables are a convenient way to build intelligent, flexible summary tables. When analyzing large amounts of data, you can look at the same information in many different ways. The way that you organize and group the data often determines whether you find or overlook important trends.

Figure 6.6 illustrates a simple pivot table that shows the count of vendors for different commodities. This pivot table has been created by counting the number of instances of vendors associated with each commodity. Figure 6.7 is a pivot table that shows the spend associated with UNSPSC commodities, along with a count of the individual payment transactions.

These pivot tables are single-dimension (commodity) pivot tables. You can also create pivot tables with nested dimensions as shown in Figure 6.8 (only part of the pivot table is shown). For each commodity, the amount of spending and the count associated with each cost center are now shown.

Cross-tabular Reports

As you start nesting more dimensions into pivot tables, they tend to become very large and cumbersome. To deal with this situation, you can use a cross-tabular report, which essentially shows the same information, but shows dimensions both as rows and columns. For example, the same above information can now be shown as a cross-tabular report as shown in Figure 6.9.

If you now want to add a third nested dimension, e.g., diversity spend, you could nest it under a cost center. The resulting cross-tabular report is illustrated in Figure 6.10.

Commodity	Vendor Count
Consignment related	272
Customer related	35
Exempt	36
Facilities	783
General and administrative	642
Human resource services	312
Logistics, shipping, and travel	380
Manufacturing	4,830
Marketing and print	47
One time	1
Professional services	208
Technology and communications	900
Uncategorized	8,336
Grand Total	**16,782**

Figure 6.6. Pivot table showing count of vendors for each commodity.

Commodity Name	Spend ($)	Transaction Count
UNSPSC (total)	1,325,399,086	389,122
Management and business professionals and administrative services	309,970,402	18,255
Food beverage and tobacco products	256,249,112	7,314
Material handling and conditioning and storage machinery and their accessories and supplies	135,846,539	10,550
Industrial production and manufacturing services	93,627,691	8,430
Travel and food and lodging and entertainment services	59,173,136	58,656
Transportation and storage and mail services	39,912,936	132,010
Farming and fishing and forestry and wildlife contracting services	32,479,210	14,307
Financial and insurance services	25,812,437	12,999
Building and construction and maintenance services	23,290,481	1,023
Engineering- and research- and technology-based services	20,354,472	1,876
Public utilities and public sector related services	19,470,703	16,618
Sum of remaining UNSPSC (total)	309,211,967	107,084

Figure 6.7. Pivot table showing spend and count of vendors for each commodity.

UNSPSC Commodity Name	Cost Center	Spend ($)	Count
Management and business professionals and administrative services	1 2 2	209,295,447 100,674,955 177,256,111	4,960 13,295 6,023
Food, beverage, and tobacco products	1	78,993,001	1,291
Material handling and conditioning and storage machinery and their accessories and supplies	1 2	70,756,391 65,090,148	1,043 9,507
Industrial production and manufacturing services	1 2	53,893,036 39,734,655	858 7,572
Travel and food and lodging and entertainment services	1 2	42,936,410 16,236,726	777 57,879
Transportation and storage and mail services	2 1	27,049,726 12,863,210	131,862 148
Farming and fishing and forestry and wildlife contracting services	2 1 2	32,445,143 34,067 24,897,006	14,299 8 12,964
Financial and insurance services	1	915,431	35
Building and construction and maintenance services	2 1	22,273,519 1,016,962	1,005 18
Engineering- and research- and technology-based services	2 1	19,084,164 1,270,309	1,860 16
Public utilities and public sector related services	2 1	17,941,732 1,528,971	16,540 78

Figure 6.8. Pivot tables with nested dimensions.

Graphical Reports

Information in pivot tables and cross-tabular reports can also be presented in a variety of graphs, including several types of 3D-bar, 2D-bar, line, area, pie, box plot, and error bar charts.

As an example, a one-dimensional pivot table such as the top six commodities by spend can be shown via a three-dimensional pie chart (Figure 6.11). A stacked bar chart can be used to visually show a pivot table with nested dimensions (or a cross-table). The top three commodity spend areas with nested cost centers are illustrated in Figure 6.12. Adding another dimension (in this case, GL) results in the stacked bar chart shown in Figure 6.13, in which the third dimension GL (consisting of three codes, GL1, GL2 and GL3) is nested under cost center.

UNSPSC Commodity Name	Cost Center 1 Spend ($)	Cost Center 2 Spend ($)	Row Totals Spend ($)
Management and business professionals and administrative services	209,295,447	100,674,955	309,970,402
Food, beverage, and tobacco products	78,993,001	177,256,111	256,249,112
Material handling and conditioning and storage machinery and their accessories and supplies	70,756,391	65,090,148	135,846,539
Industrial production and manufacturing services	53,893,036	39,734,655	93,627,691
Travel and food and lodging and entertainment services	42,936,410	16,236,726	59,173,136
Transportation and storage and mail services	12,863,210	27,049,726	39,912,936
Farming and fishing and forestry and wildlife contracting services	34,067	32,445,143	32,479,210
Financial and insurance services	915,431	24,897,006	25,812,437
Building and construction and maintenance services	1,016,962	22,273,519	23,290,481
Engineering- and research- and technology-based services	1,270,309	19,084,164	20,354,472
Public utilities and public sector-related services	1,528,971	17,941,732	19,470,703

Figure 6.9. Cross-tabular representation of a nested pivot table.

Oftentimes, there is a need to show all levels or specific levels of hierarchical dimensions. For example, a commodity dimension may have multiple levels. Each level can be nested in the pivot table. Figure 6.14 shows that the facilities commodity at level 1 (L1) breaks down into two more levels. Figure 6.14 also shows the vendor count associated with the lower-most level. This type of hierarchical data can be visually presented via the area chart option (Figure 6.15).

UNSPSC Commodity Name	Center 2		Center 1		Row Totals Spend ($)
	Nondiversity Spend ($)	Diversity Spend ($)	Nondiversity Spend ($)	Diversity Spend ($)	
Management and business professionals and administrative services	100,557,372	117583	209,161,665	133,782	309,970,402
Food, beverage, and tobacco products	177,246,573	9,538	78,993,001		256,249,112
Material handling and conditioning and storage machinery and their accessories and supplies	65,090,148		70,756,391		135,846,539
Industrial production and manufacturing services	39,039,646	695,009	53,893,036		93,627,691
Travel and food and lodging and entertainment services	16,223,227	13,4994	2,936,410		59,173,136
Transportation and storage and mail services	27,033,768	15,958	12,863,210		39,912,936
Farming and fishing and forestry and wildlife contracting services	32,445,143		34,067		32,479,210
Financial and insurance services	24,891,097	5,909	915,431		25,812,437
Building and construction and maintenance services	22,273,519		1,016,962		23,290,481
Engineering- and research- and technology-based services	19,084,164		1,270,309		20,354,472
Public utilities and public sector-related services	17,941,732		1,528,971		19,470,703

Figure 6.10. Adding more dimensions is easier in cross-tabular reports.

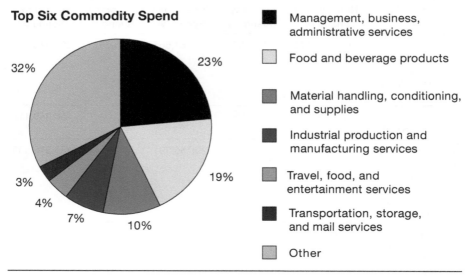

Figure 6.11. A simple pie chart.

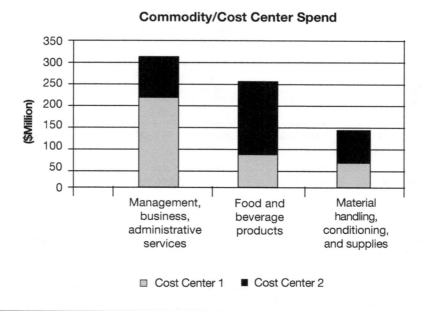

Figure 6.12. A stacked bar chart showing three dimensions.

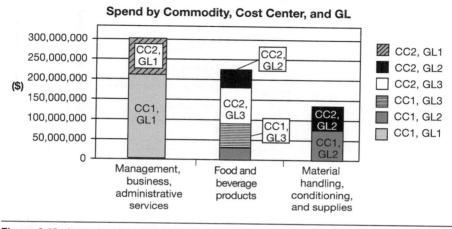

Figure 6.13. A stacked bar chart is used to show a cross-tabular report with a nested third dimension.

Count of Vendor			
Commodity: L1	**Commodity: L2**	**Commodity: L3**	**Total**
Facilities	Construction	Architectural and engineering services	4
		Construction general	13
		Construction services	7
		Construction supplies and materials	2
	Construction total		26
	Facilities management and operations	Employee business transportation	4
		Facilities cleaning	100
		Facilities maintenance	23
		Facilities management and operations general	28
		Furniture	174
		HVAC	126
		Industrial gases	33
		Landscaping	3
		Mechanical and electrical equipment	1
		Plumbing and sanitation equipment	35
		Rent	23
		Security	59
		Utilities	31
		Waste management	1
		[blank]	3
	Facilities management and operations total		644
	Food service	Cafeteria and catering services	44
		Food and beverages	66
		Food service general	3
	Food service total		113
Facilities total			783

Figure 6.14. Hierarchical information for a dimension.

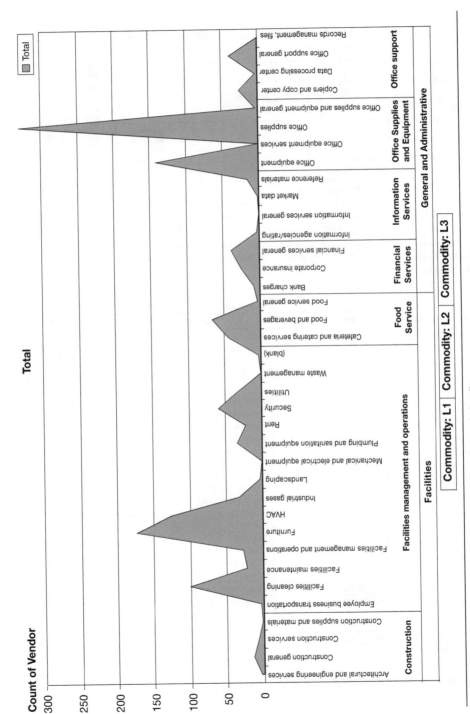

Figure 6.15. Same information as in Figure 6.14, but depicted visually.

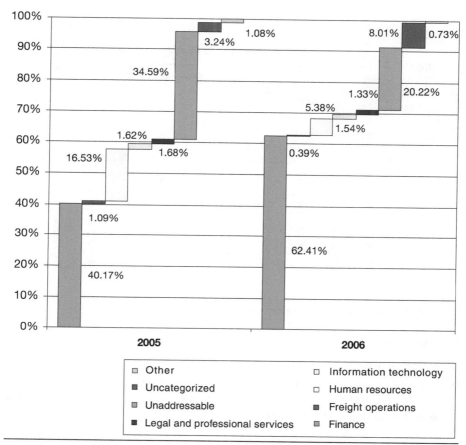

Figure 6.16. Waterfall chart showing commodity spend trend.

Specialized Charts

Some charts that are used primarily to simplify complex information will now be described.

Waterfall Chart

An example of a waterfall chart was used in Chapter 1. Waterfall charts are usually not part of the standard charts library, but they are extremely useful in depicting information in a very simplified manner. For example, in spend analysis, the chart in Figure 6.16 shows commodity spend trend in a waterfall chart. Notice how easy a visual comparison of spend between years 2005 and 2006 can be made.

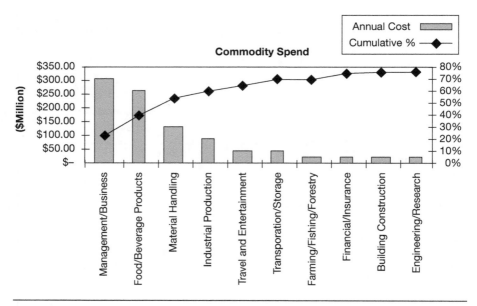

Figure 6.17. Pareto chart for commodity spend.

Pareto Chart

In spend analysis, Pareto charts are very useful in opportunity identification because they visually show the 80/20 rule, i.e., the top 20% commodities (or suppliers) that account for 80% of spend. In Figure 6.17, we show a Pareto chart for the spend cube that is shown in Figure 6.19.

Treemap

Treemapping (also TreeMap and Schneiderman diagram) is a method of visualizing hierarchical data with proportionally sized squares. For spend analysis, this plot shows relative spending by the size of a block (square). The example in Figure 6.18 shows the top N commodity spend areas. Certain treemaps can be very sophisticated and interactive. In the example below, positioning the cursor on a particular block shows the relative spend as a tool tip. If the commodity is hierarchical, then within each block, the subcommodities can be shown as sub-blocks, again, with relative spending proportional to their sizes. Treemaps can also be very powerful for visualizing the relative spend across a single dimension such as a commodity, suppliers, etc.

Note: All of the reports discussed so far can present information comprising up to three dimensions quite well. Beyond that, the information starts becoming cluttered and difficult to understand.

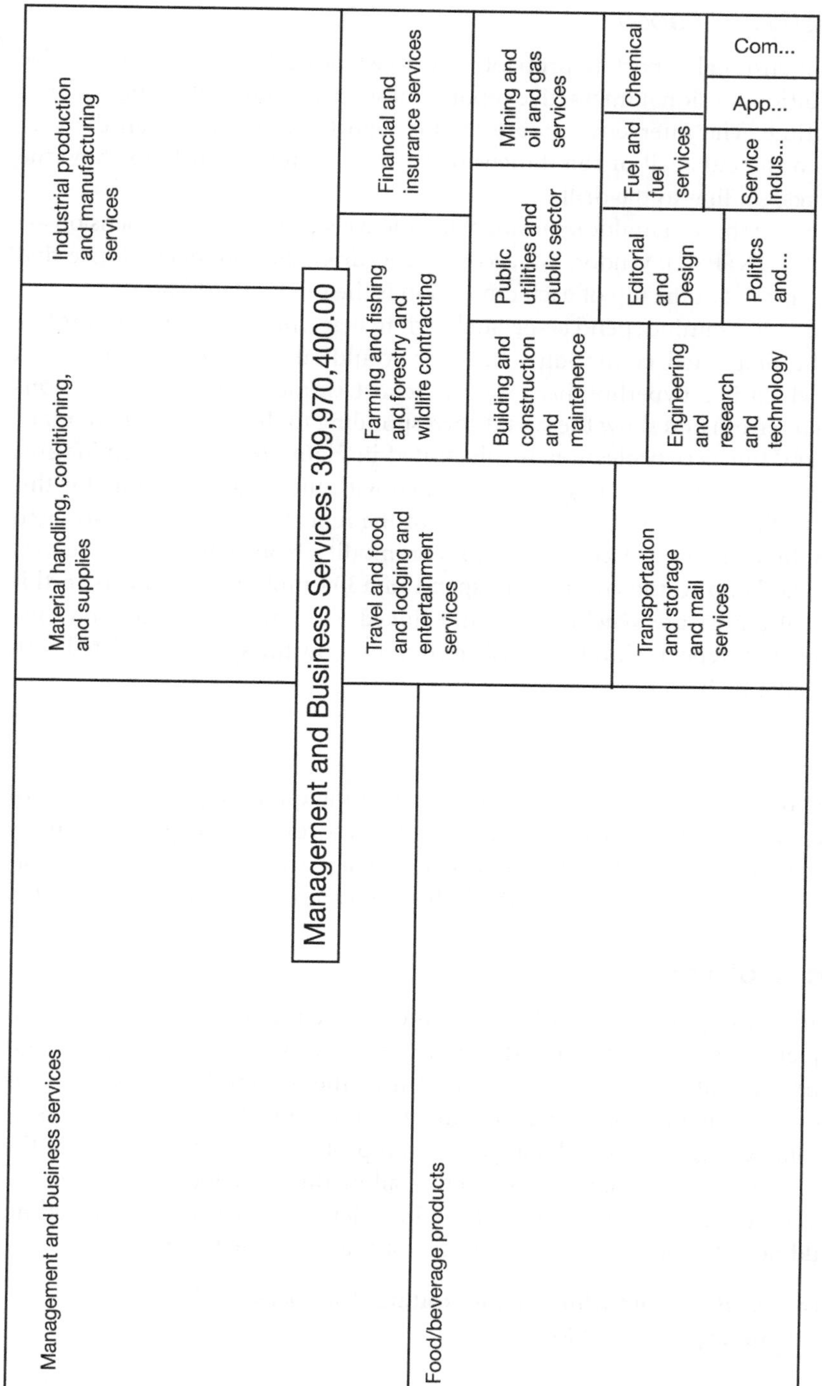

Figure 6.18. Schneiderman (Treemap) diagram showing commodity spend.

Multidimensional Report

A multidimensional report is probably the most powerful type of interactive report. Multidimensional interactive reports show spend across all dimensions at the same time. The interactive nature of this report means that when the user "drills" into the cube, all of the dimensions refresh simultaneously to show the spend corresponding to the drill point.

Figure 6.19 shows a multidimensional interactive report for four dimensions—commodity (UNSPSC), vendor, GL account, and diversified supplier. Notice that the spend amount at the top of each dimension is the same ($1.3 billion).

In order to examine spend associated with management and business professionals, the first-listed commodity, the user would simply click on the spend amount, which is a hyperlink because this report is interactive. All dimensions would then refresh and show the spend corresponding to the commodity of management and business professionals (illustrated in Figure 6.20). The vendor area of the report now shows only spend associated with the various vendors for this commodity. Similarly, the GL account area of the report shows spend associated only with the various GL accounts for this commodity. Notice that in each report, the spend adds up to the commodity spend of $309 million. All reports in this dimensional report are synchronized and linked, so if the user drills into any report, the other reports simultaneously refresh to show the spend associated with that particular drill point.

Map Report

A map report is a new type of chart that is becoming quite popular. The idea of a map report is to show spend (or any other measure) on a geographical map. Map reports are usually interactive, so clicking on a particular country or geography will open a specific chart into which the user can further drill (Figure 6.21).

Ad Hoc Analytics

One of the key requirements for business intelligence is having the ability to run *ad hoc* queries on the underlying database. For example, to analyze spend and identify opportunities, you might want to identify the commodities or vendors or transactions that match some specific criteria. Let us consider the case of consolidating your services vendors. First, you would probably want to identify all the suppliers who are providing services, across all of the commodities, and whose spend amount is greater than $10 million. In order to retrieve that information, you would need to construct a simple query of the following type:

> **Show me all vendors whose name contains "services" and whose spend > $10M.**

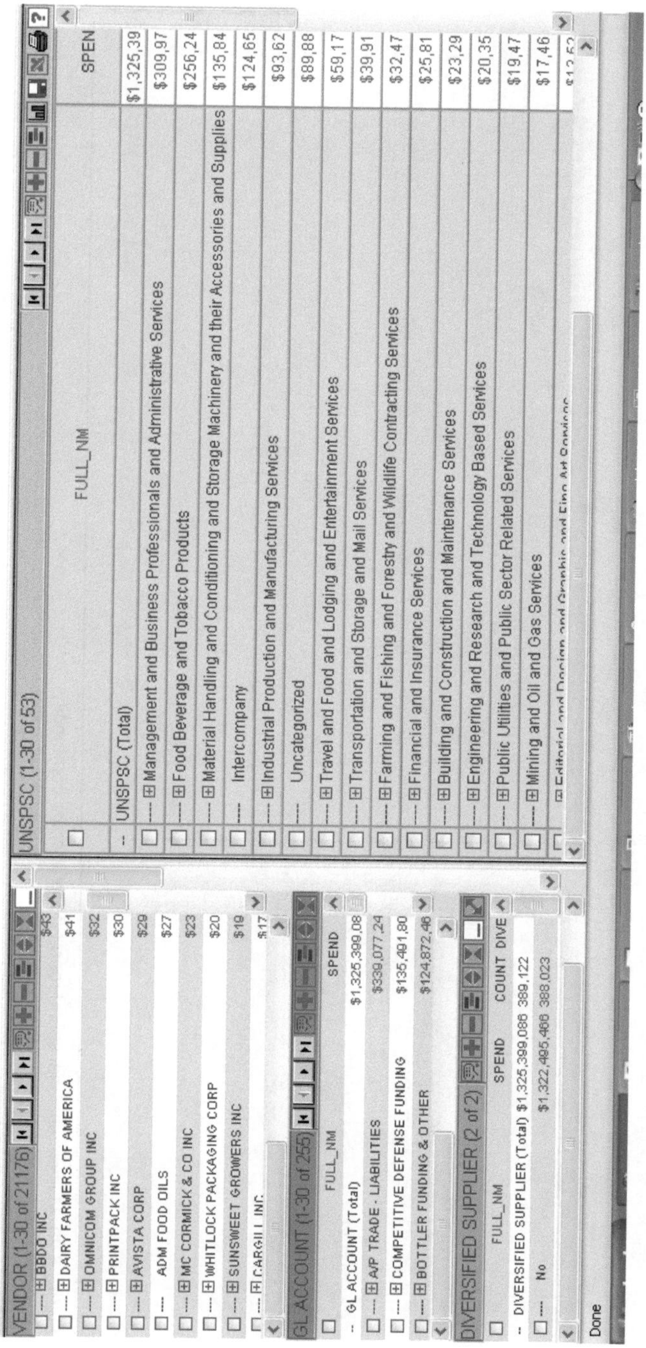

Figure 6.19. Multidimensional spend report (top of the cube).

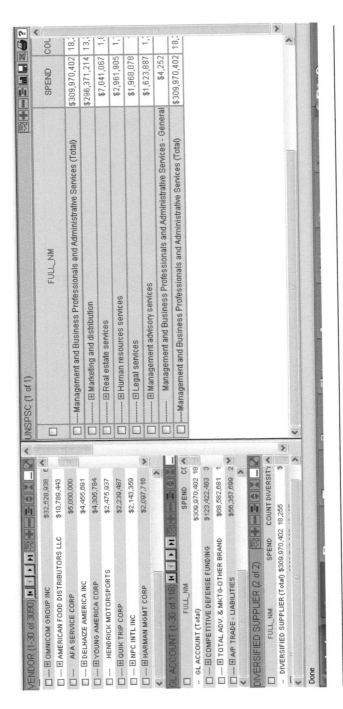

Figure 6.20. Multidimensional spend report (for a specific commodity).

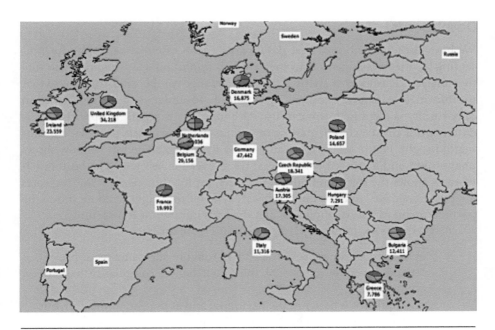

Figure 6.21. Map report.

Alternatively you could construct the query as:

> **Show me all vendors with spend > $10M and who belong to
> commodities whose name contains "services."**

The ability to easily construct such queries and receive the results within a reasonable timeframe is a key component of spend analysis.

What-If Analysis

What-if analysis is a special case of ad hoc analysis. The idea in what-if analysis is to be able to predict outcomes by changing some particular input variable. For example, if the price of corn were to go up by 15% next year, what commodity spend areas would be impacted? How would this situation affect the savings targets? The ability to perform what-if scenarios boils down to changing an input parameter in the underlying cube and recomputing the spend aggregates on-the-fly. This kind of analysis can be very expensive to perform; hence it is often not practical to allow every user to perform what-if analysis. Rather, this ability should be reserved for one or two special users who are responsible for strategic planning.

Dashboards

We have already mentioned that dashboards are an essential capability for presenting business intelligence, but they are also important as springboards to further analysis. Dashboards are used to group/arrange complex information so that the information delivers a compelling yet simple-to-understand message. Once an opportunity is identified, you can use dashboards to explain the opportunity. A dashboard is constructed by pulling in various data and charts to provide meaningful insight. Figure 6.22 is an example of a dashboard. The top window shows unapproved and approved MRO spend trend over the last year. The bottom left window shows the top commodities that account for this spend ("Yes" indicates approved and "No" indicates unapproved). The bottom right window shows the payment method that is employed and the total number of transactions.

A few things are immediately apparent in Figure 6.22:

1. On average, unapproved spend is roughly the same as approved spend (over the course of the year); hence, compliance has not improved.
2. Compliance is better in the beginning and at the end of the year, but as spending goes up in Q3, compliance suffers.
3. Supplies accounts for the majority of the spend amount.
4. Eighty five per cent (85%) of the total spend is paid with checks.

By analyzing these views, it is clear that there is an immediate opportunity in increasing compliance by increasing the usage of P-cards in the supplies commodity.

SUMMARY

Chapter 6 has explored in detail each of the four modules that comprise a spend analysis system—data design and loading (DDL), data enrichment (DE), knowledgebase management (KB), and spend analytics (SA). We have also explored in detail the two areas of data enrichment, namely, transactional and dimensional enrichment. Within each of these two areas, we have studied different approaches for enrichment—classification, clustering, and business rules. We have also presented some useful information theoretical constructs, such as the information quality index, which you can use to gauge how rich your spend information is. In the last section on analytics, we have listed various types of reports that can be used to present spend information in such a way that it is easy to understand. In many cases, basic reports such as pivot and cross-tabular reports may suffice. At other times, it is necessary to use more powerful visualization and discovery tools

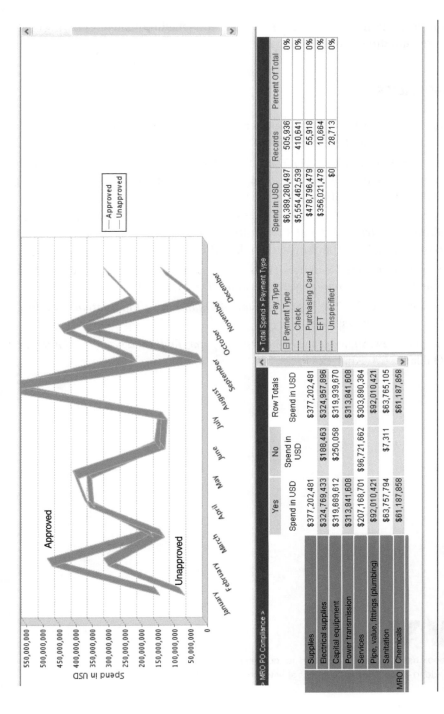

Figure 6.22. MRO spend dashboard.

such as the multidimensional report, which allows the simultaneous viewing of all measures and dimensions.

REFERENCES

1. Jiawei Han and Micheline Kamber. *Data Mining: Concepts and Techniques*. Boston: Morgan Kaufman; 2001.

2. Erhard Rahm, Hong-Hai Do. Data Cleaning: Problems and Current Approaches. In *IEEE Bulletin of the Technical Committee on Data Engineering* 2000 December; 23(4).

3. Nicola Guarino, Pierdaniele Giaretta. *Ontologies and Knowledge Bases: Towards a Terminological Clarification*. In *Towards Very Large Knowledge Bases*, N.J.L. Mars, Ed. Amsterdam: IOS Press; 1995.

4. Sergey Brin, Page Lawrence. The anatomy of a large-scale hypertextual Web search engine. *Computer Networks and ISDN Systems* 1998; 33:107-17.

5. Edward R. Tufte. *The Visual Display of Quantitative Information*. Cheshire, CT: Graphic Press: 1983.

6. Stephen Few. *Show Me the Numbers: Designing Tables and Graphs to Enlighten*. Oakland, CA: Analytics Press; 2004

TAXONOMY
CONSIDERATIONS

In Chapter 6, we laid down some ground rules for creating good taxonomies. In this chapter, we will examine some popular commodity taxonomies that can be used for spend analysis. Because most analysis is done at the commodity level, the choice of this taxonomy can play an important role in the success of your implementation.

ONTOLOGIES AND TAXONOMIES

In information science, an ontology can be thought of as a data model that describes a domain of interest. A data model typically consists of objects or sets of objects, attributes of the objects, and relationships between objects. Much of the power of the ontology comes from the ability to describe these relationships. Together, the set of relationships describes the semantics of the domain.

Figure 7.1 illustrates how a domain for transportation vehicles can be described in terms of objects and their relationships.[1] There are many ways in which such a taxonomy or a classification schema can be constructed. For example, rather than describing cars by "size"' (luxury, SUV, midsize, etc.), they could be described as having two-wheel drive or four-wheel drive, in which case a Ford Explorer would be four-wheel drive, whereas a Bronco would be two-wheel drive.

The concept of taxonomy is best illustrated through a game of "20 questions." In this game, one player is chosen to be the *answerer*. That person has an object in mind, but does not tell the other players what this object is. All other players are *questioners*. The players each take a turn asking a question which can be answered

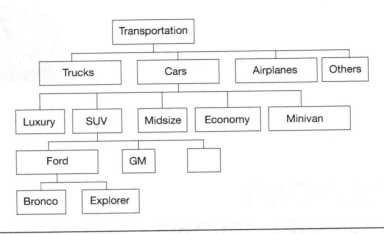

Figure 7.1. Taxonomy for classifying vehicles. (From Wikipedia®.)

with a simple "yes" or "no." The *answerer* answers each question in turn. There is a limit of 20 questions. Sample questions could be "Is it in this room?" or "Is it bigger than a breadbox?"

The answer to each question should narrow down the "solution space." Thus, a good first question might be "Is it alive?" Basic information theory suggests that each question asked should serve to divide the solution space exactly in half. Mathematically, if each question is structured to eliminate half of the objects, 20 questions will allow the *questioner* to distinguish between 2^{20} or 1,048,576 objects. If these objects were arranged in the form of a decision tree, the resulting tree would be 20 levels deep and would be split into 2 branches (or choices) at each level.

General taxonomies can have multiple choices at each level. Pictorially, these are depicted as "nodes." If at each level, say, there are 5 nodes, then a taxonomy that is 20 levels deep can differentiate between 5^{20} or 95×10^{12} objects. The English language contains a quarter of a million words. Assuming an ideal classification, such taxonomy would be able to classify each word in just nine levels.

Taxonomies are very important in spend analysis because how efficiently you group spend transactions in various dimensions determines how easily you can search and discover opportunities. For example, if your vendor master file has 100,000 vendors and you want to arrange them in a taxonomy, you could do so in several different ways. You could arrange them in a "flat" structure. Alternatively, you could create a two-level hierarchy wherein the top level represents parent organizations and the second level represents all of the subsidiary companies. Still better, you could use SIC (Standard Industrial Classification) codes as a first level, which would allow you to group similar companies. If you want to make the structure even more compact, you could have "region" as the first level, followed by SIC, which would then be followed by parent and then by children vendors. As you can see, each option would have trade-offs. The flat hierarchy uses the least number of nodes; however, searching for a vendor will take the longest amount of time. On the other hand, four-level hierarchies use more nodes, but you can reduce the search space if you know the geography and/or SIC code.

In Chapter 6, we listed some ground rules for constructing good taxonomies for analytical purposes. We will now revisit this list and expand it a bit more:

1. The depth and breadth of the tree should reflect a balanced node distribution. A low node count should be balanced against a high search speed requirement.
2. Each node should have only one parent.
3. Avoid repetition of nodes.
4. At every level, the nodes should not have any overlaps or leave any gaps. The node names should unambiguously represent the category and be sufficiently different from other node names to avoid confusion.
5. The taxonomy should have a high percentage of one/one mapping to a widely used standard taxonomy.

For spend analysis, a two- or three-level vendor hierarchy is usually sufficient. Other dimensions, such as cost centers, divisions, and organizations, can be single- or multilevel depending on organizational complexity.

The choice of commodity taxonomy is often the toughest and also the most important decision to be made. In the rest of this chapter, we will explore the common industry standard commodity taxonomies.

POPULAR INDUSTRY STANDARD COMMODITY TAXONOMIES

Taxonomies for classification of goods and services range from rough schemas such as the NAICS (North American Industry Classification System), which was meant to capture and analyze economic and customs data, to newer, more complete, internationalized schemas, such as the UNSPSC (United Nations Standard Products and Services Code®), eClass (also eCl@ss; a four-level hierarchy for classifying materials), eOTD (ECCMA Open Technical Dictionary), and RUS (Requisite Unified Schema). These schemas differ in many respects:

- Product and services class coverage
- Dictionary of properties
- Specificity of properties (i.e., properties are tied to categories)

- Currency and update frequency
- Industry adoption and sponsorships (long-term viability)
- Cross-functional use
- Associated knowledgebase (e.g., keywords, synonyms, property values)
- Internationalization

Customers wishing to implement an industry standard taxonomy must evaluate each of the above criteria before making a selection. Depending on the industry domain, the domicile of the corporation, etc., one schema may be better than another. For example, the eOTD schema has the best coverage for medical and dental products, but it has very limited coverage for earth-moving equipment, whereas the UNSPSC provides good overall coverage.

UNSPSC

The UNSPSC provides an open, global, multisector standard for efficient, accurate classification of products and services.[2] The management and development of the UNSPSC is coordinated by ECCMA (Electronic Commerce Code Management Association). The current version consists of more than 18,000 terms.

The UNSPSC classification schema was jointly developed in 1998 by the United Nations Development Program (UNDP) and Dun and Bradstreet (D&B). Initially, the schema was managed by ECCMA, but in 2001, due to competitive supplier selection mandates, UNDP took the then existing UNSPSC version and appointed D&B as an interim manager. In the meantime, ECCMA continued to expand the schema. In 2002, UNDP and ECCMA announced that the two different versions were being unified into a single code and that ECCMA was once again being appointed as the manager. ECCMA has significantly expanded the schema coverage since this unification and has published a number of new versions.

Design

The UNSPSC is a pure classification schema. Unlike other schemas such as eClass and eOTD, the UNSPSC does not define properties, either generically (i.e., applicable to all classes) or specifically (i.e., tied to a class). The schema is a four-level schema. Each level contains a two-character numerical value and a textual description as follows:

Segment (logical aggregation of families for analysis)
  Family (commonly recognized group of related commodities)
    Class (functionally similar commodities)
      Commodity (group of similar, substitutable products and services)

Examples:
Distribution and Conditioning Systems and Equipment and Components (40)
  Fluid and Gas Distribution (4014)
    Valves (401416)
      Hydraulic Valves (40141608)

Industrial Manufacturing and Process Machinery and Accessories (23)
  Industrial Process Machinery and Equipment and Supplies (2315)
    Paper Making and Paper Processing Machinery and Equipment and Supplies (231519)
      Cutters (23151901)

Drugs and Pharmaceutical Products (51)
  Central Nervous System Drugs (5114)
    NSAIDS (Nonsteroidal Anti-inflammatory Drugs) (511421)
      Ibuprofen (51142107)

Advantages of the UNSPSC

1. The hierarchical structure of the UNSPSC enables companies to focus on a level of granularity that suits their needs. For example, on the indirect spend side, companies can aggregate their spend at the class level, e.g.:
   Office Equipment and Accessories and Supplies
     Office Supplies
       Writing Instruments

   The UNSPSC defines commodities such as erasers, roller ball pens, etc. under the class "Writing Instruments," but most companies would not find it necessary to go down to this level. Visibility at the class level would be sufficient. However, on the direct or MRO side, it would make sense to categorize and aggregate spend at the commodity level.

2. The coding of the UNSPSC has been translated into many international languages. (A complete list can be found on ECCMA website.)
3. UNSPSC is one of the more complete schemas in terms of coverage across all domains.

4. The UNSPSC is very frequently updated and members are invited to submit change requests.
5. Funding is through membership fees. Currently there are in excess of 1000 members, which make the standard viable in terms of financial backing.
6. The UNSPSC is open; therefore, there is no charge for downloading and using the schema.
7. The UNSPSC has been widely adopted in North America and is proliferating in Europe and Asia.
8. The UNSPSC is well mapped to other industry standard taxonomies. For example, eOTD and RUS provide a mapping to the UNSPSC. (A publicly available eClass/UNSPSC mapping is not available to the authors' knowledge.)

Disadvantages of the UNSPSC

1. The UNSPSC does not provide a property or attribute dictionary. It is purely a classification schema. Lack of a category-specific property means limitations in how searching can be done. For example, parametric and step search engines cannot be built on the UNSPSC unless properties (parameters) are first defined. Because there are no mandatory property lists, the descriptions of products and services remain loosely worded, thus not lending them to use by engineering, operations, or material management. Oftentimes, there is a need to identify functionally equivalent parts. The only way this can be accomplished is by comparing the technical attributes of the parts. However, because the UNSPSC does not define attributes, most adopters construct their own attribute schemas or use other industry standard attribute lists such as eClass or RUS.
2. The UNSPSC commodity names are not in the classic noun-qualifier format that most material managers and systems use. For example, the very first example above, "Hydraulic Valves," when formatted as a noun-qualifier becomes "Valve, Hydraulic" which is a more widely used format because the noun, being the more dominant phrase, comes first and the qualifier, which describes the noun, comes next.
3. As in most classification schemas, there are certain industry domains that are not covered very well by the UNSPSC. For example, most pharmaceutical or chemical companies do not use the UNSPSC for their direct material classification. Many semiconductor companies also prefer to use their own internal schemas in specialized areas such as fabrication equipment. In situations such as this, the only

way to use the UNSPSC is to add a fifth level (a ninth and tenth digit)—a subcommodity level—or even a sixth level to UNSPSC.

eOTD

In 2003, ECCMA released the first version of the ECCMA Open Technical Dictionary (eOTD), which went beyond previous classifications by introducing item and attribute dictionaries to address item-level functions such as functional equivalence.[3] The ECCMA goal was to leverage the expertise and work of the members of the Federal Catalog System (FCS) taxonomy. The FSC taxonomy which was initially developed at the end of World War II and redefined by the 1952 Defense Cataloging and Standardization Act (Public Law 82-436) mandated a single federal supply cataloging system. The FCS represents over 5000 man-years invested in cataloging and is used today in over 50 countries to manage over 16 million item specifications referenced by globally unique National/NATO Stock Numbers (NSN).

Design

The exact data model has since morphed into a more generic "metadata" model. eOTD is an open technical dictionary of cataloging concepts used to create unambiguous language-independent descriptions of individuals, organizations, locations, goods, and services. At its heart, however, eOTD has the following core "dictionary" concepts:

- **Class**—A dictionary of the names and definitions for common commercial concepts used to identify individuals, organizations, locations, goods or services; also known as standard item names (SIN), approved item names (AIN), product classes or product families; a generic concept that has a defined list (template) of properties; essentially a dictionary of items, e.g., machine screw, LCD display, etc. (In the previous version of eOTD, this dictionary was structured as EGIS or the ECCMA Global Item Schema.)
- **Property**—A dictionary of property names associated with a class; properties have values associated with them that are used to describe an item, e.g., thread diameter and screen resolution
- **Features**—Property names that are associated with a class, but have no values associated with them, e.g., outer ring, second hole, and touch sensitive
- **Property value**—A dictionary of possible values which are linked to individual properties

- **Unit of measure**—A dictionary of UOMs associated with values
- **Qualifier of measure**—Currently three values: nominal, maximum, and minimum
- **Currency**—Used in conjunction with price, discounts, and other monitorial properties

These dictionaries are all linked together to form precise, meaningful constructs. For example, the item "Routers" is linked with a property called "Bandwidth" which is linked to the values 28.8, 56, and 10BaseT, and each of these is linked to the appropriate unit of measure (KBytes/second, MBytes/second, etc.).

eOTD has recently added new dictionaries for concepts such as images. The latest data model can be obtained by visiting the ECCMA website (www.eccma.org). The latest UNSPC schema can also be downloaded from this site. The ECCMA website has several utilities such as a query builder, a translator, and an item search engine.

Figure 7.2 shows several choices that were obtained when searching for a "display control" (Concept Identifier: 0161-1-01-034996). Note several things in Figure 7.2. At the top, there is a concept identifier associated with the item called a "control display unit." This identifier is:

$$0161\text{-}1\text{-}01\text{-}034996$$

The numbers in the identifier indicate the following:

0161	International Code Designator: 0161 = eOTD
1	Organization Identifier: 01 = ECCMA
01	Context Code: 01 = Class, 02 = Property, etc.
034996	Concept Code: 034996 = Control Display Unit

This item is linked to 81 properties. The chart in Figure 7.3 shows some of these property identifiers.

Are all of these properties really needed? Let us examine a typical real-life example. Figure 7.4 shows the specifications of an actual control display unit (CDU-900) by Rockwell Collins.

If you compare the attributes defined in eOTD with the attributes specified in the actual product data sheet, you will find that a majority of the technical attributes in the datasheet are very specific to the product. For example, the datasheet specifies the information bus, the I/O card, etc. The specific attributes provide extremely important information for an engineer. In the absence of these fields, an engineer will not be able to decide if two control display units are functionally equivalent.

On the other hand, one can argue that eOTD has gone overboard in defining very detailed attributes pertaining to dimensions, material composition, etc.

Terms			
Concept Identifier	Term	Language	External References
0161-1-01-034996	REGULATOR S DISPLEJI	Czech	View
0161-1-01-034996	CONTROL-DISPLAY UNIT	English	View
0161-1-01-034996	STEUERGERAET-ANZEIGEEINHEIT	German	View
0161-1-01-034996	UNIDAD DE CONTROL Y VISUALIZACION	Spanish	View
0161-1-01-034996	UNITE DE COMMANDE-VISUALISATION	French	View
0161-1-01-034996	VEZÉRLO-KIJELZO EGYSÉG	Hungarian	View
0161-1-01-034996	제어-표시 유니트	Korean	View

Definitions		
Definition	Language	External References
A component which performs the dual function of presenting visual information from other sources such as flight instruments and regulating the mode of operation of those sources. The item is essential for operation of the equipment.	English	
Un componente que realiza la doble función de presentar visualmente la información de fuentes tales como instrumentos de vuelo y de regular el modo de operación de las mismas. El artículo es esencial para el funcionamiento del equipo.	Spanish	
비행기구들과 같은 다른 제원으로부터 영상정보를 제시하고 그런 제원들의 작동형태를 제어하는 두가지 기능을 행하는 구성품이.이 품목 장비의 작동을 위하여 필수적이다.	Korean	
BAUELEMENT MIT DER DOPPELFUNKTION DER DARSTELLUNG VISUELLER INFORMATIOEIN BAUELEMENT MIT DER DOPPELFUNKTION DER DARSTELLUNG VISUELLER INFORMATIONEN VON ANDEREN QUELLEN WIE FLUGUEBERWACHUNGSINSTRUMENTEN UND DER REGELUNG DES BETRIEBSMODUS DIESER QUELLEN. DER ARTIKEL IST WESENTLICH FUER DEN BETRIEB DES GERAETS.	German	

Figure 7.2. eOTD identifier information for control display unit.

Definitions		
Definition	**Language**	**External References**
Kettos funkciót ellátó komponens, mely más jelforrásokról, pl. repülési muszerekrol jövo vizuális információkat jelenít meg, és szabályozza is ezen jelforrások üzemmódját. A cikk a berendezés muködése szempontjából alapveto jelentoségu.	Hungarian	
A component which performs the dual function of presenting visual information from other sources such as flight instruments and regulating the mode of operation of those sources. The item is essential for operation of the equipment.	English	
Article qui assure la double fonction de présenter une information visuelle de sources extérieures, tels que instruments de vol, et de réguler le mode d'opération de ces sources.	French	
Zařízení umožňující dvojí funkci, tj. dává vizuální informaci z jiných zdrojů, jako jsou letové přístroje, a dále řídí charakter činnosti těchto zdrojů. Uvedená jednotka je pro činnost těchto zařízení rozhodující.	Czech	

Figure 7.2 (continued). eOTD identifier information for control display unit.

which might not be very valuable to an engineer, but perhaps might be important to an environment and safety inspector.

The point here is that associating attributes to an item is a complex exercise—and the complexity increases with the specificity of the industry domain. It is for this reason that high-tech companies in very specialized areas such as telecommunications, test and measurement, chip fabrication, biotechnology, and others do not use industry standard schemas—instead they use their own internal material schemas.

Let us look at another example (Figure 7.5). In this example, we select from the MRO domain a typical item, namely, "machine screw" which has in excess of 80 attributes defined.

A typical commercial catalog description of a machine screw is illustrated in Figure 7.6. As you can see, only a few pertinent attributes are needed to qualify the item for purposes of functional equivalence. The technical attributes in MRO are (probably) more relevant and specific than the ones in other domains. Most of the other attributes defined in eOTD are nice to know, but probably are not necessary in 80% of use cases. On an average, good descriptions can yield about four to five properties.

Attribute ID	Term	Definition
0161-1-02-006260	MAXIMUM OVERALL HEIGHT	The maximum distance measured in a straight line from the bottom to the top of an item.
0161-1-02-006261	MAXIMUM OVERALL LENGTH	A maximum measurement of the longest dimension of an item, in distinction from width.
0161-1-02-006262	MAXIMUM OVERALL WIDTH	The maximum measurement taken at right angles to the length of an item, in distinction from thickness.
0161-1-02-012617	NUCLEAR HARDNESS CRITICAL FEATURE	An indication of the nuclear hardness criticality of the item.
0161-1-02-012992	RADIOACTIVE CONTENT	An indication of whether or not the item contains radioactive materials.
0161-1-02-014598	TERMINAL LOCATION	The position of the terminal(s) for making connection to an item.
0161-1-02-014785	CASE MATERIAL	The element, compound, or mixture of which the case is fabricated, excluding any surface treatment.
0161-1-02-015189	PRECIOUS MATERIAL	Identification of the precious material contained in the item.
0161-1-02-015191	PRECIOUS MATERIAL AND LOCATION	An indication of the precious material and its location in the item.
0161-1-02-015192	PRECIOUS MATERIAL AND WEIGHT	An indication of the precious material contained in the item and the amount per a measurement scale.
0161-1-02-016047	CUBIC MEASURE	A measurement of volume taken by multiplying the length by the width by the height of an item and rendered in cubic units.
0161-1-02-016066	CURRENT RATING IN AMPS	The electrical current rating, expressed in amperes.
0161-1-02-016377	EXTERIOR CONTAINER CUBIC MEASURE	A measurement of volume taken by multiplying the length by the width by the height of the exterior container and rendered in cubic units.
0161-1-02-016378	EXTERIOR CONTAINER WEIGHT	The measured weight of the exterior container.
0161-1-02-016505	FREQUENCY IN HERTZ	The cycles per second (hertz) of the alternating current.
0161-1-02-016967	MAGNETIC FORCE	The magnetic force measured at a specified distance.
0161-1-02-017207	MAXIMUM VOLTAGE RATING IN VOLTS	The maximum voltage rating at which the item is designed to operate in an alternating current and/or direct current circuit, expressed in volts.
0161-1-02-017214	MAXIMUM WATTAGE RATING IN WATTS	The maximum rated power that an item can safely consume or provide, measured in watts.
0161-1-02-017470	OPERATING RANGE	The minimum and maximum operating limits of the item.
0161-1-02-017475	OPERATING TEMPERATURE RANGE	The minimum and maximum limits of temperature at which the item is rated for operation.

Figure 7.3. eOTD property identifiers for control display unit.

Display and Keyboard	Screen size 3.25 in. x 2.60in.
	8 lines, 22 characters/line
	220 x 170 graphics capability
	8 line select keys
	7 generic function keys
	Full alphanumeric plus dedicated keys
Qualification	MIL-E-5400, Class 1A
	MIL-STD-461 EMI (Incl 200 V/M)
	1500V/M Design

Enhanced I/0 Card	
Two (2) – Dual MIL-STD-1553B	Bus control, backup bus control, or RT
ARINC 429	Two fully independent channels
	On-card programmable controller
	Dual-port RAM interface to processor
	Baud rates software selectable
Discrete	16 input, 4 output
Memory	128 KB EEPROM – NVM for application use MO

Commercial Standard Data Bus (CSDB) (676-2956-002)

CSDB/RS422	4	CSDB/RS422 transmit and receive programmable data rates
Discrete	4	28 v/open inputs
	4	28 v/open outputs
	16	GND/open inputs
	4	GND/open outputs

Synchro Driver

Synchro Driver	1	3 Wire Synchro Output
	2	AC Analog Outputs
Discrete	3	GND/Open Outputs

Figure 7.4. Example of a control display unit by Rockwell Collins.

Terms		
Term	**Language**	**External References**
ŠROUB, MONTÁŽNÍ	Czech	View
VITE PER METALLO	Italian	View
SCREW, MACHINE	English	View
SCREW, MACHINE	French	View
SCHRAUBE, SCHLITZKOPF-	German	View
SCHROEF, MACHINE	Dutch	View
WKRĘT,MASZYNOWY	Polish	View
TORNILLO, MECANIZADO	Spanish	View
나사,기계용	Korean	View

Definitions		
Definition	**Language**	**External References**
An externally threaded fastener whose threaded portion is of one nominal diameter, No. 0 (0.060 in./1.5 mm) or larger, designed to be held or driven with either a wrench or an inserted driver or both (excluding internal socket or internal multiple spline types), in sizes below No. 10 (0.190 in./5 mm). No. 10 and larger sizes must have a head designed for any type inserted driver (excluding internal socket or internal multiple spline types), but may also be designed for external wrenching. A locking feature may be incorporated in the design of the head or threads. Excludes BOLT: CLEVIS, BOLT: EXTERNALLY RELIEVED BODY, SCREW: EXTERNALLY RELIEVED BODY, and SCREW: ASSEMBLED WASHER. See also, SCREW: INSTRUMENT, BOLT: MACHINE, BOLT: INTERNAL WRENCHING, and SCREW: CAP; SOCKET HEAD.	English	

esci	Field3	Term/Content	Definition/Content
014850	0161-1-02-000198	COLOR	A characteristic of light that can be specified in terms of luminance, dominant wavelength, and purity.
014850	0161-1-02-000810	STRENGTH GRADE DESIGNATION	A numeric and/or alpha-numeric designator which indicates the strength rating of a threaded fastener.
014850	0161-1-02-001149	ASKEWED HEAD ANGLE	The angle of the head bearing surface in relation to the longitudinal axis of the item.
014850	0161-1-02-001708	BOTTOM COUNTERSINK DIAMETER	Smallest diameter of the countersink head.
014850	0161-1-02-002315	CHAMFER ANGLE	The included angle of the chamfer(s).

Figure 7.5. eOTD example of a machine screw.

014850	0161-1-02-002624	COUNTERSINK ANGLE	The included angle of the countersink.
014850	0161-1-02-003298	DISTANCE FROM HEAD LARGEST BEARING SURFACE TO SHANK HOLE CENTER	The distance from the shank hole centerline to the largest bearing surface of the head.
014850	0161-1-02-003785	EXTENDED WASHER DIAMETER	Diameter of the bearing element of the item.
014850	0161-1-02-003786	EXTENDED WASHER THICKNESS	Thickness of the washer face portion of the item.
014850	0161-1-02-003868	FASTENER LENGTH	The dimension, measured along a line parallel to the longitudinal axis, from the largest bearing surface of the fastener head to the extreme opposite end, or as specifically designated for other types of fasteners.
014850	0161-1-02-004963	HEAD DIAMETER	The length of a straight line which passes through the center of a circular head and terminates at the circumference.
014850	0161-1-02-004963	HEAD DIAMETER	Definition under development.
014850	0161-1-02-004968	HEAD HEIGHT	A measurement from the bottom to the top of the head, in distinction from depth.
014850	0161-1-02-004968	HEAD HEIGHT	Definition under development.
014850	0161-1-02-004971	HEAD LENGTH	A measurement of the longest dimension of a head, in distinction from width.
014850	0161-1-02-004978	HEAD MINOR DIAMETER	Minor diameter of the head.
014850	0161-1-02-005072	HOLE DIAMETER	The length of a straight line which passes through the center of a hole and terminates at the circumference.
014850	0161-1-02-005526	KEY LENGTH	A measurement of the longest dimension of a key, in distinction from width.
014850	0161-1-02-016611	HARDNESS RATING	A numeric value that reflects the hardness of an item when used in conjunction with a hardness rating scale.
014850	0161-1-02-017323	MINIMUM TENSILE STRENGTH	The maximum rated load in tension applied in a longitudinal direction, per unit of cross-sectional area, that the material can withstand without rupture.
014850	0161-1-02-020560	LOCKING FEATURE	An element inserted into the fastener, or a design feature, that enables the fastener to effectively resist vibration and rotation.
014850	0161-1-02-020602	MANUFACTURER CODE	The identifying numeric code of the originator that controls or manufactures the item.

Figure 7.5 (continued). eOTD example of a machine screw.

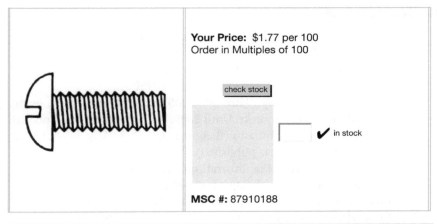

Description:	Machine Screws Head Type: Slotted Round Head Thread Size: 8-32 Length Under Head: 1/2 Material: Alloy Steel Finish/Coating: Zinc Plated
Head Type:	Slotted Round Head
Thread Size:	8-32
Length Under Head (Inch):	1/2
Material:	Alloy Steel
Finish/Coating:	Zinc Plated
Big Book Page #:	1897

Figure 7.6. A catalog description of a machine screw. (Adapted from the MSCDirect online catalog.)

Advantages of eOTD

1. eOTD primarily addresses the two limitations of the UNSPSC—namely, that the UNSPSC is not a noun-qualifier formatted schema and does not have an attribute dictionary.

2. eOTD has defined crosswalks or mapping to the UNSPSC, so categorizing to eOTD will also automatically enable categorization to the UNSPSC with minimal effort.

3. The ECCMA organization also supports mapping to other ECCMA-supported standards such as eCl@ss, CPV (common procurement vocabulary), HS (harmonized system), NAICS, and FCS. (Whether or not these mappings are publicly available is unclear to the authors. Interested users should inquire with ECCMA.)

Disadvantages of eOTD

1. By itself, eOTD is a flat schema, i.e., the concepts are not linked together in a hierarchical manner. Therefore, for purposes of spend analysis, for which hierarchical grouping is necessary, eOTD can and should be used in conjunction with the UNSPSC.

2. eOTD is still evolving. Through 2005, new versions were being released once every 4 weeks. Until 2005, eOTD versions had unequal coverage in various domains (these may have been largely addressed by the time this book is published).

3. As can be seen from the illustrations given above, there are a large number of attributes defined for each commodity and not all of them are necessary to adequately define the product. Ideally, some of these should be labeled as "mandatory"' and others should be labeled as "optional" attributes, but this distinction has not yet been made. One reason could be that engineering, purchasing, operations, and other departments will use different attributes and the ECCMA prefers to keep the schema neutral. However, for purposes of spend analysis and sourcing, functional equivalence is an important requirement, and it becomes easier to identify functionally equivalent parts by comparing mandatory attributes which are not defined in eOTD.

eCL@SS

In the following sections, eCl@ss and eClass are used synonymously. Similar to the UNSPSC, the eClass consists of a four-level hierarchy for classifying materials, products, and services.[4] eClass is developed and maintained by eCl@ss e.V., a nonprofit organization started in 2000 by a group of large German companies, and is supported by members that include corporations, associations, and institutions. eClass has widespread adoption in the European Union countries. Information about eClass can be obtained at http://www.eclass-online.com.

Design

The four-level hierarchy is arranged as segments, main groups, groups, and commodity classes. A two-digit code is associated with each level, similar to the UNSPSC. In addition, and unlike the UNSPSC, eClass also has defined attributes or properties for each commodity. eCl@ss is currently available in eight languages—German, English, French, Italian, Spanish, and Chinese, as well as Czech and Portuguese (currently only in the older 4.1 version).

Figure 7.7. eCl@ss example of a machine screw.

Let us explore eClass using the previous example of a machine screw. The screen shot in Figure 7.7 shows part of the taxonomy when the commodity for "machine screw" is searched (based on version 5.13). When clicking on the first link "machine screw," the screen shot in Figure 7.8 shows the results. Machine screw has been classified as:

Segment (23)	Machine Element, Fixing, Mounting
Main Group (23-11)	Screw, Nut
Group (21-11-01)	Screw, with Head
Commodity (21-11-01-01)	Hexagon, Head Cap Screw

Note: In Europe, the same part is referred to differently. "Machine screw" is entered as a keyword, not as the actual definition of this particular part. The label "SSP" in the figure is an acronym for "standard set of properties." SSP tells us that properties have been defined for this commodity.

The information displayed in Figure 7.9 is also associated with the "machine screw" commodity. Each property is explained in greater detail. In Figure 7.10, the property "Thread diameter" is further specified.

In Figure 7.10, no values are listed for "Thread diameter." However, a large number of possible values are associated with the property "Material" as can be seen in Figure 7.11 (only a few values are shown).

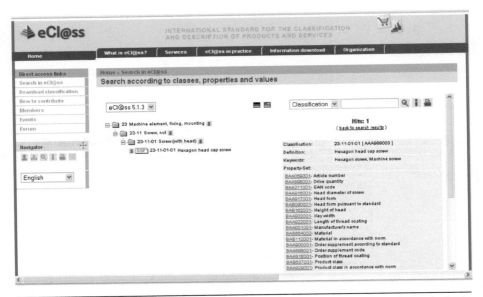

Figure 7.8. Properties associated with machine screw in eCl@ss.

A quick examination of Figure 7.11 reveals that some of these material values cannot be associated with machine screws. For example, wood, solution, quartz, and many others cannot be possible material values. Therefore, the possible values should be carefully selected and associated with the particular commodity.

Advantages of eClass

1. Like the UNSPSC, eClass provides a four-level classification taxonomy which can be customized by adding a fifth or sixth level if needed. eClass is also available in multiple international languages.
2. The latest version of eClass has 25 segments, 514 main groups, 4,658 groups, and 25,083 commodities. Over 50% of the commodities have SSPs already defined.
3. eClass provides extensive attribute lists with possible values, which have been used for many years and have widespread acceptance in Europe.
4. eClass also provides over 50,000 keywords that can be used as alternate product names.
5. eClass has teamed up with Requisite Technology, Inc. (now part of Click Commerce, Inc.) to provide bidirectional mappings.

Classification:	23-11-01-01 [AAA988003]
Definition:	Hexagon head cap screw
Keywords:	Hexagon screw, Machine screw
Property-Set:	

BAA059001- Article number
BAA898001- Drive quantity
BAA271001- EAN code
BAA916001- Head diameter of screw
BAA917001- Head form
BAB090001- Head form pursuant to standard
BAB162001- Height of head
BAA932001- Key width
BAA922001- Length of thread coating
BAA001001- Manufacturer's name
BAB664002- Material
BAB112001- Material in accordance with norm
BAA900001- Order supplement according to standard
BAA899001- Order supplement code
BAA918001- Position of thread coating
BAB637001- Product class
BAA929001- Product class in accordance with norm
BAA316001- Product name
BAA002001- Product type description
BAB010001- Publication date (year-month)
BAE162001- Requirement in accordance with
BAA919001- Screw length
BAB165001- Standardized letter as designation of form
BAB101001- Surface protection
BAB150001- Surface protection in accordance with norm
BAB618001- Thread design according to standard letter
BAA907001- Thread diameter
BAA908001- Thread direction
BAA997001- Thread length
BAA909001- Thread pitch at nut end
BAB341001- Thread size
BAB072001- Tolerance
BAA936001- Tolerance information in accordance with norm

Figure 7.9. eClass properties associated with machine screws.

6. eClass has been used in conjunction with several SAP implementations. There are a number of qualified consultants (primarily in Europe) to support such integration.

Disadvantages of eClass

1. eClass commodity names are sometimes different from names in North America. For example, "machine screw" is referred to differ-

Property	BAA907001 - **Thread diameter**
Abbr.	
FieldFormat	NR2..3.3
FormulaSign	
Unit	mm
Definition	Diameter which indicates the size of the thread and is used to designate the thread.
Synonyms	
Values:	
Classification	
Connected Classes: 250	

Figure 7.10. eClass values for thread diameter.

ently in Europe. In general, eClass has not been implemented as much in North America as in Europe, perhaps due to the popularity of the UNSPSC.

2. Attributes in eClass are associated only at the commodity level and not to any intermediate level, which can sometimes be a limitation because the implementer is forced to assign a part to the commodity level before being able to use the attribute lists.

3. Mapping (crosswalks) to other popular taxonomies are not publicly available (eClass e.V. also does not offer this as a service).

4. As with eOTD, eClass has defined a large number of properties for each class, without distinguishing between mandatory and optional attributes. Thus, this "last mile" of schema customization is often left to the implementation team.

RUS

RUS (Requisite Unified Schema) is the proprietary schema pioneered by Requisite Technology, Inc. (now part of Click Commerce, Inc.). RUS, along with the search engine "BugsEye" that sits on top, played a significant role in e-procurement expansion during the Internet boom by being SAP's preferred catalog search engine.[5] For a number of years, the SAP Enterprise Buyer came bundled with the BugsEye search engine and the eMerge toolset for maintaining the underlying catalog.

Property	BAB664002 - **Material**
Abbr.	
FieldFormat	X..32
FormulaSign	
Unit	
Definition	Material composition that a single component comprises as the result of a manufacturing process whereby the raw materials are given their final shape by means of extrusion, molding, welding, etc.
Synonyms	
Values:	

AAA005001 - 10CrMo910
AAA004001 - 13CrMo44
WPA381003 - 14.435
AAA003001 - 15Mo3
AAA007001 - 15NiCuMoNb5
WPA182003 - 18/8 steel
WPA113001 - 70 NBR/803
WPA114001 - 72 NBR/803
BAC020001 - ABS
WPA310003 - Acrylic
WPA269003 - Agate
WPA010001 - Aluminum
WPA216003 - Borosilicate glass
WPA006001 - Brass
WPA327003 - Brass CU2 (CuZn37) or brass CU3 (CuZn39Pb3)

Figure 7.11. eClass values for property "material."

Some e-procurement vendors still use BugsEye/RUS as the underlying catalog schema for procuring goods and services. The fact that it has been deployed in 100+ SAP implementations has given RUS a life of its own. The authors believe that this schema will continue to survive for the foreseeable future.

Design

RUS is a flat, single-level schema based on an "IS-A" (also a "what is") model. Category assignments are made by asking simply "What is it?" instead of "Where is it used?" or "How is it used?" For example, there are many ways to describe a pen—ballpoint, felt tip, etc. RUS uses the category of pen, with many attributes to describe the type of pen, which is slightly different from the noun-qualifier

Short/Text	RUS_Category
SWITCH PROX #IGK2008B-ABOA/SL/LS-100AK	Proximity Switches
SCREW SET 4492U-K-5 IT.12	Set Screws
CABLE POWER FIELD BETA TECH #CC-TPWR-02	Electrical Cable
POWER SUPPLY 1746-P1 SLC500 ALLEN-BR	Power Supply Modules
RACK 4-SLOT 1746-A4 ALLEN-BRADLE	Electronic Equipment Rack Systems
MODULE INPUT 1746-IA16 ALLEN-BRAD	Input/Output Modules
RELAY OUTPUT SOURCE 1746-OB16 AB	Relay Modules
SUPPLY POWER 1746-P2 SLC-500 ALLEN-BRADL	Power Supply Modules
RELAY 8-POINT OUTPUT CARD 1746-OW8	Relay Modules
RACK EXPANSION 1746-A10 AB	Electronic Equipment Rack Systems
PROCESSOR SLC-500 5/03 16K 1747-L532	Microprocessors
CABLE 5 MT RIGHT ANGLE C04-BEC-00-VY-050	Sensor Connector Cables
MOTOR CONTACTOR TYPE:3-TF-4022-0BB4	Electrical Contactors
MOTOR CONDENSOR#024-25050-700	Capacitors
CONNECTOR 804001A09M050 BRAD HARRISON	Circuit Board Connectors

Figure 7.12. RUS classification examples.

approach to categorization. The "qualifier" in this case is modeled as an attribute called "type."

The RUS structure is flat, similar to a dictionary whose entries are not alphabetized, which contains categories with definitions, attributes, and aliases and is created in accordance with a formally defined methodology. RUS is currently available in 16 languages. The chart in Figure 7.12 shows some real-life examples of RUS categories and how these categories are used in classifying products.

The examples in Figure 7.13 show the attributes associated with two specific categories, namely, time delay fuses and limit switches. RUS has defined four to eight attributes per commodity. This simplicity is what has driven RUS adoption. Rather than associate 50+ attributes, RUS has narrowed this list down to a few highly essential attributes that are necessary for purposes of functional equivalence.

Advantages of RUS

1. RUS is a flat schema based on a "what is" concept. RUS is really a search-centric schema that is best used in conjunction with BugsEye, its proprietary search engine.
2. RUS has defined a set of necessary but sufficient attributes associated with each class, which makes identifying functional equivalents from a purchasing standpoint easy. RUS is fairly well adopted among the SAP customer base in North America and Europe.

Short/text	RUS_Category	Param1	Value1	Param2	Value2	Param3	Value3	Param4	Value4	Param5	Value5
FUSE-TIME DELAY™ FRS-R-100	Time Delay Fuses	Current		Interrupting Rating		Voltage Rating		Model Compatibility			
FUSE TD 150A 600V FRSR150 TRS150A	Time Delay Fuses	Current	150 A	Interrupting Rating		Voltage Rating	600 V	Model Compatibility	TRS150A		
FUSE TD 200A 600V FRS-R-200	Time Delay Fuses	Current	200 A	Interrupting Rating		Voltage Rating	600 V	Model Compatibility			
FUSE-TIME DELAY™ FRS-R-70	Time Delay Fuses	Current		Interrupting Rating		Voltage Rating		Model Compatibility			
FUSE TD 80A 600V	Time Delay Fuses	Current	80 A	Interrupting Rating		Voltage Rating	600 V	Model Compatibility			
FUSE TD 90A 600V FRSR90 TRS90R	Time Delay Fuses	Current	90 A	Interrupting Rating		Voltage Rating	600 V	Model Compatibility	TRS90R		
SWITCH-LIMIT SQD#9007-C52D 1 N.O.-1 N.C	Limit Switches	Current Rating		Number of 2		Voltage Rating		Number of Throws		Operating Force	
SWITCH-LIMIT * 9007-C52A2 COMPACT B	Limit Switches	Current Rating		Number of Poles		Voltage Rating		Number of Throws		Operating Force	
SWITCH LIMIT PART# 9007-C54A2	Limit Switches	Current Rating		Number of Poles		Voltage Rating		Number of Throws		Operating Force	
SWITCH LIMIT 2NO-2NC CW&CCW 9007-C52B2	Limit Switches	Current Rating		Number of 4		Voltage Rating		Number of Throws		Operating Force	
SWITCH LIMIT 9007 A012 SQ D NO/NC	Limit Switches	Current Rating		Number of Poles		Voltage Rating		Number of Throws		Operating Force	

Figure 7.13. RUS attribute examples.

3. RUS is fairly stable and offers good coverage in the areas of indirect and MRO spend.

Disadvantages of RUS

1. RUS was created as a search engine schema, so it does not lend itself naturally to spend analysis which requires a hierarchical schema. Requisite Technology rectified the problem by building mappings to the UNSPSC and other schemas.
2. These attributes are very "purchasing"-centric, i.e., they enable searching for an appropriate product using attributes. The attribute dictionary does not extend support to operational, engineering, and environmental areas.
3. RUS is a private, not a public taxonomy. The only way to access RUS is to be a customer.
4. SAP has announced discontinuation of BugsEye as a preferred/bundled product.

QUANTITATIVE COMPARISON OF TAXONOMIES

Hepp, Leukel, and Schmitz have done an analysis of UNSPSC, eClass, eOTD, and RNTD (*Rosettanet Technical Dictionary*).[6] The following sections will use their findings, which, although dated, provide valuable comparative insight into the strengths and weaknesses of these taxonomies. Rather than use these findings "as is," the reader is urged to use them as guidelines for conducting further research on each of the available taxonomies.

Also note that a number of schemas, such as eClass and eOTD, have been offering more frequent updates to their taxonomies in the last 2 years; therefore the reader is urged to use the analysis that follows merely as guidance in the selection of an appropriate taxonomy. The analysis will not cover RUS because RUS is a proprietary taxonomy. The original analysis included RNTD. Note: RNTD has not been discussed in this chapter because RNTD is very particular to the high-

	Version	Total Number of Classes
eCl@ss	4.1	15315
	5.0	24814
	5.0SP1	24919
	5.1beta	25585
	5.1de	25658
eOTD	01-17-2003	58973
	10-01-2003	58898
	11-01-2003	58901
	03-01-2004	58975
	06-01-2004	58970
	08-01-2004	58970
UNSPSC	6.0315	19778
	6.0501	20212
	6.0801	20498
	6.1101	20683
	7.0401	20739
	7.0901	20789

Figure 7.14. Total number of classes in various schemata.

tech dictionary and therefore has seen little adoption for spend analysis. Interested readers can visit the Rosettanet website to obtain more information on their freely available technical dictionary.

Size and Growth

The absolute size of a schema is the most basic metric available (Figure 7.14), but size does not reveal the amount and frequency and maintenance; size can be biased by a large number of categories in one domain; and size also does not place importance on properties. Nevertheless, important to note is that eOTD has the largest set of concepts, whereas eClass grew by 280 and the UNSPSC grew by 230 new classes per month (in 2005) (Figure 7.15).

Hierarchical Order and Balance of Content

The chart in Figure 7.16 compares the amount of concepts contained in the largest and the three largest top-level sections. One can see that in all standards, the biggest share of categories stems from a few branches. The largest segment in eOTD is more than 50 times as large as the median.

The chart in Figure 7.17 summarizes the distribution of elements along the hierarchy. This metric reveals how the number of subconcepts varies among the levels of the hierarchy. One can see that the coefficient of variation per top-level category for eOTD is about twice that of the others. This points to very diverse top

	Release	Previous Release	New Classes per 30 days	Mean	Modified Classes per 30 days	Mean
eCl@ss	5.0	4.1	865	279.6	157.4	1271.4
	5.0SP1	5.0	47.8		10.2	
	5.1beta	5.0SP1	131.6		4918	
	5.1de	5.1beta	74.1		0.0	
eOTD	10-01-2003	01-17-2003	6.1	6.2	0.0	0.0
	11-01-2003	10-01-2003	4.8		0.0	
	3-01-2004	11-01-2003	18.3		0.0	
	8-01-2004	06-01-2004	1.6		0.0	
	08-01-2004	06-01-2004	0.0		0.0	
UNSPSC	6.0315	5.1001	907.8	233.9	135.6	47.5
	6.0501	6.0315	304.5		53.0	
	6.0801	6.0501	97.5		15.0	
	6.1101	6.0801	69.1		50.2	
	7.0401	6.1101	13.8		29.4	
	7.0901	7.0401	10.8		2.0	

Figure 7.15. New and modified classes per month.

level sizes for eOTD. The smallest top-level category (corresponding to tractors) contains only 7 descendents, while the largest has 14,189.

Quality of Property Libraries

The chart in Figure 7.18 shows the size of property libraries in the schemas except for the UNSPSC (which does not have properties). Also shown are how many of these properties have enumerative data types. For example, the property "modem bandwidth" can only take on specific values such as 28.8KB/second, 56KB/second, 1MB/second, etc. The amount of enumerative properties is a good indication of specificity of properties because it requires good domain knowledge to define enumerative product properties.

The chart in Figure 7.19 shows the size of property lists and the specificity of properties in terms of classes with specific property assignment, i.e., they contain at least one property that is not assigned to more than 75% of all classes.

Lastly, the chart in Figure 7.20 shows how the number of properties per class varies between the schemas. A huge variation between different classes indicates only partial progress in development of property assignments. As can be seen, eClass has a higher variation than eOTD.

	Release	Percent of Classes in Largest Category	Percent of Classes in Three Largest Categories	Largest Category/ Median of Category Size
eCl@ss	4.1	23%	44%	814%
	5.0	21%	40%	731%
	5.0SP1	21%	40%	731%
	5.1beta	21%	39%	732%
	5.1de	21%	39%	732%
eOTD	10-01-2003	24%	40%	5255%
	11-01-2003	24%	40%	5255%
	03-01-2004	24%	40%	5255%
	06-01-2004	24%	40%	5255%
	08-01-2004	24%	40%	5255%
UNSPSC	6.0315	12%	30%	1128%
	6.0501	12%	29%	1134%
	6.0801	12%	30%	1134%
	6.1101	12%	30%	1108%
	7.0401	12%	30%	1107%
	7.0901	12%	30%	1107%

Figure 7.16. Chart showing the top-level distribution of classes in the various schemata.

Taxonomy	Release	Min	Max	Median	Q1	Q3	STD	Percent Coefficient of Variation
eClass	5.1de 09-28-2004	203	5,312	726	432	1216	1064.6	104
eOTD	08-01-2004 08-01-2004	7	14,189	270	148.5	590.5	1764.3	236
UNSPSC	7.0901 09-01-2004	49	2,480	224	120	370	483.3	128

Figure 7.17. Distribution of nodes (elements) along the hierarchy for top-level categories.

	Release	Number of Properties (Including Unused)	Number of Properties with Enumerative Data Type	Percent of Properties with Enumerative Data Type
eCl@ss	5.1de	5525	1064	19
eOTD	08-01-2004	21129	555	3

Figure 7.18. Chart showing the total number of properties, the number of properties that have enumerative data types, and the percentage (%) of such properties.

	Release	Total Number of Properties	Number of Classes with Specific Property Assignment	Percent of Classes with Specific Property Assignment
eCl@ss	5.1de	5525	10930	43
eOTD	08-01-2004	21129	920456	35

Figure 7.19. Chart with amount of specific property lists.

		Number of Properties in Specific Property Lists					
	Release	Min	Max	Mean	Median	STD	Coefficient of Variation
eCl@ss	5.1de	1	156	32.3	44	15.2	47%
eOTD	08-01-2004	7	417	50.3	47	19.5	39%

Figure 7.20. Chart with distribution of properties.

CONCLUSION AND SUMMARY

The selection of target schema for spend analysis should be carefully chosen based on several considerations:

1. Are your domains (direct, indirect, MRO) adequately represented in the schema?
2. Will your schema be evolving to support a centralized product information management system? If so, you need a schema that has defined properties and you should find out how many of these properties are specifically assigned to the various classes of interest.
3. Is your company global? Is internationalization an important requirement?

4. Is any taxonomy already implemented at a division level? If so, you need to consider mapping (crosswalk) requirements between that schema and the target standard schema.

5. Has the schema been maintained in recent months? Have incomplete or sparely populated domains seen growth? Are the property lists frequently updated?

REFERENCES

1. See the Wikipedia® section on ontologies.

2. See the UNSPSC website (www.unspsc.org).

3. See www.eccma.org for information on eOTD.

4. See http://www.eclass-online.com for information on eClass.

5. See http://rusportal.requisite.com for information on RUS.

6. Martin Hepp, Joerg Leukel, Volker Schmitz. *A Quantitative Analysis of eCl@ss, UNSPSC, eOTD, and RNTD Content, Coverage, and Maintenance.* IEEE International Conference on e-Business Engineering, Beijing, China; October 18–20, 2005.

TECHNOLOGY CONSIDERATIONS

There are two categories of technological challenges that the implementation of a spend analysis program needs to address. The first category addresses issues associated with the SA (spend analytics) module discussed in Chapter 6. This category includes the size of the data; the ability of the solution to scale in terms of data size and user load; the responsiveness of the OLAP (online analytical processing) queries; the quality of the graphical representations in reports; and other usability, performance, scalability, and security considerations. The second category relates to the technologies that underlie the capabilities of the DE (data enrichment) module. There are several technologies that are appropriate for item and vendor classification, dimensional clustering, and for the enforcement of business rules. It is important to understand these technologies and the differences between the various options that are available. Even if you are not the implementer of the spend analysis program, having a basic understanding of these technologies is important for assessing the business value of the various vendor offerings in the area.

TECHNICAL CONSIDERATIONS IN THE SA MODULE

Online Analytic Processing (OLAP)

The OLAP engine is the core feature of the SA module. It is the enabling technology that provides answers to the most rudimentary analytical questions in spend analysis. The OLAP capabilities of your spend analysis vendor can be categorized based on whether the product is endowed with its own OLAP engine or it relies on third-party analytical services—and therefore it solely acts as a presentation layer on top of the third-party OLAP engine. A number of third-party vendors offer excellent OLAP capabilities. However, comparing vendors explicitly is not one of the goals of this book. Instead, we will delineate the key elements that you should know before you make your selection.

To begin with, we should emphasize that the variables that influence the choice of an OLAP engine are many and there is no single clear winner among the available options (circa 2007). A third-party solution may work superbly well as an OLAP engine for one application and completely fail to satisfy the success criteria for another. In light of that aphorism, let us now proceed with the specific metrics that you should consider.

What Is Your OLAP Schema?

Several OLAP schemata are in use today, but in general you should be able to assign your schema to one of the following three categories:

Star schema. The star schema is the simplest schema possible. It is the base for nearly all of the other OLAP schemata. It consists of a table that contains the facts (transactions) and a number of dimensional tables that are built around it, by means of foreign keys. You can imagine the fact table as being in the center of a graph with the dimensional tables positioned around it and being connected to it by a line, hence the name "star" schema.

Constellation schema. A constellation schema, as you might suspect, is a number of star schemata that are interconnected. Thus, you can navigate one cube and "tele-transport" yourself into another cube as you deem fit.

Snowflake schema. The snowflake schema is a star schema, or a constellation schema, in which dimensional tables contain associated secondary tables. This schema is useful when you have a lot of information associated with your dimensional tables and it would be penalizing—in terms of maintenance and performance—to maintain that information in a single table.

Each schema category has its advantages and disadvantages. The fundamental trade-off is nearly always between schema complexity and the combination of OLAP query performance, schema maintenance cost, and data enrichment cost. In general, the larger the amount of data that you analyze, the simpler your schema should be. (See Chapter 4 for an operational definition of the term "large data set.") You should not use metrics such as the total amount of spending that is included in the cube when you want to compare the capacity and efficiency of an OLAP engine for the purpose of spend analysis. From a business perspective, it is a legitimate metric, but from a technical perspective, it can be misleading and inappropriate for comparing different spend analysis vendors—even though the vendors themselves tout the maximum amount of spend that they handle for their marquee customers. For example, product A claims that it can handle very large data sets because it is deployed for customer X whose total spend is approximately $20 billion. On the other hand, product B maintains that it also has deployed its product for customer Y whose total spend is approximately $20 billion. It would be erroneous to assert that the two products are equivalent in terms of their capacity. The total amount of spend is irrelevant for that purpose because there is an enormous variety of cubes in which the total spend is equal to approximately $20 billion. The four metrics that we provided in Chapter 4 are preferred for that purpose.

What Do Your Dimensions Look Like?

The nature of the data in your dimensional tables is pivotal to your decision about your schema. It will determine, at least, the size of the tables, the number of the tables, and the number of attributes that each table should contain. A bad data structure is not only hard to maintain, but it also has a direct effect on the performance of the OLAP queries. There have been cases when customers complained to third-party vendors about the unacceptable performance of the OLAP engine. In some of these cases, the culprit turned out to be a bad data structure that was needlessly enforcing computational work, which would not incur otherwise, for the vast majority of the queries.

An OLAP solution should support a large number of dimensional nodes and a large number of dimensions. For example, there are OLAP engine offerings that will not support more than 32,000 nodes in a single dimension or they will not support more than 8 dimensions in a single schema (i.e., no more than 8 dimensions can be associated directly with a fact table) or both. Nowadays, it is common to have between 12 and 14 dimensions in a single star schema. It is also common to have one or more dimensions with tens of thousand of nodes. In fact, quite often for large corporations, the dimension that corresponds to the corporate vendors (suppliers) contains a number of nodes that is on the order of hundreds of thousands. For these corporations, it is critical that the OLAP engine can handle that volume of data in a single dimension. An additional complication with these dimensions is that they might contain a large number of attributes that should be available during the analysis. This situation presents the dilemma of whether one should keep the attributes in the primary dimensional table of a plain star schema, if the OLAP engine can support them, or trade database schema complexity for OLAP and reporting efficiency.

Precooked Data or On-the-Fly Calculations?

Another distinguishing feature of some OLAP engines is their ability to evaluate roll-ups on-the-fly. The alternative is to evaluate roll-ups ahead of time and store them in a data store—this is also known as "data precooking." The obvious problem of the latter approach is the enormous amount of data that need to be evaluated and stored, ahead of time, as the size of the OLAP cube grows. Typical large cubes have about a dozen dimensions and their cardinality (defined as the product of the number of dimensional nodes for all dimensions) reaches some astronomical numbers, e.g., 10^{60} or even 10^{70}. The cardinality of a cube provides us with a lower bound on the number of possible *ad hoc* queries that we can perform. Hence, the number of queries that can be evaluated and stored *a priori* is a negligible fraction of the total number of possible queries that can be asked. As you would expect, most of the solutions employ a hybrid approach in order to achieve a fine balance between physical memory and database storage.

Another complication that may occur, with respect to the choice of "precooking" versus on-the-fly calculations, is the possibility of updating the cube data in an *ad hoc* manner. Typically, a spend analysis cube is updated every quarter. Historically, one of the basic differences between an OLTP (online transaction processing) and an OLAP system is the dynamic versus the static nature of the data, respectively. The data in OLTP systems change frequently and are stored into complex schemata. Long, complicated queries are infrequent. Conversely, the data in OLAP systems change infrequently and complicated queries are basic functional elements of their operation. Nevertheless, the demand for changing the data more frequently in OLAP systems continues to drive innovation in this field. It should be clear that precooking has a serious disadvantage in this case. The requirement of changing the OLAP cube on a weekly or even on a monthly basis can have a significant impact on an OLAP system that employs precooking.

In our opinion, there is no need for a frequent update of the cube. A quarterly or a monthly refresh, depending on your needs, and a small number of subsequent iterations, that would surgically alter the distribution of the measures in the cube or the structure of a dimension, should be sufficient for a thorough and successful spend analysis program. If you find that a monthly publication of a cube requires a significant number of changes thereafter, then you probably need to reevaluate your processing at an earlier stage—this situation frequently indicates that there are inefficiencies in the data cleansing or data enrichment modules.

Continental or International Deployment?

Most large corporate deployments of a spend analysis program are international. That is a fact that should be taken into consideration in the early stages of OLAP vendor selection. Can the solution be internationalized? This is a question with multiple dimensions. In how many languages is the application available? In addition, does the vendor have the capabilities to handle internationalization at the content level? For example, if your transactions contain item descriptions in English, Chinese, Japanese, and Portuguese, can enrichment processing handle all of the data equally well? Can the OLAP engine support UTF-8 (the 8-bit UCS/Unicode Transformation Format) encoding?

Moreover, an equally important aspect of an international deployment is the fact that the users of the system are geographically dispersed and therefore their Internet connection bandwidth can vary significantly. Does this affect the response time of the OLAP solution? Here, clearly, the possible issues are related to the number of data that are sent to the client browser. Does the solution support data compression during the HTTP request/response trip? Quite often, proper system configuration can address these concerns, but they are issues that you should be aware of.

The ability of an application to support internationalization (often referred to as I18N) should be taken for granted today. The number of locales that can be supported out-of-the-box is a good measure for the extent that a product will be able to handle users that are dispersed around the globe at the application level.

Pivoting or Multidimensional Navigation?

There are two prevalent modes of navigating an OLAP cube. The first is called "pivoting." Pivoting is an operation that rotates the data axes in order to present a different view of the data. The presentation of the data typically involves a single dimension each time that you execute a query. The other mode, which we will call multidimensional navigation, presents all of the dimensions of the cube and it updates the measure information on all of these dimensions, each time that you execute a query. This is a sophisticated approach and computationally very expensive. It involves more than one basic OLAP operation executing with every "click" of the end user. It would be inappropriate to compare two spend analysis solutions, in terms of OLAP efficiency, if they operate with a different mode of navigation. Pivoting requires a single roll-up (to be defined shortly) for each query, whereas multidimensional navigation requires, at least, N roll-ups, where N is the number of the visible dimensions of the cube. Although pivoting is faster, the trade-off is the lack of context that the rest of the dimensions offer. The choice depends on your analytical requirements.

Let us digress here, for a moment, to clarify a few technical OLAP terms such as "pivoting" and "roll-up," which we have used here and in earlier chapters, but which we have not yet formally defined. The basic operations in OLAP are the following:

Roll-up. Typically, the roll-up operation refers to the aggregation of the values for all measures in the cube, at each level of a dimension. The values are added at each level, starting from the leaf nodes, of a dimensional hierarchy in order to provide the total sum of a node's descendents. The term roll-up is also used in the context of *dimension reduction*, i.e., the removal of one or more dimensions from an OLAP cube.

Drill-down. The drill-down operation is considered to be the inverse of a roll-up operation. Drill-down refers to the selection of a subset of data from the current view, so that the view is restricted to nodes that are at a higher depth in the dimensional hierarchies. It is the multidimensional analogue of the "zoom in" operation on a geographic map or an image; here the levels of the dimensional hierarchy are the spatial scales that are supported by the map or the image.

Slice. The slice operation also refers to the selection of a subset of data from the current view, but the selection can be arbitrary, and no restriction to deeper levels of the dimensional hierarchies is necessary.

Dice. The dice operation refers to the selection of a subset of data from the current view in an arbitrary manner and across two or more dimensions. Hence, the slice operation is a degenerate case of the dice operation. Notice that some products support the dice operation in a single query ("one click"), while others require a combination of queries, i.e., a chain of queries in which each dimensional selection corresponds to a query.

Typically a thorough spend analysis program relies heavily on multidimensional navigation. After all, the primary purpose of OLAP is the support of *ad hoc* queries on a multidimensional set. If you employ the pivoting navigation model, then your options to execute any query, from any given point in the cube, are limited in comparison to the multidimensional navigation model; in fact, they are limited exponentially with respect to the number of dimensions.

Whether we use pivoting or multidimensional navigation, the OLAP engine should scale well with respect to dimensional views. By the term scaling, we mean that, as the number of dimensions increases, the response time of the OLAP solution does not degrade, provided that the increase in dimensional views is compensated by an increase in computational resources. The global performance of a multidimensional navigation is limited by the slowest performing roll-up.

TECHNICAL CONSIDERATIONS IN THE DDL MODULE

There are a number of technical issues that any spend analysis program should tackle in the DDL (data definition and loading) module. In this section we will review a number of these issues and suggest best practices for dealing with them.

Representative Sampling

In the preliminary phases of your spend analysis program, you will conduct a pilot project, either with the candidate vendors or internally, in order to ascertain your ROI. It is important that the sample of the data that will be used in this phase is representative of your entire dataset. Quite often this issue is handled in an empirical manner. One way to approach this problem mathematically is to examine whether the set of all of your (currently) available data and the sample data for the pilot project are drawn from the same distribution function. Formally speaking, you can never prove that two data sets come from the *same* probability distribution. However, you can prove that two data sets do come from two *different* probability distributions. The easiest approach is to treat the distributions of each dimension individually. Furthermore, notice that we always want to compare two different data sets, i.e., the global and the pilot data sets. We cannot presume that we know the probability distribution itself.

Even when we restrict ourselves to a single dimension, two special cases need to be considered, namely, the case of discrete and continuous data values. The established statistical test for identifying differences between two sets with discrete data is the *chi-square* test. For the case of continuous data, as a function of a single variable, the established test is the *Kolmogorov-Smyrnov* (KS) test. The interested reader can refer to any good statistical text for more details on these tests.

We should mention that we have treated the probability distributions as being totally independent. This assumption might or might not be true. However, the independent tests should be sufficient to provide a measure of the overall differences between our two data sets. The reason for treating each dimension separately is that, for continuous data, the cumulative probability distribution is not well defined in two or more dimensions. Alternative tests do exist, but they involve sophisticated techniques, such as Monte Carlo integrations, and they should be investigated on a data specific manner.

Missing Values

You will almost certainly encounter missing values in your data. There are many reasons why these values are not present. For example, the data schemata across the various source systems are not the same; hence, for certain attributes, what one schema possesses, another will not. Another example, at the field level, is the case of optional fields in the various applications across the source systems. If a field is optional, and the application does not provide a default value for it, then the value for that field will be missing from the data. Missing values can cause significant headaches and should not be ignored. This is especially true if the missing values appear in fields that participate in the enrichment process. From an analytical perspective, there is a difference between "missing" values and "empty" values. An empty value means that there is no corresponding value in the real world for the field of this specific fact entry. A missing value means that a corresponding value does exist, but it was not captured. Hereafter, we will refer to both cases as "missing" values, with the understanding that there is a difference, in the context of analysis, between these two cases. For all of the above reasons, it is important that we study carefully the missing values in our data set before we employ any of the replacement methods that we describe below.

Once you identify that you have missing values, there are a number of replacement options that are available to you. Let us consider the most fundamental and commonly occurring options:

Ignore the missing values. If the missing values appear in fields that are not relevant to the enrichment process, then ignoring the missing values is the recommended option. The missing values themselves, in the context of the fact that they appear, convey a significant amount of information. It is important that this information is not distorted unless it is necessary to fill in the missing values.

Define a default value. Defining a default value is the most common fix to the issue of missing values. In the case of discrete categorical data, it is common to use a value such as "Not Available." In the case of numerical data, whether discrete or continuous, you should carefully select the default value. If there are algorithms that employ this value, it is possible to get erroneous results in your analysis for certain choices of replacement, e.g., "$-\infty$" or "∞." Moreover, it is important to take into account the possible effects that the change of a default value might cause in the outcome of the entire spend analysis life cycle.

Manual entry. Manual entry is not really an option for large data sets. Even for small data sets, manual entry can be tedious and error prone. You are discouraged from using this option.

Substitution with the global mean value. This option refers to the substitution of all missing values by the statistical mean value of the field that they belong to. The substitution with the global mean value option should be used with caution, especially in the case of cubes that have many dimensions.

Substitution with the local mean value. Substitution with the local mean value refers to the substitution of all missing values by the statistical mean value of the field that they belong to, wherein the mean is taken not for all of the values of the field, but only for those values that correspond to the same class with the fact at hand. For example, a pseudoalgorithm for this would be as follows:

- While there are facts with a missing value do the following:
  - Identify a set of facts that belong to the same class (class here is defined by the dimensional keys of the facts, in one or more dimensions).

- If that set is empty or the number of elements in the set is below a configurable threshold, then augment the definition of the class by reducing the constraints of the class (drop the check on one or more dimensions)
- Obtain the mean value for the set that was selected above.

Substitution with the most probable value. Substitution with the most probable value is simply a generalization of the previous option. Any classification algorithm or regression formula can be used, if we have a model for the data or a certain belief that the values can be identified based on the remaining information. This option is, of course, the most time consuming and computationally intensive, but in certain cases, it is highly recommended. For example, consider the case in which the field that contains the missing values is a decision variable in some report or a subsequent analysis of the data. The results of that analysis can be inaccurate or entirely fallacious; hence, it is very important that the substitution of the missing values is as accurate as the available information allows it to be.

The principal precept, with regard to missing values, can be summarized with the phrase *"primum non nocere"* (i.e., "first, do no harm"). Replacing missing values can significantly increase the value of the data, but it can also add bias, or distort the data, if it is applied improperly.

Balanced Dimensional Hierarchies

The definition of a dimensional hierarchy is of paramount importance to the subsequent analysis, and it can also have significant impact on the performance of the OLAP operations. In previous chapters, we have listed some requirements for a good taxonomy. Here we will provide a quantitative approach for analyzing the quality of taxonomies.

The term "balanced" refers to the following properties:

1. The root has M children.
2. All non-leaf nodes have between 2 and $2 \times M$ children.
3. All leaf nodes are at the same depth, which we will denote by D.

Please note that although the definition resembles a B-tree, it is not quite so; for example, a B-tree would have, for all non-leaf nodes, between $M/2$ and M children. In addition, we should strive to keep the number of children for the root to a reasonable size. What is reasonable depends on the dimension, but generally speaking, any number greater than a thousand is usually too large. Recall that we are using tree structures; hence, the number of nodes grows exponentially with the height of the tree. If the structure of the dimension is balanced, in just a few levels of depth, we can store billions of nodes.

If we use the above as our working definition, then we can also define a metric of *breadth imbalance*, by the ratio $(X - 1)/M$, where X is the number of different number of children for all the nodes at a specified level. In addition, we can define a metric of *depth imbalance*, by the ratio Y/D, where Y is the maximum difference of depth among all leaf nodes. Finally, we can define a metric of *node imbalance*, by the ratio Z/M, where Z is the number of children for a non-leaf node. An example of a very well-balanced dimension is the case of a time dimension:

- 2005
  - Q1
    - January
    - February
    - March
  - Q2
    - April
    - May
    - June
  - Q3
    - July
    - August
    - September
  - Q4
    - October
    - November
    - December
- 2006
  - ...
- 2007
  - ...

The above metrics are with respect to the internal structure of a dimension. However, equally important is to balance the facts across the dimensional nodes. Let us consider a dimension that has a total of N leaf nodes and we also have F facts. If each leaf node had F/N facts (we assume here, for argument's sake, that the facts are only associated with dimensional leaf nodes; more general cases can be treated similarly, but they do not help to elucidate the basic idea), then the distribution of facts across the dimensional nodes would be, in some sense, perfect.

Hence, it is reasonable to suggest that a measure of the *fact distribution imbalance* (ϑ) is the following:

$$\vartheta = \sqrt{\sum_i \left[\frac{f(d_i)N}{F} - 1 \right]^2},$$

where $f(d_i)$ is the number of facts for the i-th dimensional node, N is the total number of leaf nodes, and F is the total number of facts as mentioned above. This measure has the following properties:

1. If each leaf node has F/N nodes, then the fact distribution imbalance (ϑ) for this dimension is zero.
2. The fact distribution imbalance (ϑ) is always positive.
3. A large imbalance on a single node is as important as a smaller imbalance on a number of nodes.

Detection of Systematic Errors

In 1881, Simon Newcomb, a Canadian astronomer and mathematician, observed: "That the ten digits do not occur with equal frequency must be evident to any one making use of logarithmic tables, and noticing how much faster the first pages wear out than the last ones. The first significant digit is oftener 1 than any other digit, and the frequency diminishes up to 9."[1] Newcomb stated correctly that the "law of frequency" of significant digits (base 10) satisfies the following distribution:

$$P(d) = \log_{10}(1 + d^{-1}), \forall d = 1, 2, \dots, 9;$$

where $P(d)$ denotes the probability that the first significant digit is equal to d.

A similar expression holds true for other significant digits as well. Benford (1938) investigated thoroughly the validity of Newcomb's observations and provided ample empirical evidence based on frequencies of significant digits from 20 different tables that among others included the specific heats and molecular weights of thousands of chemical compounds, the surface areas of 335 rivers, the street addresses of the first 342 persons listed in *American Men of Science,* and entries from a mathematical handbook.[2] The aggregated data from his tables came surprisingly close to the frequencies that were predicted by Newcomb's formulae. These formulae are commonly known today as Benford's law. Raimi (1976) has written a great review of the literature that relates to Benford's law.[3] In 1995, in an article in the *Wall Street Journal,* Berton (1995) reported that the district attorney's office in Brooklyn detected fraud in seven New York companies by using a statistical test to ascertain that a significant part of the companies' accounting data had been fabricated.[4]

In the context of spend analysis, a large amount of empirical data shows that the distribution of the first significant digit in many real world data sets follows Benford's law. Hence, the above-mentioned logarithmic distribution can be used as a benchmark to detect systematic errors as well as malicious activity (see Chapter 10 on compliance reporting). For the mathematically inclined, we should note that Benford's law is the only probability distribution that is invariant under changes of scale, e.g., converting from metric to English units; or under changes of base, e.g., replacing base 10 by base 8 or 2, in which case the logarithm base 10 is replaced by a logarithm to the new base.

TECHNICAL CONSIDERATIONS IN THE DE MODULE

As we have seen so far, there are a number of areas that need particular attention when you consider the technologies that underlie a spend analysis program. This is especially true for the technologies that are involved in the DE (data enrichment) module. In this section we will identify a number of these areas, but it should be clear from the outset that we can only present a cursory review of these issues. The interested reader can refer to the specialized literature on each of these areas.

String Matching

String comparison is one of the fundamental tools used in data enrichment. String comparison is used to identify like vendors by comparing their names (given two vendor names A and B, does A refer to the same vendor as B does?) or to identify equivalent parts by comparing the descriptions. This process is not as straightforward as you might think. The subject of matching strings has been studied in a number of areas, ranging from statistics and databases to artificial intelligence (AI) research. In statistics literature, work that relates to string matching falls into the general category that is called probabilistic record linkage. The seminal paper by Fellegi and Sunter (1969) formulated string matching as a classification problem.[5] Most work in that area has been based on similar ideas and extensions of their work. In the database community, string matching falls in the general category that is called record matching. Knowledge-intensive approaches have been proposed for record matching by Galhardaset al. (2000)[6] and Raman and Hellerstein (2001),[7] whereas Monge and Elkan (1996, 1997)[8,9] have proposed the use of string-edit distances as a general-purpose *record matching* scheme, and Cohen (2000)[10] has proposed the use of a TFIDF-based (term frequency inverse document frequency) distance metric for the same purpose. In the AI community, supervised learning techniques have been employed extensively for learning the coefficients of string-edit distance metrics (Ristad and Yianilos, 1998)[11] and combining the results of different distance functions (Cohen and Richman, 2002).[12]

Let us briefly examine a few issues that might occur. To begin with, the notion of string matching depends strongly on what the strings represent. For example, if the strings represent the names of physical persons, then the entries "John, Smith" and "Smith, John" should match (ignore name overloading for the moment). On the other hand, if the strings represent the names of corporate entities, then the entries "Gold Partners" and "Partners of Gold" might or might not be a good match. Another example concerns the fact that even when two strings are similar in a lexicographic sense, they are not similar in their content, e.g., "band" versus "bank." In comparing strings, we are interested in what the strings represent, not what the strings are. This is a very important point, which is pervasive in spend analysis because each dimension, almost certainly, will require a different semantic representation. If a vendor offers a product that matches vendor names very accurately and efficiently, you should not infer that it will also match item descriptions with the same accuracy or efficiency, and *vice versa*.

If we consider two values of a numerical field, let us say one of the cube's measures, the meaning of "closeness," "similarity," or "equivalency" of distance between two values is clear. The same holds for an array of values (also called a vector). Each coordinate in the vector belongs to a different field in a fact entry or in a dimensional node entry. We can use a Euclidean space, or any other metric space, and unambiguously define the distance between two vectors. However, strings are neither pure numbers nor vectors, thus the answer to the above simple question requires special treatment. The problem is complex enough in a single language. The presence of more than one language can be tackled by *metadata tagging*, which will result in a fragmentation of the data depending on the language, but a comparison of strings that belong to different languages requires *semantic tagging* across the language dictionaries.

Classification

Earlier in this book (see Chapter 6), we encountered classification from an operational perspective and the value that adds in a spend analysis program. In this section, we will provide a general orientation in the technical aspects of classification.

So, what is classification? Classification is the process of assigning a label, which denotes a specific *class*, to an *object*. A class contains objects that are similar, in some sense, whereas objects that belong to two different classes are dissimilar, in exactly the same sense. Hence, the notion of similarity is crucial in defining the process of classification. In fact, widely different definitions of similarity will lead, almost certainly, to different classification results. In order to define similarity, we assume that the objects can be characterized by a set of *features* that describe them adequately for our purposes. Features fall into two broad categories—quantitative or numerical features and qualitative or categorical features. The former category is further divided into continuous-valued features (e.g., temperature, time) and discrete-valued features (e.g., number of contracts, number of commodities sourced by a vendor). The latter category is further divided into ordinal-valued features (e.g., position in the organizational hierarchy) and nominal-valued features (e.g., vendor name, general ledger description). These are working definitions, of course. There are cases in which the definition depends largely on our conventions. For example, a discrete-valued feature with a large number of possible values may be treated as a continuous-valued feature or an ordinal (qualitative) feature may be mapped into the natural numbers and be treated as a discrete-valued (quantitative) feature.

Most classification algorithms require a numerical representation; hence, the values of qualitative features must be translated somehow into numbers. The methods that are used to attain such representations are, typically, based on heuristics and depend largely on the specific case under study. Nonnumerical algorithms do exist for qualitative features, but they are not as general as numerical algorithms.

Classification, in the context of spend analysis, is usually implemented in the form of *supervised machine learning*. This implies that there is some *a priori* knowledge about the classes that you want to assign. That knowledge is usually represented in the class structure and a set of object assignments to that structure, typically referred to as the *training set*. Because training is involved, during the phase of classification, an evaluation process is required, in order to qualify the degree of learning that has been achieved. However, it is crucial to understand the difference between the training data and the testing data. If you qualify your classification operator based on the same data that you used to train it, then you will probably encounter what is called *overfitting*. Overfitting refers to a high bias of the classifier toward the set of data that was used for training. In these cases, the prediction error of the classifier can be very low, but its ability to generalize (i.e., to classify objects that were not present in the training set) will also be very low. In the context of spend analysis, overfitting is not always bad news! If you are confident that your training set includes the vast majority of assignments that can possibly occur, then overfitting might be good news. Nevertheless, be aware of overfitting and select a consistent methodology that ensures a high degree of accuracy while maintaining some degree of generalization.

Let us now look into the various algorithms that are available for classification. Of course, we will not present in detail these algorithms, but rather we will describe the various kinds of algorithms and their usefulness in the context of spend analysis. The interested reader can find much more information in the specialized literature on this subject, e.g., a nice book, with many references, is Dunham (2003).[13] We will divide the classification algorithms into five broad categories:

- Statistical algorithms
- Distance-based algorithms
- Decision tree-based (DT) algorithms
- Neural network-based (NN) algorithms
- Rule-based algorithms

Statistical Algorithms

There are two basic groups of statistical algorithms—regression and Bayesian. Regression algorithms, in essence, are based on the idea of finding the best fit of a particular numerical formula, in which a number of features participate, for a given data set. Let us denote the participating features as X_i, and the value of the regression formula as Y. The simplest regression formula would be linear regression, which would take the following form:

$$Y = c_0 + \sum_i c_i {}^* X_i,$$

where c_i represents the regression coefficients. If the weighted terms are not linear, but rather nonlinear functions of the X_i features, then we have a case of nonlinear regression. The regression formula divides the space of X_i values into two subspaces, which can be used for classification. Hence, regression algorithms are suitable for *binary classification*, i.e., the rudimentary case of classification, in which there are only two classes. Regression algorithms are usually ineffective for qualitative data, which is very reasonable given the nature of these algorithms. For example, a linear regression may be a fairly good representation of the actual data in a limited region of the coordinate space, but it might be completely inadequate to describe the data that are outside that domain. It is possible to get around these limitations, e.g., a number of regression models may be used, in which each model covers a specific region of the coordinate space and interpolation is used at the boundary surfaces between different models; however, this is not always straightforward.

Bayesian algorithms are based on a theorem of probability that is known as the *Bayes rule* or *Bayes theorem* which you may have studied in high school.[14] The underlying concept is also known as *conditional probability*, i.e., what is the probability of item description A belonging to class X given that historically N similar descriptions were classified to class A? These algorithms perform very well in a variety of contexts, including spend analysis. Although they rely, in principle, on the probabilistic independence of the participating features, it has been shown that they can be fairly effective in cases in which that independence is not maintained. It should be noted that the simplest Bayesian algorithm, i.e., *naïve Bayes*, does not perform well in the automatic text classification problem. Nevertheless, some empirical heuristics that have been proposed perform very well in standard benchmark collections. Bayesian algorithms themselves may not be completely adequate for your purposes, but they are often used in the design of more complicated classifiers. As we shall see, state-of-the-art classification relies on the combination of various classifiers rather than on a single classifier over the entire domain.

Distance-Based Algorithms

In distance-based algorithms, we introduce the notion of a similarity measure that gives us the "distance" of a given object from a given class. The class that is closest to the object is assigned to that object. You can think of this as a generalization of the usual notion of geographic distance. It is equivalent to searching for the restaurant that is closest to your house, but the distance is, typically, evaluated in a space with many other dimensions, not just two. This is the most intuitive classification approach, but it can also be grossly misleading. The reason for this lies in the fact that many of the features that describe an object are not directly, or linearly, related to each other. As a result, in most of the cases, a single similarity measure cannot capture efficiently the knowledge that is required for the distance-based algorithm to be successful. Nevertheless, in many low dimensional cases, with low complexity, these algorithms perform well and are fairly simple to implement. The most common classification scheme in the distance-based algorithms category is the *K nearest neighbors* (KNN).

Decision Tree-Based Algorithms

In *decision tree-based (DT) algorithms*, we build a tree that models the classification process. This approach to classification divides the domain of inquiry into disjoint sets. An object will be classified based on the set to which its "coordinates," i.e., the values of its defining features, belong. DT algorithms have several advantages. They are easy to use and they are very efficient. Their scaling properties do not depend on the number of objects that we need to classify. The time that it takes to process all objects is proportional to the height of the tree, which is fixed during the training phase. However, DT-based algorithms also have several disadvantages. For example, they are not very good choices when we deal with continuous features. The continuum of the feature values must be divided into a finite number of bins in order to construct the tree. Furthermore, overfitting may easily appear because the DT is built based on the training data alone. Thus, it is very hard for these algorithms to correctly generalize and properly classify unseen data for many kinds of data that appear frequently in a spend analysis program. This is especially true for data that are characterized primarily by nominal valued features. Additionally the performance of this kind of classifiers can degrade because correct branches in the tree cannot be accessed when some data are missing.

It is worth mentioning some of the most common DT-based algorithms. ID3 is based on information theory. ID3 attempts to minimize the expected number of comparisons that leads to correct classification of a given object. This is an idea that might be familiar if you have ever read Charles Dickens' *A Christmas Carol*. In the game described in the book, "Yes and No," Scrooge's nephew had to think of something and the others had to find what it was, but the nephew could answer only "yes" or "no," depending on the question asked. (Incidentally, this game is fairly popular among children in Spanish-speaking countries, where it is known as "veo veo." The game was also popular in the United States in the 1940s because of a radio panel quiz show.) Similar to these familiar games, ID3's strategy is to ask questions that have answers which will eliminate as many candidates as is possible based on the provided information. This strategy can be formalized by using the notion of *information entropy*. We suggest that interested readers explore this topic, in more detail, by studying the technical literature on the subject (e.g., see McKay, 2003).[15]

Two classification algorithms, C4.5 and C5.0, improve the performance of ID3 by gracefully handling missing data, using ranges for continuous data, employing effective pruning strategies, introducing rules, and by using "splitting" in order to maximize the information gain at each step of the decision flow. C5.0 (on Unix machines; or See5 on Microsoft Windows machines) is a commercial version that is used in data mining products. The RuleQuest website (http://www.rulequest.com/see5-comparison.html) offers a direct comparison between See5/C5.0 and C4.5 which is quite instructive. The *classification and regression trees* (CART) algorithm generates a binary decision tree. CART also relies on the information content gained as a criterion of choice for choosing the best splitting attribute. However, CART differs from ID3 in that it limits the number of children to two. Finally, the *Scalable PaRallelizable Induction of Decision Trees*, or simply SPRINT, employs the CART algorithm, but it can be applied in cases in which there are constraints in the available main memory. In addition, as the name suggests, SPRINT facilitates parallelization of the execution.

Neural Networks-Based Algorithms

Classification algorithms that rely on *neural networks* (NN) are highly proprietary. Their operation and results are not as obvious, or intuitive, as those of the other aforementioned algorithms. The interested reader is referred to the vast specialized literature on the field. A good starting point would be Dreyfus (2004).[16]

Rule-Based Algorithms

Last but not least are classification algorithms that are *rule based*. In order to achieve good results from a spend analysis program, we are collecting and leveraging knowledge from various sources. One way of collecting knowledge is by accumulating business rules, also known as "feedback requests." These rules are of the if-then form (technically known as "productions"). For example, a rule might be stating: "If the vendor is IBM then the commodity should be set to IT Services." A problem that you might face over a period of time is that the number of rules increases so much that the processing of these rules for your entire dataset becomes very slow. In the AI community, this situation is known as the *utility problem*—the larger the number of rules, the slower the performance of the system.

The most efficient forward chaining production systems use the Rete algorithm that was introduced in the OPS-5 production system or one of its variants.[17] Rete is the basis for well-known libraries such as CLIPS, Jess, and Soar. There are also object-oriented implementations of Rete, e.g., the JBoss rules library (formerly known as Drools). We strongly recommend employing a Rete-based rules engine in order to efficiently process your data.

Clustering

In Chapter 6, we noted that clustering and classification are the two most important operations of dimensional enrichment. We also described the areas in which the clustering operation can be useful in our context. It should be clear, however, that clustering algorithms can be used effectively for transactional enrichment, as well as for advanced analytical reports. In this section, we will take a closer look at the technical aspects of clustering. Clustering is similar to classification, in the sense that our data are assigned to a group that is distinguished from all other groups on the basis of certain criteria. The basic distinction between clustering and classification is that in clustering, the groups are not known *a priori*, whereas in classification, the groups are the concepts of our reference schema. Hence, from that perspective, clustering can be considered as a special case of classification, i.e., a self-referential classification. A clustering algorithm may divide the original set of data into partitions (partitional clustering) or it may divide it into a number of sets that are hierarchical in structure (hierarchical clustering). In partitional clustering, the number of partitions can be given as an input to the algorithm or the number can be determined dynamically. In hierarchical clustering, both the number of sets and the number of hierarchy levels can be given or be determined dynamically.

In the context of spend analysis, clustering outliers are frequently encountered. An outlier is an element of the original data set with attribute values that are much different from any other element and therefore cannot be grouped with any other element. For example, during vendor clustering, you should expect a large number of vendors that are single, independent, entities—these are often called *vendor singletons*—which do not belong into any other corporate entity and therefore should remain at the top level of the vendor hierarchy. This property of the data makes the qualification of the vendor clustering, also know as vendor "familying," fairly challenging. However, this property can be used intelligently to create a superior structure for your vendor hierarchy. For example, upon identification of the major vendor groups, you may proceed by clustering the remaining, unclustered, vendors based on the amount of spend that they represent in your data, either as a percentage or in absolute terms, e.g., "vendors with spend greater than 100K" or "vendors with spend greater than 2% of total spend." You could do this by using one-level partitions based only on spend or by using hierarchical algorithms that are based on spend and corporate characteristics or by employing a combination of these options based on your specific structure needs. The understanding of how to use secondary clustering for the initial clustering of outliers can significantly improve the structure of your vendors.

Let us now explore, in some detail, the various clustering algorithms that are available and are relevant to spend analysis. Consider a set of dimensional nodes $D = \{d1, d2, \ldots, dn\}$ that we want to cluster under certain criteria and assume that the notion of the "closeness" between the members of a group can be specified by a similarity measure S. The tuple (D, S) must define a metric space that allows us to distinguish whether an element di is closer to another element dj, for any di and dj in D. Mathematical jargon aside, the important aspect of this is having the ability to unambiguously and consistently compare any two entries in D. If we can do that, then we can tell whether they "belong" together. There are two major categories of clustering algorithms—graph-based algorithms and pure metric space algorithms.

The first kind of algorithms would be most appropriate when considering D as a set of nodes in a graph. In the context of spend analysis, a large number of relationship graphs are defined implicitly through the OLAP schema relations. These graphs can be analyzed to reveal hidden structures among dimensional nodes or plain transactions. You can think of the second kind of clustering algorithms as a set of techniques that allows you to determine geographic regions based on the proximity of villages or cities on a map. In a geographic map the number of spatial dimensions is just two, but the main idea is the same in higher-dimensions as well. However, even though the underlying concepts are identical, computational complexity increases dramatically with the number of dimensions, depending on your specific clustering algorithm.

The simplest graph-based clustering algorithm is the *single link algorithm*, which is also known as the *nearest neighbor* clustering algorithm. More compact clusters can be created by using the *complete link algorithm*. Another popular and quite effective clustering algorithm is called RObust Clustering using linKs (ROCK). We should note that clustering algorithms based on genetic algorithms, as well as neural networks, do exist and have been applied with various degrees of success. In particular, an abundance of algorithms, based on the Kohonen self-organizing map, are known in the literature and are available in commercial products. For more implementation details and additional clustering algorithms the interested user can peruse the review sections on clustering in Hastie et al. (2003)[18] and Han and Kamber (2001).[19]

Classifier Evaluation

The evaluation of classification engines is not as trivial as you might think. You might be shocked about the credibility of certain claims that are often made during the sales cycle. A fully automated classification of your data is not possible by any known method or algorithm. There are actually fairly strong theoretical reasons that can explain the inability of any one classifier to predict correctly an arbitrarily selected corpus of descriptions. Nevertheless, as we described earlier in this book, it is desirable to leverage automation to the largest extent possible in order to lower the overall cost and increase the overall value of a spend analysis program.

Let us now see, in more detail, the means that are available to our disposal for the purpose of judging the credibility of certain claims when we consider the results of an automated classification. To begin with, you should know that there are two major learning techniques, namely, supervised and unsupervised learning techniques. Nearly all the classifiers in the market today are based on supervised learning techniques. The supervision refers to the fact that the classifier undergoes a process of training before it is deployed in the field. As you can imagine, the relation of the training data to the actual data in your deployment will be crucial for the success of classification. Hereafter, we will tacitly ignore the evaluation of clustering techniques and unsupervised classification techniques because neither the research in that field is conclusive (i.e., there is no consensus as to the preferred method of evaluation among academicians) nor is there a ubiquitous established practice in the industry.

For the purpose of clarity, let us introduce a few terms. We will consider the standard binary classification problem. In more concrete terms, we are trying to discern whether a particular description, say, "Dell Latitude D600," belongs to the commodity category of "Computers" or not. The most basic tool we have is called the confusion matrix. A confusion matrix is a simple matrix, in which the rows refer to the category that the classifier assigns and the columns refer to the actual

Actual Predicted		
	True Positives (TP)	False Positives (FP)
	False Negatives (FN)	True Negatives (TN)
Column Totals	P	N

Figure 8.1. A typical confusion matrix for a simple binary classification problem.

category to which an instance of a description belongs. In this case, a description either belongs in a class or it does not, but a general case does not differ drastically in its fundamentals from this simple case. A confusion matrix is illustrated in Figure 8.1.

This simple chart captures the possible outcomes of the classification of a given description and a given classifier. That is, we are asking the classifier: "Does this description belong to class (category) X?" If the classification assigns the description to class X, then we would call that classification "positive." Otherwise, the classification would be "negative." Of course, the classification itself could be right ("true") or wrong ("false"). Thus, as shown, the matrix must contain four possible outcomes.

Based on the values of Figure 8.1, we have the following definitions:

1. FP rate = FP/N
2. TP rate = TP/P (this quantity is also known as "Recall")
3. Precision = TP/(TP + FP)
4. Accuracy = (TP + TN)/(P + N)
5. F-score = Precision × Recall

These are very valuable quantities in evaluating a classifier. In addition, a well-known classifier evaluation technique is based on ROC (receiver operating characteristics) graphs.

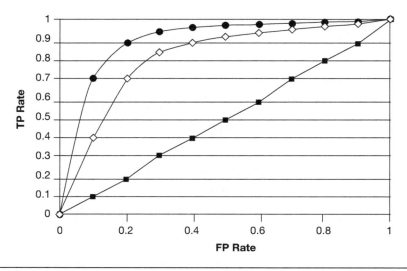

Figure 8.2. A typical ROC graph that compares two classifiers.

ROC Graph Details

ROC graphs have been used in signal detection theory for a long time. ROC graph analysis has also been applied to medical diagnosis systems, e.g., see Thurner et al. (1998)[20] and Swets et al. (2000).[21] Since the late 1980s and early 1990s, ROC graph analysis has been adopted in machine learning. ROC graph analysis has been demonstrated to be extremely valuable in evaluating machine learning algorithms. ROC graphs are two-dimensional graphs in which TP rate is plotted as a function of FP rate. The beauty of a ROC graph is that it visualizes the trade-offs between value extracted (true positives) versus value lost (false positives).

Figure 8.2 depicts a typical ROC graph that compares two classifiers. Classifier A is shown with the top curved line, whereas classifier B is shown with the middle curved line. The diagonal line depicts a "random pick" classifier.

Any classifier with a ROC curve that appears below the diagonal line would perform worse than a classifier that randomly assigns the descriptions to a class. Of course, if you should ever get a graph such as that in Figure 8.2, you should simply reverse the final assignment of your classifier! Hence, in the ROC graphs that you see in classification, the lower right triangle is typically empty. In Figure 8.2, classifier A (the top curved line) is performing better than classifier B (the middle curved line). In general, the more the ROC plot is squeezed in the upper left corner of the ROC space, the better the classifier performance is going to be.

Now, let us turn our attention to the following scenario. Suppose that we find out about a classifier with a TP rate, as defined above, of 85%. What does this mean? You should always remember that this result is only an estimate and that in statistics an estimate is only as good as the context in which it is derived. A statement such as the above implies that there is a set of descriptions for which the classifier accurately assigned the proper commodity category to the descriptions; here we tacitly assume, without loss of generality, that we are classifying item descriptions. If you enlarge the set of descriptions, or you use an entirely different set, the TP rate of the same classifier is going to change. Intuitively, we understand that if the estimate was obtained with a very large number of descriptions that cover all, or nearly all, of our categories and the descriptions that were used for the training of the classifier are characteristic of the entire set of descriptions that we have, then the 85% estimate should be robust. However, how close to the true TP rate of the classifier is our estimate? To get a better idea of what is involved, we will answer that question by considering a Bernoulli process, i.e., a process that describes a sequence of independent events that either succeed or fail. In other words, we will consider the process of binary classification as a Bernoulli process. Let us denote the true TP rate as TP*; then the following question can be asked: "How good an estimate of TP* is the TP rate?"

In order to answer that question, we can use, as you may recall from your knowledge of statistics, the notion of a *confidence interval*. That is, TP* must be within a specified interval with a certain degree of certainty. For example, if our TP rate is 85%, in a set of 100 descriptions, our confidence cannot be very high. However, if our TP rate is 85%, in a set of 100,000 descriptions, our confidence should be much higher. As the size of the set increases, the confidence interval shrinks. The mathematically inclined reader can consult any good textbook in statistics for more details, e.g., see Papoulis and Pillai (2002).[14]

Association Rules

The use of association rules, which identify correlations between entries in a data set, has received considerable attention in the area of market basket analysis. In the context of spend analysis, association rule mining can help you achieve the main goals of your program and add insight into your analysis. In market basket analysis, association rule mining is used to understand purchasing behavior for the purpose of targeting market audiences more effectively. For example, in a store chain, the analysts would seek strong correlations between the purchase of merchandise A and B, in the hope that customers who purchased merchandise A were also likely to purchase merchandise B. Hence, a marketing campaign should focus on those customers who purchased A, but did not purchase B. In essence, these rules represent knowledge about purchasing behavior. Thus, it should be clear that association rule mining can have a significant impact on any spend analysis program because one of the main goals of such a program is the study of purchasing behavior, perhaps not at the level of an individual buyer, but certainly at the level of a cost center or purchasing unit.

Association rules should be novel, externally significant, nontrivial, and actionable, e.g., see Roddick and Rice (2001)[21] and Hilderman and Hamilton (2001)[23] and the references therein. Today, the fundamentals of association mining are well established and understood. The majority of current research involves the specialization of known algorithms in order to include additional semantics, such as information that belongs to a specific ontology. Association mining involves two steps. First, we identify the sets of items, also known as itemsets, within the dataset. Second, we derive inferences based on these *itemsets*. Most current research is related to the efficient discovery of itemsets because the computational complexity of the first step is significantly greater than that of the second step. For example, if there are N distinct items within our data set, there are 2^N possible combinations of these items that we must explore. The problem is that N is typically very large; hence, brute force techniques are not realistic. Intelligent sampling, efficient pruning strategies, careful selection of data structures, and compression techniques can offer significant improvements when N is large, as it is often the case in practice.

In the context of spend analysis, a number of options are available. For example, the values of certain dimensions, say, X, Y, and Z, can be used to identify the value of some other dimension W. If W were, say, commodity, its value might have been "uncategorized;" however, the association rule might indicate an appropriate category for the commodity of the transactions that are specified by certain values of the dimensions X, Y, and Z. Another example of an association rule would be the enrichment of a missing dimensional attribute value based on information at the dimensional node level or on the set of transactions that corresponds to that particular dimensional node.

It should be noted that the use of these rules, like any rule that is applied during the data enrichment stage, should be subject to review. In the interest of efficiency, the rules can be reviewed in a sorting order of decreasing spend.

The coverage, or support, of an association rule is the number of instances for which the application of the rule would lead to the correct assignment of values in a dimensional node or a transaction. The accuracy, or confidence, of an association rule is the number of instances for which the application of the rule would lead to the correct assignment of values in a dimensional node or a transaction expressed as a proportion of all instances to which it is applicable. It is common to specify threshold values for both coverage and accuracy while seeking candidate rules. In addition, for a spend analysis implementation, we should specify threshold values that relate to the amount of spend that is affected by a rule. Because the number of possible rules is enormous, only rules that meet these criteria should be considered as candidate association rules for review.

It is beyond the scope of this book to delve into the intricacies of the specific algorithms. However, the interested reader can find a recent survey of the field in the comprehensive review by Ceglar and Roddick (2006).[24]

SUMMARY

Whether you build you own spend analysis application or you license one, be aware of certain technology challenges and trade-offs that exist in each of the components of the application. For example, in the SA (analytics) module, the type of OLAP schema, the structure of the dimensions, and whether roll-ups are precomputed or not, are all important considerations that determine performance. In the DDL (data definition and loading) module, there are various statistical techniques that can be used to improve the IQI (information quality index) of the data. The notion of balanced hierarchies is also covered in the DDL section. In the DE (data enrichment) module, how efficiently and accurately you can classify spend transactions is of paramount importance. Therefore, we have presented a set of commonly used classification algorithms—statistical, distance-based, decision tree-based, neural network-based, and rule-based algorithms. We also have provided an overview of string matching and clustering techniques which are typically useful for vendor enrichment, although they can be used to enrich any other dimension as well.

REFERENCES

1. Newcomb, S. Note on the frequency of use of the different digits in natural numbers. *American Journal of Mathematics*; 1881: 4, 39–40.

2. Benford, F. The law of anomalous numbers. *Proceedings of the American Philosophical Society*; 1938: 78, 551–572.

3. Raimi, R. The peculiar distribution of first significant digits. *Scientific American*; 1969 December: 221, 109–120.

4. Berton, L. He's got their number: scholar uses math to foil financial fraud. *Wall Street Journal*; 1995: July 10.

5. Fellegi, I.P., Sunter, A.B. A theory for record linkage. *Journal of the American Statistical Society*; 1969: 64, 1183–1210.

6. Galhardas, H., Florescu, D., Shasha, D., Simon, E. An extensible framework for data cleaning. In *International Conference on Data Engineering*; 2000: 312.

7. Raman, V., Hellerstein, J. Potter's wheel: an interactive data cleaning system. *The VLDB Journal*; 2001: 381–390.

8. Monge, A., Elkan, C. The field-matching problem: algorithm and applications. In *Proceedings of the Second International Conference on Knowledge Discovery and Data Mining*. Simoudis, E., Han, J., Fayyad, U., Eds. Menlo Park, CA: AAAI Press; 1996.

9. Monge, A., Elkan, C. An efficient domain-independent algorithm for detecting approximately duplicate database records. In *The Proceedings of the SIGMOD 1997 Workshop on Data Mining and Knowledge Discovery*. Tucson, AZ: 1997 May: 23–29.

10. Cohen, W.W. Data integration using similarity joins and a word-based information representation language. *ACM Transactions on Information Systems*; 2000: 18(3), 288–321.

11. Ristad, E.S., Yianilos, P.N. Learning string edit distance. *IEEE Transactions on Pattern Analysis and Machine Intelligence*; 1998: 20(5), 522–532.

12. Cohen, W W., Richman, J. Learning to match and cluster large high-dimensional data sets for data integration. In *Proceedings of the Eighth ACM SIGKDD International Conference on Knowledge Discovery and Data Mining* (KDD-2002); 2002.

13. Dunham, M.H. *Data Mining: Introductory and Advanced Topics*. Upper Saddle Ridge, NJ: Prentice Hall; 2003.

14. Papoulis, A., Pillai, S.U. *Probability, Random Variables, and Stochastic Processes, Fourth Edition*. New York: McGraw-Hill; 2002.

15. McKay, D. *Information Theory, Inference, and Learning Algorithms*. Cambridge: Cambridge University Press; 2003.

16. Dreyfus, G. *Neural Networks: Methodology and Applications, Second Edition*. New York: Springer-Verlag; 2004.

17. Russell, S., Norvig, P. *Artificial Intelligence: A Modern Approach*. Upper Saddle Ridge, NJ: Prentice Hall; 1995.

18. Hastie, T., Tibshirani, R., Friedman, J. *The Elements of Statistical Learning: Data Mining, Inference, and Prediction*. New York: Springer-Verlag; 2003.

19. Han, J., Kamber, M. *Data Mining: Concepts and Techniques*. San Francisco: Morgan Kaufmann Publishers; 2001.

20. Thurner, S., Feurstein, M.C., Lowen, S.B., Teich, M.C. Receiver-operational-characteristic analysis reveals superiority of scale-dependent wavelet and spectral measures for assessing cardiac dysfunction. *Physical Review Letters*; 1998: 81(25), 5688–5691.

21. Swets, J.A., Dawes, R.M., Monahan, J. Psychological science can improve diagnostic decisions. *Psychological Science in the Public Interest*; 2000: 1(1), 1–26.

22. Roddick, J.F, Rice, S.P. What's interesting about cricket?—on thresholds and anticipation in discovered rules. *SIGKDD Explorations*; 2001: 3(1), 1–5.

23. Hilderman, R.J., Hamilton, H.J. Evaluation of interestingness measures for ranking discovered knowledge. In *Proceedings of the 5th Pacific-Asia Conference on Knowledge Discovery and Data Mining (PAKDD '01)*, Hong Kong, China. Cheung, D., Williams, G.J., Li, Q., Eds., *Lecture Notes in Computer Science, Volume 2035*. Berlin: Springer-Verlag; 2001: 247–259.

24. Ceglar, A., Roddick, J. F. Association Mining. *ACM Computing Surveys*. 2006: 38(2), Article 5.

PART III

TRACKING AND MONITORING

INTRODUCTION

So far, we have discussed how spend analysis can be used as a "front end" or a "window" into strategic sourcing—by consolidating demand, aggregating spend, and identifying opportunities for cost reduction. These opportunities are then addressed by leveraging reverse auctions, optimized bidding, e-procurement, and other modules. In many cases, savings programs are created for various commodities or cost centers which are systematically tracked on a monthly or quarterly basis.

Spend analysis can also be effectively used for tracking and monitoring of the bottom line progress in achieving these savings targets. Many companies refresh their spend cube either monthly or quarterly. These successive cubes capture the spend in the last period and can be used to flag those programs that are on track and those that are lagging behind. Thus, spend analysis can also serve as a window at the back end to monitor the progress of cost reduction strategies.

In order to enable such closed-loop programs, the spend information needs to flow through to the various sourcing modules and then back to the spend module in a periodic manner. In other words, spend analysis needs to be integrated into the other modules that make up the strategic sourcing solution. Such an integrated offering from Emptoris is shown in Figure 9.1.

At a high level, the information (and decisions) flows in the following manner:

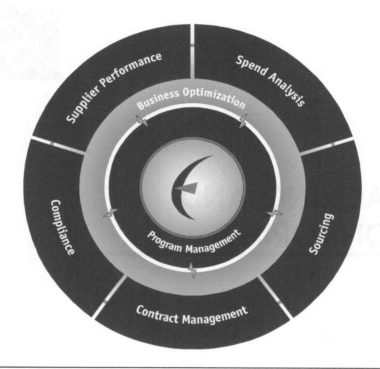

Figure 9.1. An integrated supply management solution from Emptoris.

1. Historical spend (purchasing transactions data) originating in accounts payable, purchasing, and e-procurement systems is first analyzed in spend analysis and opportunities are identified.
2. Sourcing events are then designed to capture the savings. These events, such as reverse auctions and complex multistage negotiations, are designed to capture the best value, not just the best price, from your supply base by factoring cost, risk, and performance drivers into decision making.
3. The parameters (price/quantity, delivery, quality) that are finalized with suppliers in the sourcing (negotiation) events flow into the contract management application which automates and optimizes the management of contracts from creation and execution through performance monitoring, analysis, and renegotiation.
4. The contract information, along with purchasing information, flows into the compliance modules which monitor operational and regulatory compliance across the supply base by analyzing spend, contracts, and controls.

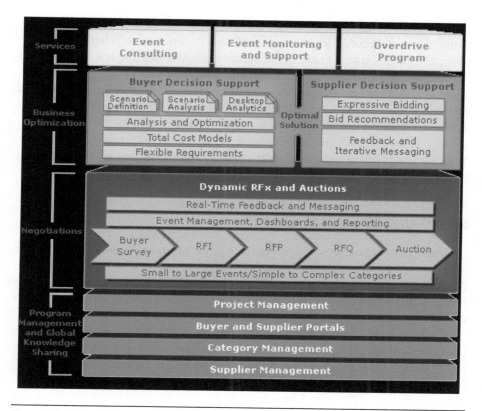

Figure 9.2. Sourcing module from Emptoris.

5. The supplier performance module receives information from spend, sourcing, and contracts and marries all three information feeds for the purposes of evaluation and tracking of supplier performance through a central repository of key performance indicators and scorecards and a robust assessment capability that identifies root cause performance drivers.

6. The cycle repeats for the next period, in which new spend data are captured and presented in the spend analyzer. The historic spend data now forms a baseline against which the efficiency and effectivity of the new cost savings programs can be measured in hard dollars.

The program management module ties the suite together with integrated dashboards and portals that offer cross-suite visibility.

Because the sourcing module is where all of the event modeling and execution happens, it is prudent to examine this area in more detail (Figure 9.2). In

Figure 9.2, the dynamic RFx module includes all of the features and functionality to manage and execute auctions and multistage negotiations efficiently and effectively. The optimization-based buyer decision support module empowers buyers to make the right business decisions and to realize the best value from their supply base. The supplier decision support module extends the optimization-based decision support capabilities to suppliers by empowering them with recommendations to improve their bids and win more business.

Events are run and monitored within the context of a category or a supplier. Multiple events can be integrated into a project and monitored via the buyer and supplier portals and dashboards.

SPEND UNDER MANAGEMENT

An important notion in strategic sourcing is the amount of spend under active management. Active management means that on an ongoing basis, the corresponding commodities are being analyzed (for cost reduction and compliance), segmented, and benchmarked and savings opportunities are being targeted through the various sourcing events.

During each successive period, through acquisitions and expansions, new (unapproved) suppliers/commodities are added, with spend that will need to be pulled under active management. Spend analysis always captures (or should capture) 100% of spend, but only a subset of that spend might be under active management. For example, spend associated with office supplies might not be under active management. However, as this spend grows in size, it might make sense to target the top ten suppliers of these commodities and bring them under active management (e.g., via P-cards), so that they can be benchmarked for price, and the supply base can be rationalized with preferred supplier status and entered into contracts with pricing and other terms. Ideally, companies should strive to bring 100% of spend under active management.

Integrated Supply Management

In order to iteratively get 100% spend under management, it is essential to have information visibility and integration across the entire supply management suite, i.e., each module within the suite must be tightly integrated into other modules so that relevant information is available at all times and whenever needed. Spend information plays an important part in this:

- Data from e-procurement and purchasing systems should be available for spend analysis on an ad hoc basis. Ideally, the refresh period should be zero, meaning that completed transactions should be immediately available for spend analysis. In reality, because of data quality and enrichment requirements, the refresh period may vary from a few days to a few weeks. Forecasted spend information from MRP systems should also be made available for spend analysis so savings can be tracked.

- Historic spend information, which, when combined with forecasts forms the baseline for cost reductions, should be pervasive and visible at each step of the sourcing process—during supplier selection, during modeling and running events, during contract creation and negotiation, and in supplier performance monitoring—to enable answering the following questions:
  - During supplier selection:
    - How much did we spend with this supplier? Can we expect to get better deals because we have done business with this supplier historically?
    - What price per unit did these suppliers charge us? Did we receive price breaks as we increased volume?
    - Did a supplier have multiple contracts for the same commodity. If so, did each contract have different price points?
    - Did we have quality and delivery problems with this supplier? What is the supplier's credit rating?
  - During events:
    - What starting price should be entered in the auctions? (The starting price should be derived from the historic average price.)
    - Because we have a large spend with supplier A, should this supplier be allowed to creatively bid, given that this supplier is not in the top three suppliers from a pure price standpoint?
    - So far, how much have we saved with this event?
  - During contracts:
    - What is the historical spend with this supplier?
    - What are the average unit price and the payment terms?
    - Has the supplier met quality requirements?
    - Has the supplier met delivery date requirements?
  - In supplier performance:
    - What was the performance score, and what was the corresponding spend with this supplier?
    - What was the weighted average performance (weighted with spend) across my top $X\%$ suppliers?
- Information related to various events (in process and completed) should be available in spend analysis in order to estimate future savings. This

information should also be available in contracts, so that if, say, a contract is up for renewal, the purchasing manager is aware that a new auction/negotiation event is under way, the results of which could impact whether or not this contract should be renewed.

- Information from contracts should be available within spend analysis for purposes of "spend-to-contract" visibility. This integration can provide much needed visibility to enable answering several (simple to complex) questions:
  - Which suppliers and commodities are on-contract?
  - What did we spend relative to the contract size? Have we exceeded the contracted amount?
  - What was the contract amount variance and the contract price variance?

External Integration using Web Services

Web services can be used for transferring information between the various modules. Web services, which are HTTP calls, specify the exact format in which information can be requested by the source application. For example, a spend analyzer, when supported by Web services, can respond to a request of the type: "Send me the spend associated with Vendor IBM in Q1, 2006 for the commodity 'consulting services.'" Once the applications support Web services, they can be externalized to other native applications, which may benefit from such information. For example, PLM (product life cycle management) or EAM (enterprise asset management) systems may want to request spend data from the spend analyzer.

USING SPEND ANALYSIS FOR MEASURING BENEFITS

Cost savings can be generated through either cost reduction and/or cost avoidance. Cost reduction is easier to measure because the baseline (forecasted) and actual cost figures are readily available. For example, say the forecasted spend for commodity "office supplies" was $50 million and the actual spend came out to be $45 million; thus a cost reduction of $5 million was achieved. On the other hand, say the cost of electricity (power) was $20 million last year and was forecasted to be $30 million this year due to an estimated 50% rise in the cost per watt. However, by careful selection of suppliers and using green energy credits, the actual (post-tax) cost this year came out to be $25 million. Although this represents an increase in $5 million compared to last year, it also represents a cost avoidance of $5 million, which should be included in calculating total benefits. Because cost avoidance is calculated using forecasted pricing, the credibility of the

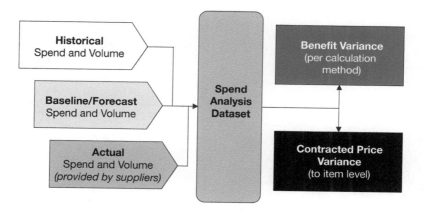

Figure 9.3. Benefits tracking via variance analysis.

Benefit Type	Objective	Category Applied
Unit price saving	Benefit analyzed by difference in baseline, actual, and target unit prices	Stationery Graded contract labor Permanent labor
Percent reduction in management fee	Reduction in management fee versus passed-through costs (i.e., cost of labor resource)	Ungraded contract labor
Weighted average cost per case	Calculation of weighted average unit price benefit per contract item across a collection of invoice transactions	Legal
Percent discount reduction	Benefit of a flat percent discount on the baseline unit cost	Event management

Figure 9.4. Cost savings basis can be different for each category.

savings is often questionable. Nevertheless, not using cost avoidance in the overall savings calculations can also be unfair to the managers who are responsible for that commodity.

In order to use spend analysis for tracking benefits for specific categories, historical, forecasted, and actual spend information for that category must be available in the spend cube (shown in Figure 9.3).

The actual basis for cost savings depends on individual categories. The chart in Figure 9.4 shows a few category examples.

Historical and forecasted spend can be combined to create a baseline spend. Based on the savings target, a "targeted spend" can be established. The actual

Commodity (4 of 4)								
Commodity	Actual Volume	Actual Spend	Baseline Spend	Target Spend	Expected Benefit	Actual Benefit	Benefit Variance	Contri Price Varian
‒ Commodity (Total)	229,036,778	$698,307,106	$553,392,067	$548,446,157	18,141,616	138,014,208	119,872,591	-57,82?
⊟ People	127,512,114	$118,466,022	$202,554,992	$197,997,731	5,357,195	134,629,255	129,272,059	-129,73?
⊟ Recruitment	127,408,234	$81,089,018	$170,471,863	$167,717,236	3,212,608	132,123,813	128,911,204	-129,14?
Permanent Staff	121,765,113	$17,461,759	$142,273,443	$140,932,738	1,704,144	131,164,509	129,460,364	-129,64?
Temporary Staff	5,643,121	$63,627,259	$28,198,420	$26,784,498	1,508,463	959,304	-549,159	50?
⊟ Travel	101,954	$33,273,428	$29,729,614	$28,443,068	1,640,850	2,023,223	382,373	-56?
Accommodation	57,702	$9,149,160	$3,627,071	$3,372,524	287,474	-156,655	-444,130	42?
Travel Management	44,252	$24,124,268	$26,102,543	$25,070,544	1,353,375	2,179,879	826,503	-98?
⊟ Employee Benefits	1,925	$4,103,576	$2,353,515	$1,837,426	503,736	482,218	-21,518	-3?
Outplacement	1,925	$4,103,576	$2,353,515	$1,837,426	503,736	482,218	-21,518	-3?
⊟ Communications & Logistics	100,349,233	$514,035,368	$305,735,122	$304,654,212	1,357,122	1,088,139	-268,982	68,96?
⊟ Communication	76,183,816	$467,672,427	$292,441,275	$287,692,861	0	11,509	11,509	70,12?
Print Commercial/Proprietary	73,379,006	$16,927,533	$28,452,505	$25,650,295	0	11,509	11,509	-21,37?
Creative	2,055,234	$30,602,929	$11,245,759	$9,496,983	0	0	0	8,30?
Media	643,044	$419,735,852	$252,460,633	$252,263,204	0	0	0	83,24?
Publishing	106,531	$406,114	$282,379	$282,379	0	0	0	-4?
⊟ Logistics	24,165,417	$46,362,941	$13,293,847	$16,961,352	1,357,122	1,076,629	-280,492	-1,15?
Stationery & Warehousing	24,102,429	$39,036,920	$11,974,525	$14,699,114	1,275,754	1,084,968	-190,785	-2,63?
Removalists	54,386	$4,226,644	$628,333	$565,381	81,368	-8,338	-89,707	8?
Cash Movement	8,106	$2,624,582	$459,283	$1,206,932	0	0	0	1,41?
Couriers	495	$474,794	$231,706	$489,924	0	0	0	-1?
⊟ Professional Services	886,546	$64,423,748	$45,010,493	$45,728,765	11,401,287	2,270,801	-9,130,485	2,94?
⊟ Financial Services	630,454	$4,191,002	$3,169,597	$1,787,235	1,121,073	1,120,657	-415	
Banking Services	630,454	$4,191,002	$3,169,597	$1,787,235	1,121,073	1,120,657	-415	
⊟ Corporate Risk	256,092	$60,232,746	$41,840,896	$43,941,530	10,280,213	1,150,144	-9,130,069	2,93?
Legal	256,092	$60,232,746	$41,840,896	$43,941,530	10,280,213	1,150,144	-9,130,069	2,93?
‒ Uncategorized	288,882	$1,381,969	$91,460	$65,449	26,011	26,011	0	
‒ Commodity (Total)	229,036,778	$698,307,106	$553,392,067	$548,446,157	18,141,616	138,014,208	119,872,591	-57,82?

Figure 9.5. Calculation of benefits.

spend can then be used to calculate the actual benefit versus the estimated benefit, where:

Estimated benefit = targeted spend – baseline spend

Actual benefit = actual spend – baseline spend

Benefit variance = estimated benefit – actual benefit

The sample report shown in Figure 9.5 can now be generated. This report shows actual spend in dollars. The same metrics can be shown as percentages as well.

Benefits can also be calculated using contracted and approved spend baselines. If such information is available in the spend cube, contract amount variances and approved spend variances can be calculated and shown in the spend cube.

SUMMARY

In this chapter, we have described how spend analysis can be integrated within an end-to-end supply management process, so that savings opportunities identified by spend analysis can be passed on to the sourcing modules for running events. The pricing and other terms optimized in the sourcing module can be passed on to the contract module for final agreement. The pricing, delivery, payment terms, and other parameters in the contract now form the baseline for the next period. Spend analysis can thus be used at the front end to identify opportunities and at the back end to measure savings relative to the baseline. We have also presented an example of a complete supply management system from Emptoris. In addition to being a front window to strategic sourcing, spend analysis can also be used as a rear window to monitor and track savings. Additionally some examples have been presented describing how savings can be calculated based on baseline, target, and actual spend, in which baseline spend can be constructed from historical and forecasted spend information.

SPEND ANALYSIS AND COMPLIANCE

INTRODUCTION

Studies in the literature reveal that the Sarbanes-Oxley Act (SOX) of 2002 is the most widely implemented compliance initiative today and also the most expensive. Additionally most multinational companies have other multiple, concurrent compliance initiatives underway such as those of the U.S. Department of Labor's Fair Labor Standards Act (FLSA) and the Health Insurance Portability and Accountability Act (HIPAA) of the U.S. Food and Drug Administration; the European Union's Restriction of Hazardous Substances Directive (RoHS); and others.

CFOs and COOs strive to optimize these multipronged initiatives under one umbrella and to squeeze as much value from them as possible. Three key metrics CFOs and COOs look for are:

Value. On average companies are spending $5 million on compliance and supply risk initiatives.[1] Large companies are spending much more. SOX accounts for roughly a one fifth share of the cost. AMR predicts that in 2007, companies will have spent $29.9 billion on governance-, risk-, and compliance- (GRC) related activities.[2] Not surprising is that CFOs are requiring a higher return on invested capital. This required return forms the basis of the other two metrics:

Heightened risk awareness and measured risk management. By quantifying the risk associated with various processes and activities, and implementing controls for monitoring the risk, a quantitative framework can be developed for real-time or near real-time risk analysis. Such reports can be used by executive management and boards of directors for improving corporate governance and reporting. The COSO (Committee of Sponsoring Organizations of the Treadway Commission, 1992) model for enterprise risk management is widely endorsed as a framework for analyzing and managing risk.[3]

Efficiency. A simple control alerting a category manager about excessive inventory levels can lead to the discovery of a "leaky" process, e.g., one that causes two suppliers to ship parts at the same time. It is perhaps impossible to measure the value of identifying a critical supplier who is about to declare bankruptcy or a supplier who is identified on the U.S. government watch list for terrorist organizations. Yet, many companies today do not follow proper supplier assessment processes. Correcting inefficient processes directly translates to lower risk and higher profitability.

According to the findings of a survey of large, midsize, and small companies in 2006, procurement compliance is being pursued by the largest percentage of surveyed customers.[4] Spend analysis can be used very effectively to analyze purchasing transactions for control violations in the procurement process. The following sections will explore how this can be done.

CONTROL VIOLATIONS IN THE PROCUREMENT PROCESS

It is useful to examine the end-to-end procurement process in order to understand where process control violations might occur, and the impact of those violations on financial accuracy and efficiency. In Figure 10.1, a similar diagram to Figure 5.2 in Chapter 5 has been reproduced. Figure 10.1 shows a complete procurement "program," starting from supplier assessment and moving to selection and requisition and payment. Let us examine violations associated with each activity.

Supplier Assessment

The buyer first goes through a supplier assessment phase to determine which suppliers comply with specific requirements. For example, suppliers might need to be ISO (International Organization for Standardization) and CPM (Certified Purchasing Manager) certified and also be required to comply with the FLSA in addition to local (base) country standards. The supplier might need to be audited for financial viability and references might need to be checked. The assessment phase can be done remotely, through surveys, by sending a team of experts, or by

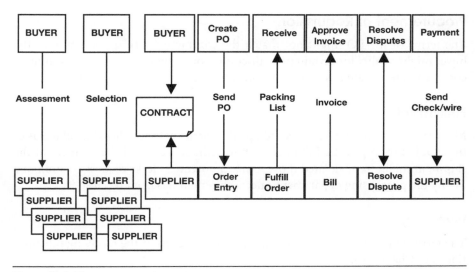

Figure 10.1. The procurement process.

relying on a third party provider of such services. In either case, there is always the risk of a supplier providing false or incomplete information (*information inadequacy*) or the risk of not collecting all of the information needed to completely qualify each supplier.

Supplier Selection

The next step is to select the supplier(s) from among the list of qualified suppliers, which is typically implemented through RFx, reverse auction, or some other variations of these. From a compliance standpoint, it is important that the award process be carried out in a fair manner so as to not violate any fair business practice laws in the host country as well as in the country in which the supplier is based. Therefore, it is important to preserve a "data trail" in the entire award process as proof of *fair selection*.

Contract

Once the award decision is made, the buyer draws up a contract that lays out the terms of the engagement. It is important that the contract reflects the terms that have been finalized in the award phase (supplier selection), including the agreed upon price, delivery, payment terms, quality, and warranty. Not doing so might again constitute unfair business practices.

Procurement or Requisition

The terms of the PO might not match the contractual terms. For example, the buyer might qualify for certain price discounts, or better payment terms, but these contractual terms are not taken into account at the time the PO is created.

Fulfillment

Many times, shipping dock clerks accept shipments without checking all terms of the PO. For example, the PO might call for adherence to shipping time, but the shipment might have violated those terms. Sometimes clerks request creation of a PO by the purchasing department once a shipment has been received.

Invoicing

The terms of the invoice might not match the PO terms or the receiving information (see Chapter 4).

Payment

The payment information entered might not be the same as the information on the invoice (see Chapter 4). Duplicate invoices can result in duplicate payments.

According to Chechetts and Bartolini (2006), supplier compliance with price, diversity, delivery, service, and quality is considered to be very important.[4] The interested reader is encouraged to review these findings.

IMPLEMENTING CONTROLS IN PROCUREMENT

Once the various types of violations are identified, controls can be implemented for monitoring and alerting when violations occur. Figure 10.2 shows the different types of controls that need to be implemented at each step of the procurement process.

In the Chechetts and Bartolini (2006) study, roughly a third of the surveyed companies admitted that their internal controls were poor.[4] About half of the participants said that their controls were good, but that big improvements were needed.

Commonly Implemented Controls

Figure 10.2 shows all of the possible controls that should be implemented and monitored for end-to-end procurement compliance. In reality, though, based on

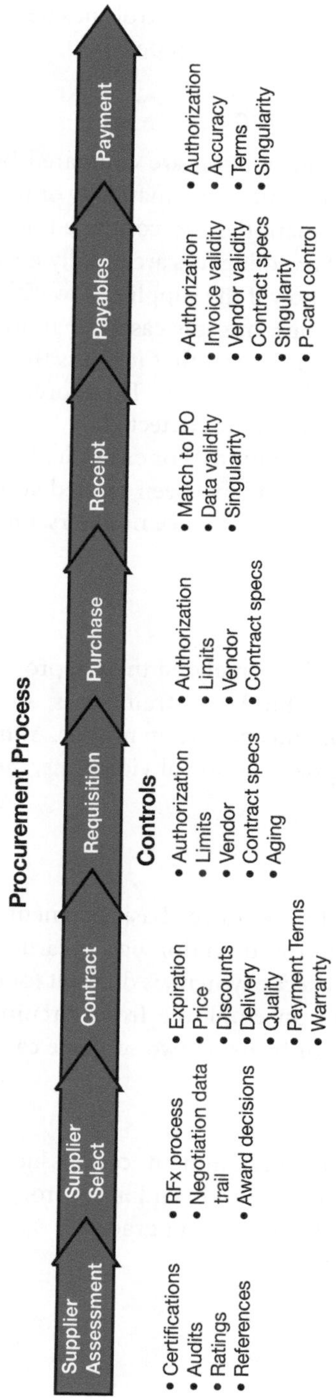

Procurement Process

Controls

Supplier Assessment	Supplier Select	Contract	Requisition	Purchase	Receipt	Payables	Payment
• Certifications	• RFx process	• Expiration	• Authorization	• Authorization	• Match to PO	• Authorization	• Authorization
• Audits	• Negotiation data trail	• Price	• Limits	• Limits	• Data validity	• Invoice validity	• Accuracy
• Ratings	• Award decisions	• Discounts	• Vendor	• Vendor	• Singularity	• Vendor validity	• Terms
• References		• Delivery	• Contract specs	• Contract specs		• Contract specs	• Singularity
		• Quality	• Aging			• Singularity	
		• Payment Terms				• P-card control	
		• Warranty					

Figure 10.2. Procurement controls.

a survey by Emptoris, only a subset of these controls has been implemented. The controls that are commonly implemented include:

Payment Controls via 3-Way Match

The PO, invoice, and receiving information are compared before the invoice is approved. This comparison can be done either manually or in an automated manner. The dates, item price, and quantities are compared across the three feeds. However, taxes and shipping and handling fees are usually never mentioned in the PO; therefore there is no way to know if the supplier is overbilling on those items. 3-Way matching has many variations. In some cases, an approval clerk only compares the total invoice amount and ensures that it is less than or equal to the PO amount, without looking at the line item details. Therefore, it is easily possible for a line item to be incorrectly priced, but not detected.

3-Way matching has certain limitations. For example, 3-way matching cannot detect duplicate POs and invoices that have been created accidentally or through fraud (e.g., those that have different PO/invoice numbers, but have the same vendor for the same item).

Authorizations

Most SOX compliant-companies have analyzed their approval processes and have instituted SOD (segregation of duty) constraints. As an example, the same employee cannot create a vendor and approve an invoice. Although such measures are an initial step in preventing basic approval violations, they are insufficient in preventing fraud.

P-Card Control

Most P-card issuing companies have enforced basic payment and vendor controls. Therefore, buying from an unapproved vendor via a P-card, or exceeding the purchasing limit or making an incorrect payment, is difficult for employees. However, P-card controls cannot prevent an employee from circumventing his limit by making two separate purchases or by using two separate cards.

Travel and Entertainment

Similar to P-cards, travel and entertainment card issuers such as American Express provide some basic payment and vendor controls, but they cannot flag suspicious travel itineraries or unapproved upgrades.

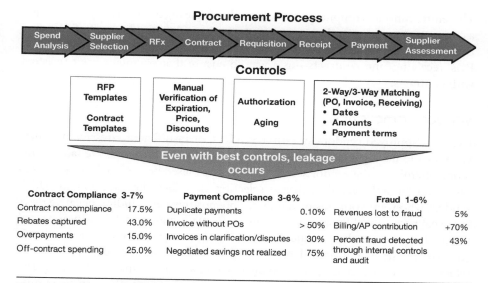

Figure 10.3. Leakage even with procurement control.

SPEND LEAKAGE

According to analysts, spend leaking out from procurement controls ranges from 2 to 17%. Figure 10.3 shows the three areas that account for the major portion of spend leakage. The chart in Figure 10.3 has been compiled from various reports.[1,2,5] An extensive library of research papers is available on this topic.

Contract Compliance

The single biggest source of spend leakage occurs in contract compliance, especially in the area of the purchase of direct materials. Yet most companies have only ad hoc processes to monitor contract compliance.

Use of expired contracts and multiple contracts with different price points is common. Chechetts and Bartolini (2006) cite that 15% of all contracts are auto-renewable.[4] Because contract expirations are not monitored, most of these contracts renew at the same price performance levels. According to this same study, 18% of purchases made by an average company are not contract compliant; more than 50% of the potential rebates and discounts are not captured by an average company; PO prices are rarely checked against the contract for volume discounts; and restrictions on delivery dates, penalties on late deliveries, product returns, warranties, and pass-through costs are very rarely monitored and enforced.

Therefore, contract compliance represents the single biggest source of savings that a company can realize in the next wave of procurement compliance. In fact, many companies are now talking about 4-way payment compliance—between invoices, POs, receiving, and contracts—as a way to ensure that payments are consistent with contracts.

Vendor Compliance

Use of unapproved vendors, one-time vendors, or insufficient assessment of new vendors and having a lack of monitoring of vendor performance are fairly common. Oftentimes, the vendor selection process is biased because of "adverse selection" and "moral hazard." Adverse selection describes the situation in which vendors who want your business only supply positive news, hiding negative news and weaknesses in RFPs, and thus create "information asymmetry." Moral hazard is the situation which is created by information asymmetry after a vendor is selected. (Note: Moral hazard has it origins in the insurance community and refers to the concept that a party insulated from risk, e.g., by insurance, will be less concerned about negative consequences and will make fewer efforts to avoid misfortune.) Vendors who fall in the category of moral hazard have less inclination to abide by best practices once the contract is signed.

Most vendors look at profit maximization strategies which can sometimes be in conflict with best practices. For example, the same vendor might have two contracts active with two different divisions and might continue to offer two different prices for the same product. Unless this pricing situation is brought to the attention of buyers, the buyer for one division will continue to pay excess amounts for procuring the same part. As another example, a vendor might show appropriate certifications for being compliant with local labor laws at the time of assessment, but might resort to unfair labor practices once delivery begins.

Supplier assessment controls need to be implemented to prevent adverse selection. Similarly supplier monitoring controls, along with contract compliance, can ensure that moral hazard situations do not occur.

Fraud

According to a 2006 report by the Association of Certified Fraud Examiners, U.S. organizations lose an estimated 5% of annual revenues to fraud.[5] Only 12% of the fraudsters had a previous conviction for a fraud-related offense, which means criminal background checks are not sufficient to weed-out fraudsters because most fraud is committed by seemingly honest employees. About 40% of this fraud can be caught through internal controls and "sniffing" for anomalies in transaction databases.

Leakage	Control	Annualized Spend
1906 instances in which the invoice was created prior to the PO	Payment/fraud	$9.6M
14 purchases that are equal to or just under approved limit	Payment/fraud	$87M
140 vendors were consistently rounding invoice amounts	Vendor/fraud	106,760 transactions
1 vendor on U.S. Government's watch list (denied person's list) for terrorist organizations	Vendor	$324K
Spend associated with invoices with missing dates	Vendor	$58M
Recurring invoices	Payment	$78M
Spend associated with nonpreferred suppliers	Vendor	$2.3M
Spend associated with poorly performing suppliers	Vendor	$2.3M
Missing vendors (in vendor master) and no description on corresponding invoices	Vendor/fraud	$58M
250 invoice payments made to an engineering company in 3 months (could have been consolidated into monthly payments)	Payment	$94K

Figure 10.4. Sample findings from a transaction data audit.

Detailed metrics on procurement compliance are hard to obtain, primarily because very few companies monitor and record them. For example, surveys conducted by research analysts in 2004 indicated that less than half of the surveyed companies monitored contract compliance on a monthly or better basis. Purchase price variance and use of preferred suppliers were also being tracked, but few companies tracked contract price compliance by line item.

CASE STUDY

The chart in Figure 10.4 provides findings from an audit performed by Emptoris, in which transactions for one quarter were analyzed for violations. Below are some of the sample findings:

Profile of Company: Fortune 500 Company
Period of Activity: 1 Quarter
Total Spend Associated with Period: $1.2 billion
Existing Controls: Common 2-way and 3-way matching
SOX Status: Certified

Implications: Significant amounts of leakage were occurring despite existing controls. The total opportunity was estimated to be 10% of total spend.

THE FUTURE OF PROCUREMENT COMPLIANCE

Measurement

The first wave of compliance monitoring focused on accuracy—were the financials accurate? In the last 2 years, we have seen the focus shifting from accuracy to efficiency. CFOs and CEOs are now looking for answers to questions such as:

1. How much spend is leaking out due to inefficient processes?
2. How risky are our procurement and payment processes for fraud?
3. How efficiently are we managing our supply base?
4. Are we getting the lowest prices at the highest quality?
5. Are we managing supply risk appropriately?
6. What percent of spend is tied to contracts?
7. What percent of spend is contract compliant?

For accurate answers to these questions, controls will need to be implemented and monitored across the entire procurement process—from supplier selection to supplier payment. For rapid and accurate monitoring, these controls will need to be automated. The metrics obtained through continuous monitoring will give management the necessary information on whether or not the company is lagging behind or exceeding the best-in-class companies. They will also give management the basis for creating a robust supply risk management strategy.

Prevention

Violations can be prevented if errors are identified at the point of entry, i.e., when they occur as opposed to after they occur. For example, if a buyer creates a requisition order with an unapproved supplier, or does not get the necessary internal approvals, that error should be identified immediately. The workflow should not proceed until all errors are rectified. Correcting all errors before proceeding is an example of a simple transactional control.

The same buyer might accidentally assign an incorrect commodity code or a contract number to the requisition. In many companies, the commodity code "99999" (other) accounts for a big portion of spend because buyers do not bother to find out the correct code. Assigning an incorrect code can have a number of consequences. The requisition can go down the wrong "pipe" and might need to be recalled at a later time, costing the buyer several days. The requisition might also end up going through a different approval process which is not compliant with the category requirements. The spend analysis knowledgebase and autoclassifiers can be integrated into transactional controls to provide point-of-entry intelligence about the commodity codes and the contracts to which a requisition belongs. Some leading-edge companies are already doing this. With the capability of integrated transactional controls, a buyer will get real-time feedback on whether or not the assigned commodity code matches the description of the item and which contracts he should use to source that item, which will reduce transaction process errors and increase contract compliance.

SUMMARY

Spend analysis and compliance are really two sides of the same coin. Most companies do a good job at identifying opportunities and acting on them, but they do a poor job in ensuring that the negotiated savings are being realized. Poor contract and supplier compliance accounts for a large portion of spend leaking out because of faulty controls. Close to half of these noncompliant transactions can be identified through transactional data mining. Spend analysis applications can and should be used for performing such transactional audits. Not only is it important to identify opportunities, but it is also important to ensure that all of the controls are working properly to prevent spend leakage.

REFERENCES

1. Mark Hillman, Heather Keltz. *Managing Risk in the Supply Chain—A Quantitative Study*. Boston: AMR Research; January 3, 2007.

2. John Hagerty, Eric Klein. *Compliance Is Still a Priority: Total GRC Spending Approaches $30B in 2007 and Growing*. Boston: AMR Research; February 22, 2007.

3. See www.coso.org.

4. Vance Chechetts, Andre Bartolini. *Source-to-Settle: Compliance Clues for the CFO*. Boston: AberdeenGroup; October 13, 2006.

5. Association of Certified Fraud Examiners, Inc. *2006 Report to the Nation on Occupational Fraud and Abuse*. Available at: http://www.acfe.com/fraud/report.asp.

THE FUTURE OF
SPEND ANALYSIS

Over the last few years, traditional spend analysis solutions have been very effective in identifying quick-hit opportunities, such as supplier consolidation. Many low-hanging opportunities have already been addressed by companies that implemented a strategic sourcing program. These companies are now looking out for opportunities that are more elusive, more complex, and most often not readily visible. For example, in Chapter 10 (*Spend Analysis and Compliance*), we saw how contract compliance and transaction analysis can unearth myriads of addressable spend leakages. Similarly, such analyses can also identify broad-based compliance and process violations. We also saw how, at the back end, traditional spend analysis is sometimes used for rudimentary tracking of savings, but that it most often falls short on tracking and monitoring spend leakage across the entire sourcing cycle at a deeper level.

The strategic importance of spend analysis within and outside strategic sourcing is going to only increase in importance because it serves as a single source of cleansed and enriched transaction history across the entire organization and because its adoption is steadily increasing outside of the procurement department, especially in finance.

The following sections will provide some of the ways in which progressive, forward-thinking companies are pushing the boundaries of spend analysis and using spend analysis to solve other problems.

SUPPLIER DISCOVERY

As a company expands into new commodities, the company might need guidance on which suppliers it should source from. Traditionally, sourcing information has been provided by companies such as D&B. However, sourcing information is typically part of the vendor knowledgebase that is used by spend analysis for purposes of vendor enrichment. Rather than deal with different providers, a company should rely on its spend analysis provider for guidance in this area.

SPEND FORECASTING

Many companies today do material forecasting through their MRP systems. They feed their demand forecasts into their MRP systems, which use the bills of materials (BOMs) data as well as resource capacity constraints to generate a manufacturing plan and a procurement plan for all parts. This has not been a particularly optimal approach for several reasons—the information in BOMs' parts lists is often not updated regularly, resulting in incorrect parts being ordered; the existing inventory count is often erroneous; and capacity constraints are not modeled accurately. Therefore, in order to be safe, material planners game the system by creating their own procurement plans and having more material inventory available. An alternative approach that some companies are using is to forecast material spend at the commodity (and sometimes item) level by leveraging historical spend information. Such an analysis can be used as a sanity check on the MRP-based approach. When used in conjunction with what-if costing analysis (to be discussed shortly), this technique can also be used as a quick way of forecasting quarterly spend at the division or cost center level.

WHAT-IF SPEND ANALYSIS

As part of the planning process, purchasing officers are often required to do what-if analysis at the commodity, cost center, and item levels. For example, they might ask, "Assuming that my volume (billable hours) for contract labor remains the same for next year, what spend should I expect if the labor rates increase by 20%?" or "What spend should I expect for telecommunications if cell phone cost decreases by 20%, but video conferencing cost increases by 30%?"

In order to permit such analysis, new cubes or reports incorporating the changed parameters need to be created on-the-fly and made available to the user. This functionality should be carefully designed. Ideally the cube should be replicated on the user machine for purposes of making any data changes. A strict approval process must be followed for permitting changes to be made to the main cube in the form of different scenarios.

MICROANALYSIS

An extension of what-if analysis is the creation of separate microcubes for the purposes of detailed analysis and then making these microcubes available for selected users only. For example, the T&E system typically provides very detailed information on airlines, flight origin and destination, etc. This level of information might not be relevant for all users and therefore it will not be modeled in the main cube. However, there might be a few users who want to explore and audit this spend at a highly granular level. Thus, a microcube of T&E data can potentially be created and integrated into the main cube. The T&E audit team could be granted access to this cube. Such microcubes are typically much smaller than the main cube. The ability to quickly create such cubes will be a significant requirement going forward.

NEW PRODUCT TARGET COST ANALYSIS

Most companies today use sophisticated PLM (product life cycle management) systems which capture the product design, parts list, and costing information. Spend analysis can provide historical and forecasted information at the parts level which can be incorporated in PLM systems to predict would-be costing. For example, when an engineer designs a new product, she picks preferred parts from preferred suppliers. However, there might not be much visibility into the median or the average price paid for that part last year. There also might not be readily available information about whether (or not) existing contracts cover that part—and if so, what prices, volume discounts, etc. are available? PLM systems can be integrated into spend analysis systems to permit rapid retrieval of such information, so that a design engineer can select and finalize a part quickly rather than having to go through multiple iterations with purchasing.

REAL-TIME CLASSIFICATION

At the end of Chapter 10, we presented an example in which procurement compliance can improve if violations are identified at the time they occur as opposed to after they occur. Traditional spend analysis classifies transactions after the fact.

However, if these transactions can be classified on-the-fly (i.e., at the point of entering them into the requisition system), there are obvious benefits:

1. By identifying the correct commodity, supplier, and contract for the part(s), the requisition can be channeled through the correct approval process. In many instances, because the person creating the order does not know the exact commodity code, a "99999" code is created by default. A 99999 code corresponds to the commodity "others." These default transactions are either routed back to the appropriate code eventually (thus increasing processing time) or are approved anyway, without appropriate checks and validations. Over time, this "maverick" spend continues to increase. Then, during spend refresh, these transactions are remapped to the appropriate commodities. This approach solves half of the problem, namely, inaccurate spend visibility. However, it does not solve the root cause of why the 99999 code was entered. Addressing the root cause can be done by mapping a transaction in "real time." The best way to implement remapping is to suggest a choice from the top five commodities. Depending on which commodity is chosen, a list of contracts and vendors should be suggested. This "step search" approach will help the user select the most appropriate commodity and contract for the requisition.

2. Once mapped, there is no need to remap or reexamine these transactions during spend refresh, which can significantly increase the time to refresh the spend cube.

3. The exact commodity and contract chosen by the user can be used to train the classifier on that item, so that in the future similar items will be autoclassified.

RELEVANCE SEARCH

We all use Google™ to search the Web. When we search by typing a string, Google reports the top websites that match this search string. Google uses a form of relevance searching, wherein the metric for relevance (among other things) is tied to the number of links pointing to a particular website. The more links a website has pointing to it, the higher its score will be. In a similar manner, metrics can be defined while searching for commodities, suppliers, or parts. Traditional spend analysis reports are typically sorted by spend amount, transaction date, supplier name, etc. However, if the "sort by" can be based on relevance metrics defined by the customer, a whole new set of benefits start popping up. For example,

1. Show me the most frequently viewed reports.
2. Rank the reports based on how many users they are shared with.
3. Rank the commodities based not only on spend, but also on other attributes such complexity to source, strategic importance, and criticality of supply disruption.

PRICE BENCHMARKING

Many customers want to compare their key spend metrics (commodity spend, commodity fragmentation across vendors, item price) with their peers to ascertain whether or not they are best in class. Unfortunately, such a comprehensive database does not exist today, especially for MRO and direct spend. However, certain commodity price benchmark databases are available to a limited extent. For example, CAPS Research performs "market basket" surveys, in which it reaches out to hundreds of companies and asks them to report pricing data for some selected items that best represent that commodity. In the information technology commodity, the CAPS Research survey lists about 50 items such as monitors, computers, switches, telephone systems, etc. This data is subject to the limitations that are associated with surveys (such as accuracy and statistical significance); nevertheless, such market basket pricing information can serve as a rough baseline.

The authors are hopeful that over the next few years content aggregators will create such databases. This type of database will enable customers to very quickly identify commodities and individual items for which they are overpaying.

SUMMARY

In this chapter, we have listed a few areas in which spend analysis can play a larger role. Supplier discovery, target costing, product life cycle management, scenario analysis, and real-time control monitoring are some of these areas—areas which currently are underserved.

With a little work and a little imagination, spend analysis can be used to solve current and futuristic problems in these areas. What spend analysis can and cannot do is limited by your imagination. At the core, the spend analysis application is a specialized data mart that gives you full flexibility and control for extracting business intelligence. As business requirements evolve, you can morph the application to address these requirements.

INDEX

A

Access privileges, 17, 122
Accounts payable (AP), 72, 92, 94
Acquisitions, 12
Actionable information, 125
Ad hoc analytics, 144, 147
Ad hoc queries, 184
Advanced sourcing techniques, 27
Agrochemical business, 55–59
AI (artificial intelligence), 126, 190, 196
AIN (approved item name), 157
Algorithms
    classification algorithms, 192–196
    clustering, 197–198
    machine learning, 123, 128
    semantics and, 202
American Express. *See* P-cards
Analytic functions, 131–132
AP (accounts payable), 72, 92, 94
Application provider. *See under* Software
Ariba, 11, 95
Artificial intelligence (AI), 126, 190, 196
ASCII file, 102
Association rules, 201–203
Attribute
    described, 127
    directory, equivalent parts, 156
    selection phase, 104
Authorizations, 224
Autoclassification, 100
Autogenerated PO, 91
Automated spend analysis, 11
Automatic text classification, 194

Automotive industry, roots of spend analysis
    in, 10
Award. *See* Contract

B

Balanced dimensional hierarchies, 187–189
Balance sheet, 86
Banks, merger case, 40–44
Baseline spend, 215–216
Bayesian algorithms, 123, 193–194
Benchmarking
    information, leveraging of, 54
    for price, 235
Benefits
    calculation of, 216
    measurement of, 214–216
Benford's law, 189–190
Bernoulli process, 201
Best in class
    goals, 48
    sourcing principles, 55
Big bang approach, 51, 52
Bills of materials (BOMs), 96, 232
Binary classification problem, 199
BOMs (bills of materials), 96, 232
Boot camp workshops, 62
Business event management, 132
Business intelligence key capabilities,
        131–133
    analytics, 131–132
    business event management, 132
    dashboards, 132
    reporting, 131
    scorecarding, 132

Business release scoping strategy, 51, 52
Business rules
    data enrichment and, 116, 117
    feedback requests, 196
    in knowledge assimilation, 129
    transactional enrichment and, 120–123

C
Capability requirements, 133
Cardinality, 182
CART (classification and regression trees),
    195
Case studies
    global procurement, identifying savings
        opportunities and supplier
        compliance, 31, 34–38
    global procurement, multiple locations
        and, 61–62
    highly decentralized purchasing, 30–31,
        35
    merger planning and integration, of
        financial services, 39–44
    procurement transformation, in a spin-
        off company, 55–59
    provider of products, services,
        technology for healthcare industry,
        59–61
    spend leakage, with controls, 227–228
Category, cost savings and, 215
Category schema, 14, 215
Category segmentation, 80–81
Center of excellence, 54
Certified Purchasing Manager (CPM), 220
Change management, 21
Charts. *See also* Specialized charts
    pie chart, 70, 71, 135, 138
    stacked bar chart, 135, 138, 139
    waterfall chart, 31, 141
Chemical companies, UNSPSC and, 156
Chi-square test, 185
Classification
    algorithms, five categories, 192–196
    association rules and, 201–203
    binary, 193
    classifier evaluation, 198–201
    clustering and, 196–198

    decision tree-based (DT) algorithms,
        194–195
    distance-based algorithms, 194
    engine evaluation, 198–201
    features of objects and, 192
    neural networks-based algorithms,
        195–196
    real-time, benefits, 233–234
    rule-based algorithms, 196
    state-of-the-art classification, 194
    statistical algorithms, 193–194
    supervised machine learning and, 192
Classification (of data), 115–116
Classification and regression trees (CART),
    195
Classification schema, 151, 154, 156
Classifier evaluation, 198–201
Cleansed item descriptions, 99
C-level executives. *See* Executive
    management
Client browser, 183
Clustering, 116, 120, 196–198
    algorithms, 197–198
    classification and, 196
COGS (cost of goods sold), 86, 87
Committee of Sponsoring Organizations of
    the Treadway Commission (COSO),
    220
Commodities
    classification of, 50
    cost reduction and, 24
    indirect, 50
    top ten by spend, 8, 9
    trend report, 36
    vendor consolidation and, 26
Commodity codes
    assignment of, 14
    classification and, 50, 115
    cleansing of, 13
    incorrect, consequences of, 228–229
    internal rationalization and, 60–61
    internal system, 57, 97
    in material master files, 14
    transaction fields and, 97–98
Commodity names, noun-qualifier format,
    156
Commodity schema, 13, 50

mapping from old to new, 50
materials management and, 95
Commodity structure, 14, 18
in analysis, 40–41
custom, 41
enriched, 113
industry standard schema, using, 97
modifying, 132
in project plan, 56
rules and, 18
Commodity taxonomies. *See* Taxonomies
Communication, Webinars, 54
Competency center, 49
Compliance, 219–229
by commodity, 37
initiatives, 219
violation prevention, 228–229
Compliance multiplier, spend leakage,
23–25
Conditional probability, 193
Confidence interval, 201
Confusion matrix, 198–199
Consolidation, 12
Content providers, 11
Contract, 221
agreement in, and P2P, 89
compliance, 24, 25, 225–226
historic spend and, 213
manufacturer data, 96
visibility and, 214
Contractual term opportunities, 72–76
delivery date violations, 76
quantity violations, 74, 75
unrealized discounts and rebates, 73–74,
75
Control
implementation, procurement, 222–224
violations, procurement, 220–222
Control display unit, 158, 159, 160, 162
Core team, 54
Corporate P-cards, 96
COSO (Committee of Sponsoring
Organizations of the Treadway
Commission), 220
Cost analysis, 233
Cost avoidance, 214–215
Cost center, 6, 99–100

Cost of goods sold (COGS), 86, 87
Cost savings basis, 215
CPM (Certified Purchasing Manager), 220
CPO. *See* Executive management
Credit cards, 88–89, 93
Cross-company planning teams, 42
Cross-tabular reports, 133, 136, 137, 139
Crosswalk mapping, 107, 170
CRUD application (create, read, update,
delete), 126
Cube. *See* Spend cube
Currency formats, 97
Custom taxonomy, 107. *See also* Taxonomies

D
D&B (Dun and Bradstreet), 154, 232
Dashboards, 132, 148, 149
Data
cleansing, 105–106
compression of, 183
default value, 186
empty values, 185–186
missing values, 185–187
Data assessment, 108–110
Data cleansing, structure and enrichment.
See Data enrichment
Data definition and loading (DDL), 15–17,
101–102, 103–110
balanced dimensional hierarchies,
187–189
considerations, for module, 107–108
data assessment, 108–110
data cleansing and, 105–106
missing values, 185–187
representative sampling and, 185
state-of-the-art modules, 108
systematic error detection, 189–190
Data enrichment (DE), 17–19, 50, 101, 102,
110–124
association rules and, 201–203
business requirements and, 50
business rules and, 116, 117
change methods, 113–114
classification and, 115–116, 191–196
classifier evaluation, 198–201
clustering and, 116, 196–198
data deficiencies and, 57, 111

dimensional enrichment, 116–120
goal of, 112–113
internal rationalization, 60–61
manual operations, 114, 116, 117
outsourcing and, 53
string matching and, 190–191
transactional enrichment, 120–124
Data error categories, 106
Data extracts and source systems, 94–97
Data mining, 14, 195
Data privacy, 53
Data quality, 97
cost center and GL code, 99–100
item description, 98–99
vendor name, 99
Data sheets, 98
Data types, enumerative, 175, 177
Data warehousing
global data warehouse, 57
limitations of, 12
spend analysis and, 12–15
static metadata schemes and, 14
DDL. *See* Data definition and loading
DE. *See* Data enrichment
Decentralized purchasing
methodology, 31
overview and objectives, 30–31
Demand aggregation, 67
DE module. *See* Data enrichment
Depreciation expense, 86
Dictionary concepts, 157–158
Dimensional classification, 115–116, 123
Dimensional cube, 120
Dimensional enrichment, 113, 116–120
anti-patterns and, 118
classification and, 119–120
clustering and, 120
hierarchical depth and, 117
structure in, 118–119
Dimensional hierarchies, 187–189
Dimensional modeling, 16–17, 100
dimensional nodes, 104
drill points and, 16
star schema and, 17, 104
Dimensional nodes
association rules and, 202
balancing facts across, 188

classification and, 119–120
clustering and, 120
dummy dimensional node, 129
fact distribution imbalance, 189
Dimensional tables, bad data structure, 181
Dimension reduction, 184
Direct shipping, 93
Direct spend, 85–86
Discounts and rebates, 73–74, 75
Diversity compliance, 50
Diversity spend compliance, 70, 71
Domain. *See* Industry domain
Drill-down, 184
Drill points, 16
Dun and Bradstreet (D&B), 154, 232

E

80/20 rule, 52, 142
EAM (enterprise asset management), 214
Earnings per share (EPS), 3, 10
ECCMA (Electric Commerce Code
Management Association), 154, 158.
See also eOTD
eClass/eCl@ss, 127, 153, 166–170, 171
design of, 166–168, 169, 170
example, machine screw, 167, 168, 169,
170
Efficiency metric, 220
EFT (electronic funds transfer), 72
e-invoicing system, 92
Electric Commerce Code Management
Association. *See* ECCMA
Electronic funds transfer (EFT), 72
Emptoris, 11, 209–211, 227–228
End user feedback, 19
Enriched item descriptions, 98–99, 183
Enrichment. *See* Data enrichment
Enterprise asset management (EAM), 214
Enumerative data types, 175, 177
eOTD (ECCMA Open Technical
Dictionary), 127, 153, 157–166
advantages of, 165
concept identifier, control display unit,
158, 159, 160
design of, 157–165
dictionary concepts in, 157–158
disadvantages of, 166

example, machine screw, 160, 163–165, 167
property identifiers, control display unit, 158, 161
e-procurement, 209
  benefits, 28, 33, 65
  in MRO, 87
  systems, 94
  RUS and, 170–171
EPS (earnings per share), 3, 10
ERP systems, 12, 57
Errors in data
  categorization of errors, 106, 108
  risk in correction of, 109–110
  systematic, detection of, 189–190
e-sourcing, 58–59
ETL (extraction, transformation, and loading), 105–106
ETLA approach, 10, 13–15
  Analyze, 13–15
  Extract, 13
  Load, 13
  spend analysis components and, 15
  Transform, 13–14
Euclidean space, 191
Excel. *See* Microsoft Excel
Executive management, 49, 54
  best in class goals, 48
  C-level executives, role in implementation, 54
  CPO, role in implementation, 49
  decentralized purchasing objectives, 31
  metrics and, 54, 219–220, 228
Executive steering committee, 48–49
External data sources, 96–97
External integration, 214
Extraction, transformation, and loading (ETL), 105–106

F

Federal Catalog System (FCS), 157
Federal compliance initiatives, 219
Feedback requests, 122–123, 196
Financial statement, direct spend, 85–86
FLSA (Fair Labor Standards Act, U.S. Department of Labor), 219–220
Forecasting, 214–215, 232

Foreign languages, 166, 172
Formula, risk evaluation, 109–110
Fortune 500 companies
  analysis of transaction violations in, 227
  case study, banking industry, merger planning and integration, 40–44
  case study, provider of products, services, technology for healthcare industry, 59–61
  savings opportunities identified by spend analysis, 65, 66
Fraud monitoring, 93, 227–228
Freight transactions, details of, in process control violations, 95
Fulfillment, 222
Future, spend analysis, 231–235
Fuzzy mapping techniques, 95

G

General ledger (GL) codes, 6, 99–100
Global procurement challenges, 31, 34
  methodology to identify opportunities, 34–35, 36–38
  multiple locations and, 31–34, 61–62
  results of spend analysis, 35
Goal setting, 48
Graphical reports, 135, 136, 138–140

H

Healthcare industry, case study, of provider of products, services, technology
  challenges to strategic sourcing, 59–60
  implementation of spend analysis solution, 60
  key drivers of spend analysis, 60
  results, 61
Heterogeneous data sources, 15
Hierarchical clustering, 196
Hierarchical information, 136, 139, 140
Hierarchy and dimensional editing, 18
Historical spend, 5, 210, 213
HTTP calls, 214
Hybrid operations. *See* Man-in-the-loop operations
Hyperbolic projection, 128
Hypercube. *See* Spend cube

I

I18N (internationalization), 183
ID3 algorithm, 195
Ideal spend analysis application, 15–22
Implementation
    80/20 rule and, 52
    application provider and, 55
    center of excellence, 49
    data quality and, 53
    evaluation of choices, 50
    executive management support, 48–49
    metrics, reporting of, 54
    objectives, setting of, 48
    organizational alignment, 54
    organizational visibility, 54
    phased-rollout approach, 50–52
    sample project plan, 55, 56
    technology and, 53–54
Income statement, 86
Indirect purchasing, 94–95
Indirect spend, 86
Industry domain
    attribute association and, 160
    classification schemas and, 156
    enumerative product properties and,
      175
Industry standard commodity taxonomies,
      153–173
    eClass/eCl@ss, 153, 166–170, 171
    eOTD, 153, 157–166
    NAICS, 153
    RUS, 153, 170–173
    UNSPSC, 153, 154–157
Industry standard schemas, 14, 97
Information
    asymmetry of, 226
    content interpolation of, 113
    inadequacy, by supplier, 221
Information quality index (IQI), 104–105,
      110, 203
Information technology (IT), 53
Information theory, ID3 and, 195
Information visibility, 212–214
Instance
    described, 127
    in lexicon, 21
    -related errors, 106

Integrated supply management, 212–214
Internationalization, and spend analysis
      deployment, 182–183
Internationalized schemas, 127
International Organization for
      Standardization (ISO), 220
Internet
    connection bandwidth, effect in OLAP,
      183
    Web, for relevance searches, 234–235
Invoice
    in P2P process, 91–93
    PO terms and, 222
Invoice processing opportunities, 77–79
    consolidated payments, 77
    frequent charges and credits, 77–78
    PO approval limits, 78–79
IQI (Information quality index), 104–105,
      110, 203
IS-A schema model, 171
ISO (International Organization for
      Standardization), 220
IT (information technology), 53
Item description, 98–99
Item master files, 50, 95
Itemsets, 202

J

JIT (Just In Time) delivery, 76
Job scheduling, for spend data sheets, 19

K

KB. *See* Knowledgebase
Key capabilities, 131–133
Key performance indicators (KPIs), 132
Knowledge acquisition. *See* Knowledgebase
Knowledge assimilation, 12
Knowledgebase (KB), 101, 102, 124,
      125–129
    custom knowledge in, 125
    data elements in, 126–127
    functionality, essential, 127–129
    management, 20–21
    systems, 14
    universal knowledge in, 125
    usefulness of, 125

Knowledgebase (KB) essential functionality, 127–129
  browsing/search function, 127–128
  editing, 128
  knowledge assimilation, 128–129
Knowledge sharing, 57
Kohonen self-organizing map, 198
Kolmogorov-Smyrnov (KS) test, 185
KPIs (key performance indicators), 132

L

Languages, and schemas, 166, 172
Law of frequency, in occurrence of digits, 189
Leadership, 48–49. *See also* Executive management; Implementation
Less than truckload (LTL), as transaction detail, 95
Lexicon, 20–21
Limited-scope, phased-rollout, 50–52
  data scoping, 52
  multicube approach, 51
  refresh requirement, 52
  requirements scoping, 50–51
Logarithmic tables, 189–190
Lost opportunity calculator, 25
LTL (less than truckload), as transaction detail, 95

M

Machine learning, 200
Machine learning algorithms, 123, 128
Maintenance, repair, and operations. *See* MRO
Malicious activity, detection of, 189–190
Man-in-the-loop operations, 114
  approval process and, 119
  in classification process, 128
  data enrichment and, 114
  transactional classification and, 123–124
Manual data entry, 186
Manually created relationships, 21
Manufacturing resource planning systems, 96
Mapping (crosswalks), 107, 170
Map report, 144, 147
Market basket analysis, 201–202

Market research data, 96–97
Material requirements planning. *See* MRP
Materials management, 95
Maverick spend
  default transactions and, 234
  non-PO spend as, 69
  savings and, 23
Measurement. *See* Metrics
Merger planning and integration, 39–44
  conclusion, 43–44
  methodology, 44
  overview, 39–40
  situation, 40
  three-phase implementation, 40–43
Metadata model, 157
Metadata tagging, 191
Metrics
  constant measurement, 54
  efficiency and, 220
  procurement compliance and, 118–229
  for rejected matches in KB, 129
  for relevance, 234
  risk analysis and, 219–220
  value and, 219
Microanalysis, in spend cubes, 233
Microsoft Excel
  for assessment, 35, 55
  as data source, 107, 130, 131
  for reporting, 28, 103
Minmax principle, 117
Minority- and women-owned business enterprise (MWBE)
  corporate policy and, 70
  requirements scoping and, 51
  supplier ratings and, 71
  USDA and, 31
Modules, spend analysis implementation, 101–103
Monte Carlo integrations, 185
MRO (maintenance, repair, and operations), 11
  domain, 160
  spend, 87
MRP (material requirements planning)
  spend cube and, 95
  systems, 96, 232
Multidimensional data models, 16

Multidimensional functions, 16
Multidimensional navigation, 183–184
Multilingual product, 166, 172
Multisource errors, in data classification,106
MWBE. *See* Minority- and women-owned
 business enterprise

N

NAICS (North American Industry
 Classification System), 127, 153
National/NATO Stock Numbers (NSN), 157
Natural language (NL) relationships, 21
Neural networks (NN), 195
Newcomb, Simon, 189
Nonapproved vendors, 31
Non-PO spend
 as maverick spend, 69
 in process bypass, 66
Nonpreferred suppliers, 5
North American Industry Classification
 System (NAICS), 127, 153
NSN (National/NATO Stock Numbers), 157

O

OEM (original equipment manufacturer),
 86
Off-contract spend, 31, 69–70
OLAP (online analytical processing), 175
 basic operations in, 183–184
 continental deployment, 182–183
 cube and, 129, 182, 183
 data enrichment and, 113
 dimensions and, 181
 engine, 181
 internationalization, 182–183
 navigation in, 183–184
 on-the-fly calculations and, 182
 precooked data and, 182
 primary purpose of, 184
 SA module and, 179–183
 schema, 180–181
 tool, 103
OLAP cube. *See under* OLAP
OLAP reports, 133–140
 cross-tabular reports, 133, 136, 137, 139
 graphical reports, 135, 136
 pivot tables, 133, 134–135

OLTP (online transaction processing), 182
On-boarding, to e-procurement and P-
 cards, 61, 66, 87
Online analytical processing. *See* OLAP
Online transaction processing (OLTP), 182
On-the-fly calculations, 182
Ontologies, 126–127
 attributes in, 127
 concepts in, 126–127
 instances in, 127
 semantics and, 202
 taxonomies and, 151–153
Opportunity assessment model, 35
Opportunity identification, 65–82
 prioritizing opportunities, 79–81, 82
 spend-level opportunities, 65, 66
 transaction-level opportunities, 67
Optimized bidding, 27, 209
Organizational alignment, in
 implementation of spend analysis
 solution, 54
Original equipment manufacturer (OEM),
 86
Outsourcing, data enrichment, 53
Overfitting, in classification, 192, 194

P

P2P (procure-to-pay), 61, 77, 88
 contract agreement in, 89
 contract module in, 90
 information/approval flow in, 89–93
 invoice processing in, 91–93
 POs and, 91–93
Partitional clustering, 196
Payment controls, in 3-way match, 224
Payment term opportunities, 76–77
Payment type, of spend, 72
P-cards (purchasing cards), 88
 control of, 224
 corporate, 96
 data requirements for, 93
 indirect spend and, 86
 multicube approach and, 51
Performance. *See* Supplier performance
Pharmaceutical companies, UNSPSC and,
 156
Pie chart, 133, 135, 138

Pivoting, navigation method, in viewing data, 183–184
Pivot table, 133, 134–135
PLM (product life cycle management), 214, 233
PO (purchase order), 94–95, 222
    bypass of, 69
    contract and, 91
Precooked data, in OLAP, 182
Preferred purchasing process, bypassing, 69–70
Preferred suppliers
    identifying through spend analysis, 5
    increasing compliance with, benefits of, 51, 66
    to reduce maverick spend, 24, 25
    savings using, 35
Price benchmarking, 235
Price rationalization, merger and, 39
Printing, spend for, 71
Prioritizing opportunities, 79–81, 82
    Step 1—Conduct buyer interviews, 79–80
    Step 2—Create a segmentation framework, 80
    Step 3—Segment the categories, 80, 81
    Step 4—Assign category to implementation waves, 80–81
Probabilistic associative rules, 21
Probabilistic record linkage, 190
Probability distributions, 185
Problem scopes for errors, 106
Procurement. See Procurement process; Procurement transformation
Procurement-centric view, 6, 8, 15
Procurement process
    control implementation, 222–224
    control violations in, 220–222
    limitations to improvement, 10
Procurement transformation, 55
    background, 57
    future, supplier relationships, 59
    implementation, 57–58
    key learning, 57–58
    overview, 55–57
    sourcing program success, 58–59
    spend analysis program success, 58

spend analysis project plan, 56
Procure-to-pay. See P2P
Product life cycle management (PLM), 214, 233
Property libraries, taxonomies and, 175, 177
Pruning strategies, in classification, 195, 202
Purchase order. See PO
Purchasing (historical spend), 5
Purchasing cards. See P-cards
Purchasing/e-procurement systems, 94–95
Purchasing leverage, merger and, 39–40
Purchasing transactions data. See Historical spend

R
Raw transactional data, 12
Real-time classification, 233–234
Rebates and discounts, spend leakage and, 73–74, 75
Receiver operating characteristics (ROC) graphs, 199–200
Refresh cycle, 102, 123
Refresh requirement for data, 52, 60
Regression algorithms, 193
Relational database, 102
Relationships in lexicon, 21
Relevance search, 234–235
Remapping feedback, 61
Replenishment-related information, 96
Reports
    cross-tabulation, reporting tools and, 103
    frequent reporting, 54
    map report, 144, 147
    multidimensional report, 144, 145
    reporting engines, 131
Req-to-check process, 88, 90. See also P2P
Request for information/quote (RFx), 4, 211, 212
Requirements scoping, 50–51
Requisite Unified Schema. See RUS
Return on invested capital (ROIC), 44
Return on investment (ROI)
    calculation of, 30
    decentralized purchasing and, 30–31, 34, 35
    estimation of, 27

savings opportunity, 30, 32–33
Reverse auctions, 11, 26, 209
RFx (request for information/quote), 4, 27, 211, 212
Risk, 228
    data correction and, 109–110
    metric for, 219–220
RNTD (*Rosettanet Technical Dictionary*), 173
RObust Clustering using linKs (ROCK), 198
ROC (receiver operating characteristics) graphs, 199–200
ROCK (RObust Clustering using linKs), 198
ROI. *See* Return on investment
ROIC (return on invested capital), 44
Roll-up, in pivoting and multidimensional navigation, 183–184
Root cause of error, 109
Rosettanet Technical Dictionary (RNTD), 173
Rosettanet website, 174
RuleQuest website, 195
Rules. *See also* Business rules
    -based classification technology, 100
    probabilistic associative, 21
RUS (Requisite Unified Schema), 170–173
    advantages of, 172–173
    attribute examples, 173
    design of, 171–172, 173
    disadvantages of, 173
    as proprietary taxonomy, 173

S

SA. *See* Spend analytics; Spend analysis
SAP customer base, 172
Sarbanes-Oxley Act (SOX), 219, 224
Savings opportunity, 30, 43–44
Schema, 185–187. *See also* Commodity schema
    classification schema, 156
    common, 16
    constellation schema, 180
    evolution, 14
    flat, 171, 172
    industry standard, 50
    internal schemas, 156, 160
    internationalized, 127
    IS-A (what is) model, 171

    normalization of, 104
    number of classes in various, 174
    reference schema, 119–120
    search engine, 173
    snowflake schema, 104, 180
    star schema, 17, 18, 104, 180, 181
    target schema, considerations, 177–178
Schema-related errors, 106
Schemata. *See* Schema
Schniderman diagram, 142–143
Scope creep, 12
Scorecarding, 132
Segmentation
    metrics, 81, 82
    strategy, 80–81
Segregation of duty (SOD) constraints, 224
Semantics
    schemas and, 15
    semantic tagging, 191
Semiconductor companies, UNSPSC and, 156
SG&A (sales, general, and administrative) expense, 61
SIC (standard industrial classification) codes, 6, 50, 152
SIN (standard item name), 157
Single-source errors, in data classification, 106
SKUs (stock keeping units), 96
"Slice and dice," of data, 4, 20, 58, 103, 184
Small-value components, 58
Snowflake schema, 104, 180
SOD (segregation of duty) constraints, 224
Software
    application provider, value of feedback to, 48, 54, 55
    features, use of, 53
    search-enabled interface, value of, 103
Source systems and data extracts, 94–97
Sourcing
    strategic initiatives, 3–4
    success factors in, 58–59
Sourcing team
    data quality and, 53
    on-boarding and, 61
SOX (Sarbanes-Oxley Act), 219, 224
Specialist vendors, 11

Specialized charts, 141–144
  map report, 144
  multidimensional report, 144, 145–146
  Pareto chart, 142
  treemap, 142–143
  waterfall chart, 141
Spend analysis
  benefits to businesses, 26–27, 28–29
  defined, 5
  four required modules, 101–103
  future of, 231–235
  guidelines, 47
  high-level capabilities, 58
  history, 10–11
  ideal application characteristics, 15–21
  return on investment (ROI), 27
  supply management and, 25–26
Spend analytics (SA), 19–20, 101, 102–103
  ad hoc analytics, 144, 147
  business intelligence key capabilities,
      131–133
  dashboards, 148, 149
  OLAP and, 133–140, 179–183
  specialized charts in, 141–144, 145–147
  user expectations and, 130
  what-if analysis, 147
Spend concentration
  by commodity, 38
  P2P, 80% of spend, 88
Spend core team, 54
Spend cube
  big bang approach and, 51
  flattened, 16–17
  forecasted spend and, 95
  nodes in, 16–17
  refresh requirement and, 52
  three-dimensional, 16
Spend forecasting, 232
Spend leakage, 5
  case study, audit findings of
      transactions, 227–228
  compliance multiplier and, 23–25
  contract compliance and, 225–226
  fraud and, 226–227
  process bypass and, 69
  unrealized discounts and rebates, 73–74,
      75

vendor compliance, 226
Spend-level opportunities, 66
  bypass preferred purchasing process,
      69–70
  demand aggregation, 67
  diversity spend compliance, 70, 71
  identification of, 66
  supplier performance, 70–71
  supplier rationalization, 67, 68
Spend-to-contract visibility, 214
Spend transaction anatomy
  data quality, 97–100
  P2P, information/approval flow, 89–93
  P-cards, data requirements, 93
  procurement processes, 88–89
  source systems and data extracts, 94–97
  T&E data requirements, 93–94
  types of spend, 85–87
Spend visibility, 34, 43, 44
Splitting, in classification, 195
SRM (supplier relationship management),
      11, 59
SSP (standard set of properties), 167
Stacked bar chart, 135, 138, 139
Standard industrial classification (SIC)
      codes, 6, 50, 152
Standard set of properties (SSP), 167
Star schema, 17, 18, 104, 180, 181
Steering committee, in implementation
      leadership, 48–49, 54
Stock keeping units (SKUs), 96
Strategic planning, in what-if analysis, 147
Strategic sourcing, 10
  benefits, 5, 23, 24
  case study, provider of products,
      services, and technology for
      healthcare industry, 59–61
  challenges, 10
  objectives, 48
  reports and, 15
  savings and, 23
  spend analysis and, 10, 11, 209
  and vendor rationalization, 67
String matching, in data enrichment,
      190–191
Structured content, ontologies, 126
Success, visibility and, 54

Supervised machine learning, 192
Supplier
    assessment, 220–221
    consolidation, merger, 39
    discovery, 232
    fragmentation, 8, 9
    savings and, 30
    selection of, 213, 220
    shifting spend to approved, 30
    trend report, 36
Supplier performance, 70–72
    approved versus nonapproved spend, 71,
        73
    historic spend and, 213
    spend by payment type, 72, 74
    spend with poorly performing suppliers,
        71, 72
Supplier rationalization, 10, 51
    business unit fragmentation and, 67, 68
    preferred supplier status, 212
    sourcing events for, 52
Supplier relationship management (SRM),
    11, 59
Supply management
    integrated, 212–214
    principles, 56
    spend analysis and, 25–26

T
T&E (travel and entertainment), 88–89
    anomalies, 89
    control of, 224
    data requirements for, 93–94
    management of, 89
    microanalysis and, 233
Target cost analysis, 233
Target schema, choice of, 177
Taxonomies. *See also* Custom taxonomy
    balance of content in, 174–175, 176
    commodity, 61, 151, 153
    concept of, 151–152
    ground rules, construction of, 153
    hierarchical order and, 152–153,
        174–175, 176
    ontologies and, 151–153
    property libraries, quality of, 175, 177
    proprietary, 173

quantitative analysis of, 187–189
quantitative comparison of, 173–177
size and growth of, 174, 175
vehicle classification example, 152
Team
    cross-company planning, 42
    organizational alignment and, 54
    sourcing, 53, 61
    spend core, 54
Technology, business requirements and,
    53–54
TFIDF-based (term frequency inverse
    document frequency) distance
    metric, 190–191
Third party transportation provider, 95
3-way matching, 224
Top management. *See* Executive
    management
Tracking and monitoring, 209–217
Trade-offs, 125, 203
Trainer, role in implementation, 49
Transaction. *See also* Spend transaction
    anatomy
    AP (accounts payable), 6, 7
    default transactions, 234
    fields, 97–98
Transactional attribute, 118
Transactional classification, 18, 20
    implementation approaches, 124
    machine learning algorithms and, 123
Transactional data, 13
    controls, 229
    flow of, 103
    quality of, 13
Transactional enrichment, 113, 120–124
    business rules and, 120–123
    transactional classification, 123–124
Transaction data audit, 227–228
Transactional (fact) table, 104, 109
Transaction-level opportunities, 67, 72–79
    contractual term opportunities, 72–76
    invoice processing opportunities, 77–79
    payment term opportunities, 76–77
Transaction table, 187–188
Travel and entertainment. *See* T&E
Tree structures, 187–188, 193, 194–195
Trend reports, 36

U

UNDP (United Nations Development
    Program), 154
United Nations Development Program
    (UNDP), 154
UNSPSC (United Nations Standard
    Products and Services Code), 50, 97,
    126, 127, 153, 154–157
    advantages of, 155–156
    custom taxonomy and, 107, 113
    design of, 154–155
    disadvantages of, 156–157
    subcommodity level, 157
    top five commodities, 70
    transactional classification and, 124
UOMs, 158
User privileges, 17, 122
UTF-8 (8-bit UCS/Unicode Transformation
    Format), 183
Utility problem, 196

V

Value metric, 219
Variance analysis, benefits tracking via,
    215–216
Vendor
    for card transactions, 89
    nonapproved, 31

specialization and, 11
    of spend analysis solutions, 60
Vendor clustering, singletons and, 197
Vendor compliance, need for controls, 226
Vendor consolidation, 11, 18, 19, 26
Vendor data enrichment, 13, 14, 50, 99
Vendor familying, 197
Vendor file, 95, 152
Vendor name, 99, 100
Vendor normalization, 99
Vendor rationalization, 68
Visibility. *See* Information visibility; Spend
    visibility
Visualization tools, 15

W

Waterfall chart, top ten commodities, 34
Waves in category segmentation, 80–81, 82
Web
    -based RFI, 27
    -centric application, 17
    searches, 234–235
    services, 214
    site, 174, 195
Webinars, 54
What-if analysis, 147, 232–233
What is (IS-A) schema concept, 171, 172
WIP (work in process), 95